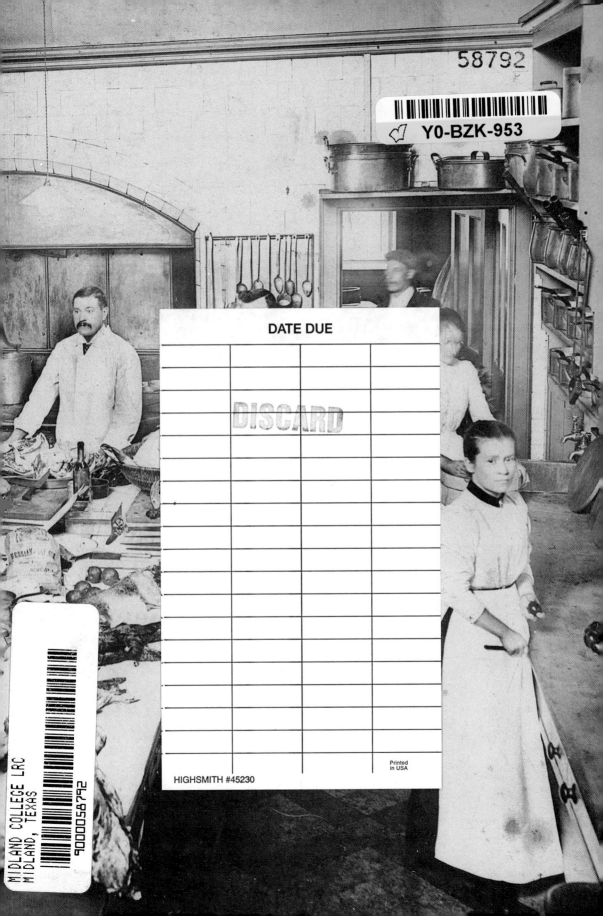

The Country House
KITCHEN
1650–1900

The kitchen at Minley Manor, Hawley, Hampshire in the 1890s. The photograph may have been taken to record the installation of the electric lights, which must have been an early example. The kitchen retains a smoke jack above the fireplace and a hastener or screen in front. The table shows what seems to have been the classic layout — table top protected by cloth, work boards placed on top, one each side for the chef and perhaps a woman cook, seasoning boxes down the middle and cooking cutlery laid out down the sides — even the wooden spoons are arranged in size order. Note also that the dresser has a cloth and the floor is sanded. (RCHME © Crown copyright)

The Country House
KITCHEN
1650–1900

Skills and Equipment for Food Provisioning

EDITED BY

PAMELA A. SAMBROOK

and PETER BREARS

ALAN SUTTON PUBLISHING LIMITED

IN ASSOCIATION WITH

THE NATIONAL TRUST

Published in association with National Trust Enterprises Ltd
36 Queen Anne's Gate · London · SW1H 9AS
First published in the United Kingdom in 1996
Alan Sutton Publishing Limited
Phoenix Mill · Far Thrupp · Stroud · Gloucestershire

British Library Cataloguing in Publication Data
The Country House Kitchen 1650–1900:
Skills and Equipment for Food Provisioning
  I. Sambrook, Pamela II. Brears, Peter C.
  D.

ISBN 0–7509–0884–X

Based on papers from the Eighth Leeds Symposium on Food History, April 1993, and the Ninth, April 1994, with several additional chapters. This is the eighth volume in the series 'Food and Society', previously published by Edinburgh University Press.

Typeset in 12/15 Garamond.
Typesetting and origination by
Alan Sutton Publishing Limited.
Printed in Great Britain by
Butler & Tanner, Frome, Somerset.

CONTENTS

LIST OF ILLUSTRATIONS

ACKNOWLEDGEMENTS

Most of the illustrations not acknowledged in their captions have been reproduced from books in the Brotherton Library, University of Leeds; the editors would like to express their sincere gratitude to the University Librarian for permission to reproduce these and also to the library staff for their helpfulness. All the line drawings not acknowledged in their captions have been specially prepared by Peter Brears. The editors would also like to thank everyone who has helped towards the preparation of this book.

INTRODUCTION

Pamela Sambrook

This book is a collection of some of the papers presented to the 1993 and 1994 Leeds Symposium on Food History. The theme of the two meetings was skills and equipment for provisioning the country house. The original papers have been supplemented by the addition of several others written by the original contributors, with the aim of making the book a more comprehensible whole than it would otherwise have been. In particular an extra introductory paper on the ideal kitchen has been included.

There is no shortage of publications on the country house; from coffee table books to hefty academic dissertations, the subject is a popular one. It is only fairly recently, however, that the domestic world of the country house has been opened up – literally in the case of the now numerous National Trust and privately-owned houses which are busy restoring and opening to the public their 'domestic offices'. After many years of neglect, the question of how a country house really worked has become a respectable one to ask. This aspect of country house administration is truly a growth industry, but it is not without its problems. We wander through a warren of kitchen, pastry, laundry, stillroom and servants' hall and it is all too easy to be bewildered by the complexity. However closely we relate to the life of the back stairs, the real world of the residential domestic servant is remote and we may find ourselves taking refuge in television fantasy.

The complexity on the ground mirrors the historical intricacy of the society itself. Even those who have been personally involved with a country house may have experienced only a partial view. A sophisticated household was a tangled web of social and physical structures and relationships which varied with individual cases and over time. In order to make sense of it we have to focus our concentration on specific themes, one of the most useful of which is food and its preparation.

The country house, of course, was a restricted environment, bounded by wealth and privilege. Many social historians would dismiss it as unrepresentative of the vast majority of human experience and therefore unworthy of study. They have a point, too. We have to be able to justify our interest in country house domestic technology and organization as something more than a limited and unhealthy introspection. The justification is easily made. Within the wider world of food history the country house has much to offer. It was here, from the seventeenth to the nineteenth centuries, that many new fashions, raw materials and techniques were adopted for practical use. Within reason, money was no object, so the potential for innovation was present, if not the actuality. The country house was one of the testing grounds for new sophisticated food tastes brought in from Europe, a process which has left tangible evidence in the shape of new stoves, new types and materials of cooking utensils, even new forms of buildings such as ice houses.

One of the fascinating issues is the extent to which households actually adopted new techniques or bought new equipment. Even where this happened, tried and trusted installations were often kept. In particular, the British cook's love affair with the roasting range lasted well into this century; at Tatton Park, as in numerous other country house kitchens, the bar grate or roasting range, an idea created in the sixteenth century and owing a debt to the medieval open hearth, stands a few feet away from the massive coal-fired range sitting in the centre of the kitchen, serviced by underground flues and representing the latest technology of the early twentieth century. It is this mix of the conceptually ancient and modern which makes a walk round the innards of a country house such unending delight.

The motivation for the adoption of technical improvements in the country house might have been complex. Owners might have wanted to be able to produce totally new things; or improve their own comfort; or reduce costs; or improve the lifestyle or working conditions of their employees. One thesis which might be interesting for the reader of this book to test is that owners were generally self-interested in their espousal of new techniques. Taking an example from a non-food technology, many owners were early to install expensive water-flushing closets, but only for their own use. Such installations represented a great increase in personal comfort for them over close-stools, chamber pots or outdoor privies. Savings in servant time would also follow, but were perhaps of secondary consideration. Owners seem to have been less concerned about the introduction of equipment whose only advantage was that it could save their servants' time and labour – until, that is, the need arose in the late nineteenth century to make a positive effort to attract and keep good servants. No doubt other insights of this nature can be debated within the area of food technology.

The country house and its way of doing things had wider relevances, too. It is a mistake to see it as an isolated ivory tower with little relationship to its neighbouring countryside. The country house after all represented not the social norm but the social target; the hierarchical structures, the systems of supply, the physical bricks and mortar presented a pattern to which middle-class households might aspire. It is an obvious truism but it still needs saying – the country house style offered the very highest quality available not only in buildings, art and furniture but also in service and administrative organization; as such it was asking to be copied. By studying the administration of domestic servants of the great houses we can make sense of some of the otherwise bizarre traditions or expectations of smaller households, just as by looking at the organization of the medieval noble household we can understand the arcane mysteries of the nineteenth century 'groom of the chamber' or 'usher of the hall'. The extent to which new ideas on hygiene or fashion did in fact 'trickle down' the social scale is a fascinating subject for further research. A comment frequently made by relatives of domestic servants is that they brought home with them new ideas of fastidiousness, higher standards of finish to linen or table, greater expectations of cleanliness, above all a better understanding of cooking; sometimes these ideas were not welcomed, were seen as fussiness or fancy new ways. But the practice of sending young girls out to the local big house until they married offered a training ground for later life, just as the same system had for young men centuries before.

In the same way, the country house system was responsible in part at least for a network of commercial retailers which could hardly be supported otherwise. It was true that most of the luxuries of life were bought from London suppliers, but there must have been numerous local tradesmen for whom the country house network provided a substantial part of their living – people like blacksmiths contracted to clean the smoke jack and repair the kitchen range, or coopers with regular seasonal work re-heading casks in the brewhouse. High quality local grocers depended on such trade, too, not only in terms of actual business, which ran on credit, but also in terms of prestige and advertising. Many an ambitious tradesman or shopkeeper must have been fired by the possibilities of being recognized as a supplier to the country house market.

Most country houses relied almost as much on part-time labour as on full-time

*Practical training. A lady (left of centre) presents a cookery book to a young woman
servant; in the foreground a young man is instructed in the art of carving; in the
background a woman servant bastes the roast while adjusting the spit drive from the
clockwork jack, here covered in a wooden case. (Frontispiece from W.A. Henderson,* The
Housekeeper's Instructor or Universal Family Cook, *6th edn, c. 1800)*

residential staff.[1] These part-timers, both regular and casual, were often members of local families who had a long tradition of service at the big house. In many ways they knew the ins and outs of the system better than the residentials and could work it to their advantage. The potential for 'leakage' through such people, particularly of foodstuffs, must have been substantial and explains in part what amounts to the paranoia of the country house proprietor. Waste and pilfering were a continual worry, and one result was the installation of a structured system of internal accounting which could be checked and supervised. In consequence, we have today copious written records of the workings of the household. Larger houses were run as businesses rather than domestic households, a feature which is reflected in the management system as well as the scale of operation. It is not accidental that resonances of the country house system can be identified in the way in which early hotels, schools and hospitals were organized.

So we can make a case for the general relevance of the country house in a study of technological change and the development of food habits. Where does this collection of papers come in? The range of the book is fairly broad and its title has been carefully considered. In a modern sense the subject matter in the papers covers more than just the kitchen, but before the commercialization of food supplies the kitchen was in some respects the end of a chain of interiors which needed to process food before it could be cooked. So larders, dairies, stillrooms, even brewhouses and ice-houses were part of this production line and thus functionally contributed to the kitchen. Similarly the book attempts to cover the skills and equipment needed; before we can begin to test out different ideas about relationships or motivations or to answer questions as to why some households were old fashioned and some forward-thinking, we need to get clear in our minds what the sequence of technical change was and which models were presented as ideal. Most of the papers offered here are concerned with this problem, and it is a particularly strong theme in some of them. Most also have deliberately gone beyond this to consider the social context, the way in which the practicalities of work fitted into the structure of the household.

In many ways this publication represents a beginning not an end, a point at which we can start to look at the domestic history of the country house in real detail. Over the last decade or more, the broad lines have been sketched in, to the point where we can articulate ideas, concepts and explanations.[2] Our job now is to test and expand these against the detailed examination of individual households. In a way our situation is not unlike that of family history, a field where broad-based theories can be tested out on a very small scale of individual research.

During the course of preparation of papers, the overwhelming feeling experienced by at least two of the contributors was that we are only just beginning to understand how much we do not know about how country houses and their kitchens were run. How, for example, was the work in the kitchen organized? How was the work table set out? How did country house cooking technology relate to that of inns or hotels? What were the relationships between chef and helper? Did they have particular clothing for particular jobs and how did this change over time? How did the servants organize their food and take their meals while on board wages (when theoretically no food was allowed from the house)? To what extent were expert chefs happy to train others and pass on their experience or was jealousy rife? Exactly what was the relationship between family and servants' food and to what extent was food used as a marker of status within the servant hierarchy? How did the individuality of families affect food type? How did the allowance system operate for servants? These and many more questions are yet to be asked and answered at the level of the individual household. This volume leaves many topics untouched, for the simple reason that in most cases little work has been done on them. This is true of, for example, the work of the scullery and the way in which washing up was handled; the poultry house; post-medieval fish stews; and table linen.

Not every house or kitchen was built to an ideal model or run by the rule book. Periods of maladministration or absence must have resulted in many a run down, neglected kitchen. The degree of regimentation depended on the personality of the cook; and as a famous historian of the domestic house, C.H.B. Quennell, has pointed out:

A place for everything, and everything in its place, is a rule more honoured in the breach than the observance. As a race, they [cooks] are prone to untidiness in their work, with a grand clear up at its conclusion, and much time and money is often expended in providing separate little compartments for each thing, with a result that they are never used for such purpose at all.[3]

Close scrutiny of individual cases is needed if for no other reason than our country houses deserve it; we must avoid the serried ranks of identically reconstructed, superficially researched country house kitchens.

Is this the real face of the country house kitchen? An unknown castle or country house kitchen. (By courtesy of Staffordshire Museum Service)

A deliberate aim has been to offer papers based on three types of sources: material culture; contemporary printed books such as manuals and recipe books; and manuscript family archives. These last are perhaps the least familiar. Sometimes they survive in enormous detail and quantity – runs of years of meal books, wages books, flour or grain books, menu books, housekeepers' and kitchen accounts, inventories, voucher books, bills, tradesmen's account books, butter books, cellar books and brewers' records. There is no quick fix to this. To make sense of it all may require years of patient transcribing, analysis and synthesis. There is ample work here for the dedicated amateur historian.

Students of the history of domestic service have used such archives, but as yet it seems that food historians have made little use of them, beyond a superficial 'pick and mix' sort of approach. The potential here is enormous, but it is important to get the approach right. By and large within the field of modern or early modern social history the documentary historians and the students of material culture have built barriers between themselves. Many an otherwise highly laudable academic thesis is marred by a technological ignorance of the most basic kind; equally writers on the material culture of the country house – whether on food or other topics – need to inject into their work some of the rigour of academic research. In this field it is important that objects and documents are seen not as rivals but as essential partners in our quest. Such an approach is well-suited to the Leeds Symposium, comprising as it does a heady mixture of cook, housewife, journalist, curator and academic.

As the subtitle indicates, the main emphasis of this book is on equipment and systems for the supply and preparation of food, not food type (menus and recipes), nor its consumption (the subject of a previous publication in this series).[4] The elaborate equipment installed was primarily for the benefit of the landed family, but the family in the context of a large supporting structure of servants. We are therefore not only considering food for the wealthy but also food for the servant and this is the main emphasis in at least the final paper.

With the notable exception of Trentham, most of the houses cited in the text still exist and are open to the public, many of them by the National Trust. The interiors described can be visited, should this book so whet the appetite, though some of them are newly restored and may not be finished at the time of publication.

Most importantly, the collection of papers presented here is rooted in a hands-on tradition. Over the years the contributors have designed, cooked and served authentic historical feasts, sweated over spits, burnt their toes on bread ovens (the ashes fall out on to your feet), given themselves headaches over stoves, fetched blood cleaning *batteries de cuisine*, shovelled ice into ice-houses and sat up all night to nurse a brew. After all that, we still would like to learn more about the country house and its food; we hope you do too.

NOTES

1. For a discussion of the role of casual labour in the country house see Jessica Gerard, 'Invisible Servants: The English Country House and the Local Community', *Bulletin of the Institute of Historical Research*, 57 (1984), pp. 178–88.

2.   For recent work on the country house and/or its food see Jessica Gerard, *Country House Life: Family and Servants, 1815–1914* (Oxford, 1994); Christina Hardyment *Home Comfort: A History of Domestic Arrangements* (London, 1992); and Sara Paston-Williams, *The Art of Dining: A History of Cooking and Eating* (London, 1993).

3.   C.H.B. Quennell, 'Kitchens and Sculleries', in Lawrence Weaver (ed.), *The House and its Equipment* (London, 1912), p. 90.

4.   C. Anne Wilson (ed.), *Luncheon, Nuncheon and Other Meals: Eating with the Victorians* (Stroud, 1994).

CHAPTER ONE

THE IDEAL KITCHEN IN 1864

Peter Brears

In order to ensure that any country house was able to receive, store, prepare and serve its food and drink as efficiently as possible, great care had to be taken in providing a well-designed and well-fitted suite of kitchen facilities. To do this, the architect had to be fully conversant with the working practices of country house domestic staff and with the particular environmental conditions which they required. In 1864 Robert Kerr, professor of the arts of construction at King's College, London, published a weighty volume entitled *The Gentleman's House* in which he explored these elements in the most comprehensive detail. In the following pages we can accompany him as he guides us through the numerous rooms of an idealized country house kitchen, noting their varied functions, their relationships with one another, and their particular fixtures and fittings.

THE KITCHEN

When planning the domestic offices of any country house, the siting of the kitchen was of primary importance. It had to be close enough to the dining room to enable the food to be served quickly and efficiently, but yet be sufficiently distant to exclude all the attendant noise, steam and odours. Ideally it was located to the north of the main house, so that the sunlight could flood into the family's apartments throughout the day, leaving the kitchen in the coolest shade. For this reason the windows ideally faced either north or east, any ceiling lights being arranged so as to avoid the direct rays of the sun. As the centre of all culinary activity, the kitchen usually had doors leading out of it into the scullery, the larders, and, preferably by way of another room or passage, the kitchen yard. A further door led towards the dining-room, but this could be replaced by a serving hatch fitted with a dresser both inside and out, so that the food might be delivered to the servants without any need for them to enter the kitchen. This arrangement also helped to prevent the spread of odours throughout the house.

An industrious kitchen. Pots boil over the roasting range grate; one chicken already roasts in front of the fire; the cook loads another on to the spit; one maid seems to be helping with the preparations while another adjusts the clockwork mechanism driving the spit; an old woman, smoking a pipe, plucks another bird and the dog helps to clean up. (Frontispiece from The Ladies' Companion, *vol. 1, 6th edn, 1753)*

Regarding the construction of the kitchen, it had to be a large room, perhaps 18 by 25 ft to 20 by 30 ft in most country houses, although some were much larger. Heights of between ten and twenty feet or more were quite usual, probably going up through two storeys. In order to increase the ventilation, air ducts might be arranged either from the ceiling, or from canopies or hoods mounted above the stoves and boilers, through the roof-space, to a louvre or a duct among the chimney flues at high level, where they could quickly and efficiently disperse steam and odours into the atmosphere. For lighting, large windows in the walls or in the ceiling admitted the maximum cool, mainly northern light, further illumination being provided by oil, gas, or eventually electric lamps hanging either from the ceiling, or from wall-mounted brackets, whichever was the most convenient. The floors were usually of stone, with the central area under and around the table sometimes being of wood, or covered with a piece of matting or carpet. Alternatively standing boards some two feet wide were laid loose around the table and along the front of the dressers for the benefit of the kitchen staff. The wall surfaces were normally of painted plaster, their lower sections being protected with boarding, hard cement, stone, tiles, glazed bricks, etc. to make them much more hardwearing, and able to withstand their frequent washing and cleaning.

This photograph of the kitchen at Kedleston Hall, Derbyshire, clearly illustrates the scale and quality of great house kitchens during the third quarter of the eighteenth century. In addition to the iron range and the roasting screen on the left, note the cosy 'snug' in the right-hand corner, where kitchen staff could dine, sheltered from the draughts by their high-backed settle.

Fittings

Fireplace	Some 5–8 ft or more in width, and 3 ft in depth, situated in the centre of one wall, where it housed a roasting range, perhaps with a boiler at the back, and an oven.
Roasting screen	A large open-fronted and shelved cupboard, lined with tinplate, which stood in front of the fireplace to keep food and dishes warm etc.
Oven	If not part of the range, standing next to the range, occupying an area of some 2 ft 6 in by 4 ft and heated from its own fire-grate and flue.
Stewing stoves	Placed close to the other cooking equipment, and in the best

natural light. Measuring about 3 ft 6 in to 3 ft wide, they were table-height masonry benches, with grates some 10 in square for charcoal fires recessed into their working surfaces.

Hot-plate and broiling-stove Probably adjoining the stoves, providing a hot iron cooking surface measuring some 6 ft by 2 ft 6 in.

Hot-closet and hot-table Both of iron, and heated by steam or water from the range boiler, used to keep the food and dishes warm ready for service to the dining table. The first occupied a space of some 4 ft by 2 ft 3 in while the latter might be some 4 ft by 2 to 3 ft.

Coppers For cooking vegetables and boiling meat, if these facilities were not available in the scullery. They measured some 4 ft by 3 ft in plan. Alternatively a set of perhaps three steam kettles heated from the range boiler could be placed on one of the dressers.

Bain-marie Also heated by steam or water from the range boiler, this shallow hot water bath some 2 ft by 2 ft 6 in was used for cooking delicate sauces, custards, etc. and keeping them hot for service.

Hot-water cistern Acting as a reservoir of hot water from the range.

Coal-box Holding supplies of fuel, perhaps fitted under the hot-plate, or in a similar position.

Kitchen dresser Some 10 to 12 ft by 2 ft 6 in to 3 ft wide, with a tier of large drawers about 10 in deep below, the space beneath them being either left open or enclosed as cupboards, to within 6 or 9 in of the floor, to provide space for cooking utensils. Lining the wall above, the dresser-backs had narrow shelves to hold ordinary crockery or copper articles, their edges having rows of small brass hooks from which jugs etc. could be hung. Further dressers might also be provided, probably without a back- or pot-board.

Mills For coffee, pepper and spice, fitted on the sides of the dresser-back, or close at hand.

Kitchen table Usually 8 to 10 ft long by 4 ft wide stood in the middle of the kitchen, perhaps with shallow drawers some 2 ft wide and an open frame beneath. One or two marble slabs might have been let into its top for the convenience of the cook.

Mortar Of white marble, mounted in a strong stone or wooden block, perhaps fixed against the wall near the dresser.

Chopping block	Similarly placed.
Shelves	Provided around the walls for the storage of utensils, as well as at a convenient height near the cooking apparatus, to receive any forks, spoons, etc. in use there.
Spit-racks	Fitted in any spare corner of the kitchen.
Pin-rails	For holding dish-covers etc., near the dressers.
Towel-rollers	

THE SCULLERY

This room was used for washing and cleaning dishes and cooking equipment, preparing vegetables, fish, game, etc. for the kitchen, and carrying out the simpler operations of cookery. One door should open into it directly from the kitchen, as close to the kitchen fireplace as possible in order to provide the most expeditious route for coal, foodstuffs, etc. A further door should proceed through a passage or covered way to the open air and the kitchen yard, coal cellar, wood house and ash-bin. In contrast, there should not be any direct communication between the scullery and the larder, dairy, pantry or other food stores, since the heat, steam and odours would damage their contents.

In general terms, the structure of the scullery should resemble that of the kitchen, a paved floor draining into a drain-trap being particularly useful here, since there was a great need for frequent washing.

Pearse's Patent Veruvolver Economic Roasting Apparatus, from the frontispiece of E. Hammond's Modern Domestic Cookery *(6th edn, London, 1826), incorporates a clockwork jack, gear-driven spits and a dripping pan, all in one convenient unit. The cook is partly protected from the heat of the fire by the movable screen or hastener which warms the dishes.*

Man servant or cook prepares the joint. The roasting fire has a spit, but we cannot see the jack.

(Frontispiece from M. Holland, The Complete Economical Cook, *14th edn, c. 1843)*

Fittings

Boiling copper	For supplying hot water for cleaning, and for boiling kitchen cloths. A further pair of boilers might also be provided for boiling meat, soup or vegetables, or steaming various foods, if these facilities were not provided in the kitchen.
Cooking range	To supplement the main kitchen range.
Sinks or washers	Placed under the light, and supplied with hot and cold water. Two might be of slate, and up to four of wood, each measuring some 3 ft to 3 ft 6 in by 2 ft 6 in, by 1 ft 9 in deep.
Stone sink	Some 1 ft 6 in by 3 to 4 ft long.
Dresser	A strong, plain table fixed in a good light, sometimes with a back and shelving to hold the servants' crockery.
Table	May be placed centrally, like that in the kitchen, but perhaps smaller.
Plate rack	Fixed above the sinks into which the water from the draining plates dripped by means of a dripboard.
Oven	May be provided here if no separate bakehouse is available.

THE PANTRY OR DRY LARDER

Originally the pantry was the bread-store, while the larder was where raw meat was larded or preserved, but by the eighteenth century the term pantry or dry larder had come to be used for the room where bread, pastry, milk, butter, and cooked meats were stored. For this purpose it was essential that it was cool, dry and well ventilated, perhaps being an entirely separate building on the north side of the house. Alternatively it could be in the outbuildings, joined to the scullery, by means of a covered way, or be incorporated in the kitchen buildings. Care had to be taken that there were no fireplaces or hot flues in any of the adjoining walls, but a hot-water circulation from the kitchen boiler could help to keep the larder above freezing point in the coldest winter weather. To ensure good ventilation, a through draught was best arranged by having a number of windows in the walls, their openings being filled with wire gauze to exclude flies, dust and leaves, etc., with glazed inner casements which could be closed in the event of severe weather.

Fittings

Dresser	A plain table 2 ft 6in to 3 ft wide and without drawers, fitted around three sides of the room, with two or three tiers of 1 ft 6 in to 2 ft wide shelves mounted against the walls above. These could all be of marble or slate.
Table	A small table may have been placed in the centre of the room.
Safe	Made of wire gauze, about 3 ft to 4 ft square, might be placed on the table, to provide additional security against insects. Alternatively individual wire gauze dish-covers were used for this purpose.
Refrigerator	This could be put in one corner, and used to chill small dishes on ice before they were served.

MEAT OR WET LARDER

Here the raw meat was stored, along with the wet fish, the fruit and the vegetables. The general construction and arrangement were similar to those of the pantry, except that the dressers and shelves were preferably of slate and the walls were protected either by glazed tiles or by hard non-absorbent cement.

Fittings

Bacon rack	Suspended from the ceiling.
Bearers	Horizontal rails suspended from the ceiling, with sliding hooks from which the meat was hung.
Balance	For weighing.
Chopping block	For butchery.
Salt pans	For salting meat.
Marble slab	For fish.
Refrigerator	
A box-sink	Provided in a window-sill or in a dresser.

The pantry and larder provided sufficient food storage space for most houses, but larger houses also required the following rooms:

GAME LARDER

Similar to the meat larder, but with a large number of bearers and hooks overhead, and a slate or marble dresser at one end, or in the centre of the room.

FISH LARDER

As the other larders, but with a broad slate or marble dresser all round, and a few hooks above.

SALTING ROOM

Located in the ground floor or basement of the house, or in the outbuildings, this room required the same coolness and ventilation as the other larders.

Fittings

Dresser	Strongly constructed for cutting up the meat.
Trays of stone	Placed along the walls to hold pieces of meat, such as sides of bacon in pickle.
Shelves	To hold pickling trays of earthenware, each with a drain-pipe to carry the brine down into the vessel beneath, ready for re-use. A supply of water, and also a drain in the stone floor were both useful.

BACON LARDER

Constructed in the same manner as the other larders, this room required racks or shelves for the bacon, as well as horizontal bearers hanging from the ceiling from which the hams were hung on sliding hooks.

SMOKING HOUSE

The smoking house could measure up to 8 to 10 ft square, and have several iron bearers running across overhead to support the meat. A wood, sawdust or peat fire burning in an external grate filled the whole room with smoke, which eventually escaped through a louvre-frame set into the roof above.

THE DAIRY

In addition to being located and constructed similarly to the meat or wet larder, the dairy might be supplied with glazed inner windows and heating pipes to maintain a temperature of 50–5°F in cold weather. The paved floor was also provided with a supply of cold water and good drainage to facilitate frequent washing.

Fixtures

Shelves One tier, made of 2 ft wide stone or slate, fitted around the walls to hold the milk dishes. Sometimes the shelves had a hollow channel around them which held water to keep them cool.

DAIRY SCULLERY

Adjoining the dairy, this scullery was used for scalding the vessels, setting them to dry, churning the butter, and similar operations.

Fittings

Copper or boiler To provide the necessary hot water.
Dresser and benches

THE PASTRY

Entered either from the kitchen or from the stillroom, the pastry was used for both making and storing pastry items. Sometimes it was provided with its own oven, but usually the baking was done in an iron oven in the kitchen or stillroom. In many houses a separate pastry was made unnecessary by having a pastry-dresser in the stillroom, and using the pantry for storage. Since dryness was essential here, the floor of the pastry was often of wood, the same material being used to cover the walls.

Fittings

Dresser	About 2 ft 3 in wide, of marble, or with at least 3 ft of marble set into it, under the light. The space beneath the dresser could be filled in with deep drawers for flour, sugar and other materials. Sometimes a flour box with a hinged lid was constructed at one end of the dresser, with a sink arranged at the other end.
Shelves	Lining the wall-space above the dresser, etc.

THE BAKEHOUSE

This room was usually only found in the larger establishments, the smaller houses making their bread in the kitchen, and baking it in the kitchen scullery.

Fittings

Oven	Of brick, some 3 to 4 ft diameter, lined with firebrick, and heated by wood burnt within it.
Table	At the window, for bread-making.
Kneading trough	Close to the table.
Flour chest	Next to the trough.
Shelves	Arranged around the walls for the storage of the bread.

THE BREWHOUSE

The brewhouse usually formed part of the outbuildings, so that its vapours did not penetrate the house. A door into the yard provided access both to the carts used to deliver and collect materials, and to the yard for the storage of casks, as well as providing a convenient route for carrying in the fuel and supplies and taking out the ashes etc. It was convenient to have the entrance to the beer cellar nearby, otherwise the beer could be run down into the casks in the cellar by means of a pipe.

Fittings

A large boiler	Set into a furnace.
One or two flat wooden coolers	

Wooden mash tun

Smaller underback Set under the mash tun.

A hand pump From the underback to the boiler.

Wooden fermenting tun

THE BEER CELLAR

There were usually two beer cellars in the larger country houses, one for the table beer of the servants, and another for the better qualities. Unless the beer was piped in from the brewhouse, a trapdoor was provided for the delivery and collection of the casks.

Fittings

Stillages or stools For casks, these usually being of wood, or of wooden beams supported on low masonry walls. There might also be drainage channels in the paved floor beneath the spigots.

THE WINE CELLAR

In order to exclude light, maintain a cool, even temperature and ensure maximum security, the wine cellar was ideally placed beneath the central part of the house, where it was convenient both for the butler and for the master. The room itself was paved, had a thick ceiling of vaulted masonry, and a strong door fitted with a proof lock.

Fittings

Wine bins A series of cupboard-like compartments 2 ft to 2 ft 6 in square by 1 ft 10 in deep, so as to take two stacks of horizontal bottles packed neck to neck. The vertical divisions were usually of brick, the three or four tiers of shelves being of slate, stone or brick arching. From the mid-nineteenth century various systems of iron wine racks were also used.

THE PACKING OR OUTER WINE CELLAR

Arranged between the exterior and the wine cellar this room was used for unpacking and washing bottles, stowing hampers, and perhaps for bottling wine from the wood.

It might be illuminated by a window, and have a trapdoor and ramp for the reception of pipes of wine, these casks being 5 to 6 ft long by 2 ft 6 in to 3 ft in diameter. There might also be racks for bottles here, these being shut in by locked doors.

THE BUTLER'S CELLAR

Sometimes this additional cellar was necessary to contain a small working stock of wine under the butler's charge, leaving the main stock in the wine cellar under the control of the master. A small lockable closet might also have been provided for the butler to lock up the wine in decanters at the appropriate cellar temperature. In addition separate cellars could be used for spirits, or for Madeira, which required a higher temperature.

THE COAL CELLAR

This cellar had to be arranged conveniently for the kitchen and wash-house, where the largest amounts of fuel were burned. Care had to be taken that there was ready access for the heavy-laden horse-drawn coal-wagon, without using the main drives through the surrounding pleasure-grounds. Similarly the coal-plate covering the chute into the cellar was best placed well out of the way of passers-by, and away from walls or doorways which could easily be soiled by the coal. Alternatively the coal could be stored either in a ground-level room in the outbuildings, or in an open shed in one of the yards. In any case, the walls and floor had to be reasonably dry, to prevent coal from absorbing water.

THE WOOD HOUSE

The wood was never stored indoors, but instead was generally stacked up outside, and brought under cover as required for splitting up. The wood house was usually in an outbuilding, supplies of small wood for firelighting being carried in as needed.

ASH-BIN ETC.

Ideally a covered way led from the scullery door to the ash-bin, which was covered by a wire screen to act as a sifter, and to the offal-bin, from which animal and vegetable refuse was collected every day or two for feeding the pigs etc.

THE UPPER SERVANTS' OFFICES

In the larger establishments, the management of the entire household was the responsibility of the steward, assisted by the butler and the housekeeper, each of whom had their own suite of offices in the domestic quarters. Where no steward was employed, the housekeeper took full charge of the culinary and general household affairs.

THE STEWARD'S OFFICE

This was the combined business-room and sitting-room of the steward. It had to be placed conveniently close to his own bedroom, to the master's room, the butler's and housekeeper's rooms, and an external door for the access of tradesmen. It should also be situated so as to control the entire men-servants' quarters, for which he was entirely responsible. In addition to general furnishings, a strongroom or safe was needed here for the storage of papers.

THE STEWARD'S ROOM OR SECOND TABLE ROOM

Here the upper servants, including the valet, butler, head cook, housekeeper, head lady's maid, head nurse, and visitors' servants of equal rank, dined with the steward. This room also served as their business room or office during the day, and sitting room in the evening, as well as acting as a waiting and refreshment room for visiting upper servants and superior tradespeople. For the above reasons, it had to be close to the master's business room, the steward's office, the back entrance to the house, and the kitchen, for the service of food. It might also have its own small scullery, for washing and putting away the upper dishes.

Fittings

Furniture   A dining table and chairs, a sideboard, probably a bookcase, and one or two cupboards or closets for storage.

THE BUTLER'S PANTRY

The modern butler fulfilled the ancient duties of the butler, who dispensed the drinks, as well as the sewer, who served the food at the master's table. His pantry needed to be close to the dining-room, the wine and beer cellars, and the steward's room (or the housekeeper's room if there was no steward). It had to be at least 12 ft square and heated by a fireplace.

Fittings

Dresser	Containing a pair of lead sinks with folding covers, and provided with hot and cold water, for washing and rinsing tableware.
Washbasin	For personal cleanliness.
Table	
Napkin-press	
Drawers	For table linen.
Hat pegs	
Closets	For glass etc, and for plate, the latter having sliding trays lined with baize.
Plate-safe	Being a strong brick enclosure fitted with an iron door and strong lock to protect the gold and silver tableware. A closet-bedstead might be provided here for one of the men-servants, so that he could guard the safe overnight. Alternatively the door to the safe could open into the adjacent butler's bedroom to give a higher degree of security.

PLATE SCULLERY

Where a large amount of plate was in regular use, a separate plate scullery could open from the butler's pantry, to provide space for cleaning the gold and silverware. It was fitted with a pair of sinks and a dresser.

SERVING OR SIDEBOARD ROOM

The process of serving meals was made much easier when a serving or sideboard room was arranged as an ante-room to the dining-room. Here the food from the kitchen, the wine from the cellar, and the tableware and glasses from the butler's pantry were all assembled ready to be carried into the dining-room by way of a door at the side of the sideboard. If the kitchen offices were on the same level as the dining-room, then the connecting corridors would be as direct as possible, some having either a covered way through the open air, or a pair of windows placed opposite each other, in order to reduce the risk of any steam or odours entering the house. If the kitchen was in the basement, however, then a dinner-stair would provide the servants with a means of access up into the serving room, while the food was carried up in a lift measuring perhaps 5 ft by 3 ft.

Fittings

Dresser	For plate, wine, dessert, etc.
Hot cupboard or hot table	To keep the dishes of hot food at the required temperature.
Lead sink and washbasin	For rinsing tableware, washing the hands, etc.

HOUSEKEEPER'S ROOM

Besides being the housekeeper's business-room and parlour, this was also the room where the upper servants took their breakfast and tea, as well as their dinner, if there was no steward's room. It was positioned close to the kitchen offices, the servants' hall, and the rooms generally occupied by the lady of the house. Since the housekeeper was the head of all the female household staff, it also had to overlook the majority of their working areas. It was generally well furnished with a dining table, chairs and rugs.

Fittings

Presses or cupboards 1 ft 6 in to 2 ft deep, filled with drawers and shelving for preserves, pickles, fancy groceries, glass, china, etc. Spicery and light groceries were contained in small drawers, linen and sugar in large drawers, and tea, sugar, cakes and biscuits in tinplate canisters.

HOUSEKEEPER'S STORE-ROOM

Adjacent to the housekeeper's room and the stillroom, this room housed the housekeeper's general groceries and stores. In smaller establishments it might also take the place of the housekeeper's room or butler's pantry for the storage of china, glass, napery and plate, in which case it could be divided into two by a high partition, the inner part being for general stores, under lock and key, while the outer part acted as a housekeeping room and china closet.

Fittings

Dresser	With drawers and cupboards beneath.
Shelves	Two or three tiers deep around the walls, with brass hooks along their front edge. Also pin-rails where a variety of goods could be hung up. In addition, part of the floor could be left clear to provide space for goods in boxes.

THE STILLROOM

Although this room received its name when distillation was a general country house activity, its use in the eighteenth and nineteenth century was as a specialized kitchen for the use of the housekeeper and her stillroom maid. For this reason it was located near the housekeeper's room and her store-room, perhaps having inter-connecting doors with each. Here preserves, cakes, biscuits and perhaps pastry work were made, tea and coffee prepared, and, in smaller houses, all the meals were cooked except luncheon and dinner, even these being cooked in the stillroom if the family were away from home. In some lesser houses it was also used as a women-servants' hall for all meals, including the men-servants' tea.

Fittings

Range and boiler	
Confectioner's iron oven	
Hot-plate	
Lead sink	Or two, with covers, and water supply.
Dresser	
Table	
Closets	
Shelving	

CHINA CLOSET

This store-room for domestic crockery not in everyday use was usually sited close to the housekeeper's room, and was preferably well lit to avoid any costly accidents.

Fittings

Table
Dresser
Lockable cupboards
Shelving   Around the walls.

CHINA SCULLERY

Usually connected with either the housekeeper's room or the china closet in the best houses, this room was used for washing and rinsing the domestic crockery.

Fittings

Dresser
Sink or washer

Having concluded this tour, it is possible to draw up a flow-chart (opposite) which explains how Robert Kerr's ideal country house kitchen should be arranged. It provides a very useful standard model against which the efficiency of real kitchens can be compared.

The Ideal Kitchen in 1864

MEN'S SIDE
WOMEN'S SIDE
Back Entrance
Tradesmen & Luggage
Bakehouse
Brewhouse
Wood & Coal
Dairy
Kitchen Court
Ash-bin
Scullery
Kitchen
Larder
Servants' Hall
Women's Room
China Closet
Steward's Room or Second Table Room
Housekeeper's Room
Store-room
Steward's Bedroom
Steward's Office
China Scullery
Stillroom
Men's Bedroom Stairs also to Bachelor's Rooms & down to Cellars
Backstairs to Nurseries & Women-servants' Bedrooms
Lift for coals, luggage, linen, Nursery dinners, etc.
Dinner Bell
Plate Safe
Butler's Bedroom
Butler's Pantry
Plate Scullery
Wine Cellar
Main Entrance to the House
Serving or Sideboard Room
Dining-room

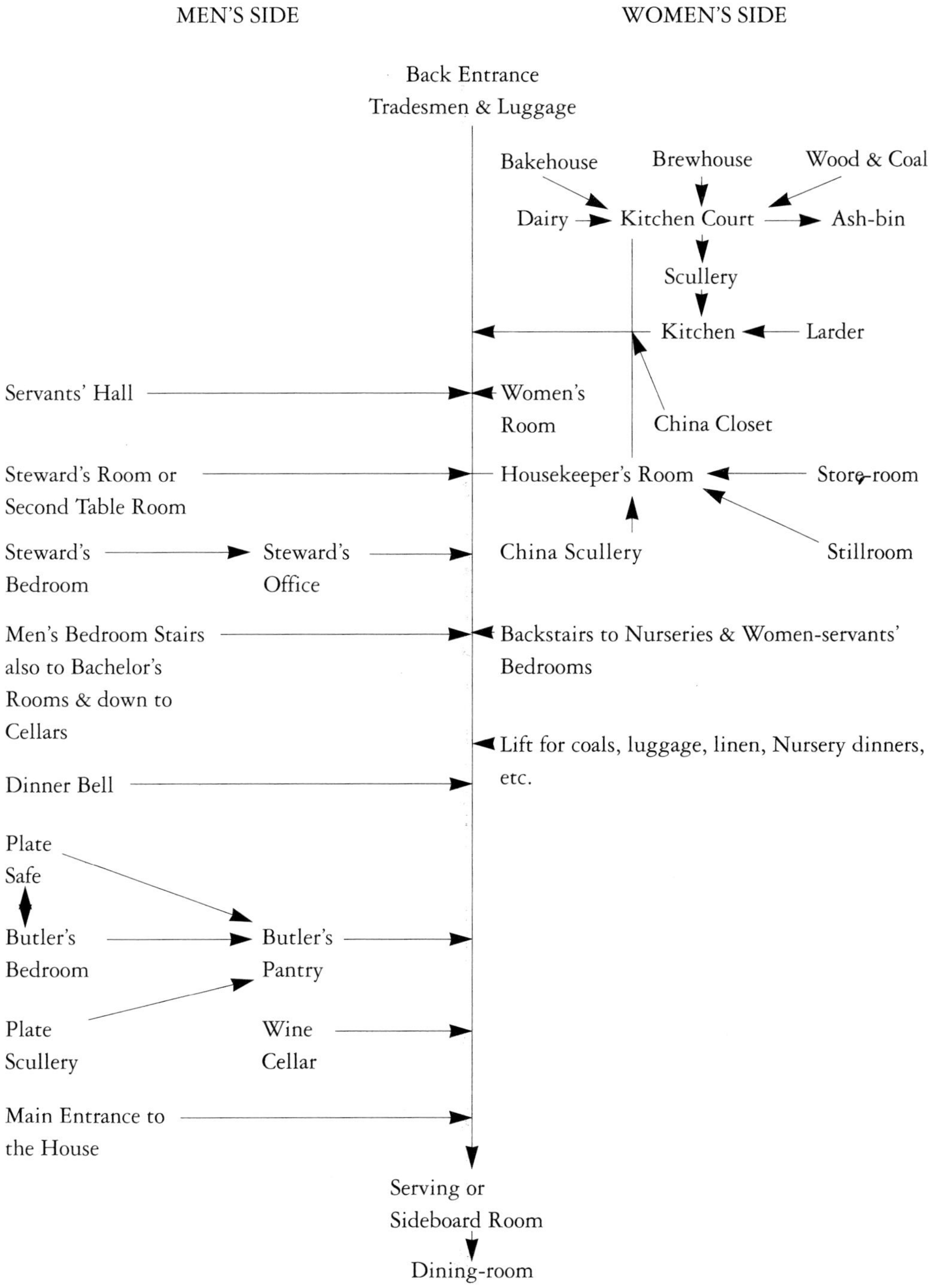

CHAPTER TWO

BEHIND THE GREEN BAIZE DOOR

Peter Brears

PLANNING THE COUNTRY HOUSE KITCHEN

In common with all other buildings, the English country house was designed to fulfil the social, economic and practical requirements of those who commissioned its creation. The works of Mark Girouard and others have enabled us to follow the development of the country house plan as it accommodated the changing needs of its principal occupants, the families of the peerage and landed gentry. In contrast, the purpose of this paper is to proceed beyond the principal apartments, through the traditional brass-studded green baize door and on into those domestic offices where food was prepared for service at the dining table.

Here efficiency was the primary concern. Just as in any industrial process, there had to be a smooth-flowing production-line, where raw materials deposited at the back entrance could be stored, prepared and finished ready for prompt delivery. This meant that there should be a minimum of congested passages, narrow doorways and contra-flows, while the different offices should be conveniently arranged to reduce the need for unnecessary carrying. At the same time, there had to be good security, to prevent the unauthorized loss of food or equipment, and good ventilation, so that any unpleasant smells would not percolate throughout the whole house. Furthermore, the domestic offices had to be divisible into distinctly male or female areas of activity, once these had become established.

Given the mass of information available in plans, inventories, architectural volumes, etc., it is first necessary to devise some relatively simple analytical process which will record the essential elements of each particular country house plan, so that it may then be compared or contrasted with others of different style and period. A flow-chart is most suitable for this purpose, one which commences at the back entrance, and proceeds to the hall or dining-room, with male areas on the left, female on the right, and common areas recorded down the centre, as follows:

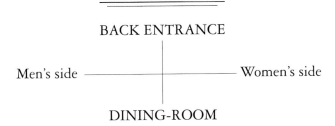

By analysing numerous house-plans in this way, it has proved possible to show how the planning of domestic offices has developed over the past four hundred years. During this period their location and complexity had changed considerably to meet the demands of different social arrangements and different architectural styles. This survey can only recognize general trends, however, since, along with every other aspect of country house life, the relative progressive or conservative nature of the inhabitants, their extravagance or penury, could lead to very individualistic arrangements.

1. Hall and Cross-passage Plans

In late medieval England, when all major landowners still retained extensive households, with numerous servants, the life of the house revolved around the hall. This large room, often of a single storey, beneath a lofty timber-framed roof, was where the household dined together and where major festivities took place. Even when the lord and his immediate family began to dine in the relative privacy of their parlours or chambers, the hall, with its hierarchy of servants and visitors, occupied an important place in the processional route by which food was carried up from the kitchens.

Most houses of this period relied on a range of outbuildings for the initial processes of food preparation, such as butchery, bakery, brewing, and dairying, so that only the essential all-male kitchen offices of the larders, bolting house and pastry, and the kitchen itself were actually within the structure of the house. From the kitchen, the food was passed through hatches at the surveying place, for inspection by the clerk of the kitchen, from where servants carried it into the screens passage, the elongated porch which ran across the bottom end of the hall. Here too were the buttery and pantry, from which supplies of drinks and bread were dispensed. The servants then proceeded through doorways cut in the screen which enclosed the passage, passed through the hall, and continued on into the

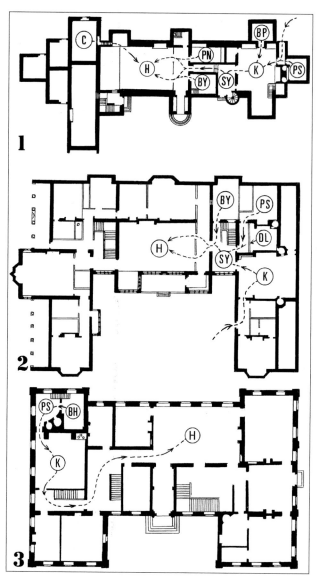

Hall and cross-passage plans. This sequence of plans shows how the traditional late medieval practice of having a large central hall, where major entertainments and the everyday meals of the household servants took place, continued to flourish in the sixteenth and seventeenth centuries, and even survived into the early eighteenth century. 1. Worksop Manor, Nottinghamshire; 2. Aston Hall, Warwickshire; 3. Newbold Hall, Warwickshire. BH bakehouse; BP boiling place; BY buttery; C cellar; DL dry larder; H hall; K kitchen; PN pantry; PS pastry; SY servery.

dining chamber itself, to serve the lord's table. Only when this task had been completed did the servants begin to serve those seated around the hierarchy of tables set up within the hall. The plans for kitchens of this period were relatively simple, since they involved only a small number of rooms, which were all on the same level as the hall, and were all staffed by men.

During the late sixteenth and early seventeenth centuries, when houses began to be built for display and comfort, rather than for defence, their architects began to explore different ground plans, and different internal arrangements. The basic sequence and number of domestic offices remained much as before, but now they had to be fitted into a great variety of locations, depending on the shape of the house, whether it be U- or H-plan, rectangular with a large courtyard, a small courtyard, or corner turrets, or hour-glass shaped. One of the architects' main considerations was the position of the hall. A favourite solution was to place it at one side of the central entrance doorway, so that visitors could enter directly into the screens passage. This left the other side of the house free for domestic purposes. There are numerous examples of this practice, but the following plans show its application to a large rectangular house, Worksop Manor; and a large courtyard house, Slaugham Place:

WORKSOP MANOR, NOTTINGHAMSHIRE, Robert Smythson (?), completed 1586

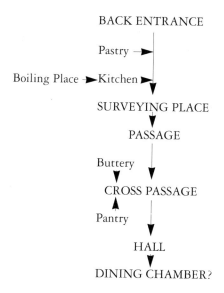

BACK ENTRANCE

Pastry →

Boiling Place → Kitchen →

SURVEYING PLACE

PASSAGE

Buttery

CROSS PASSAGE

Pantry

HALL

DINING CHAMBER?

SLAUGHAM PLACE, SUSSEX, probably before 1579

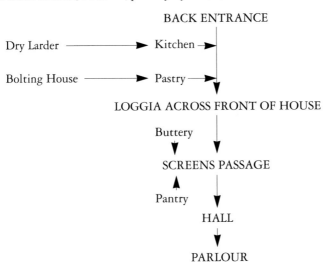

Alternatively the hall could be placed in the middle of the house, with the screens passage being entered from a porch at one end, symmetry being maintained by placing a bay window at the other, as at the U-shaped Aston Hall; and the courtyard house at Burton Agnes:

ASTON HALL, BIRMINGHAM, drawn by John Thorpe, c. 1618

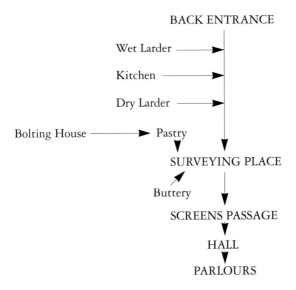

BURTON AGNES, YORKSHIRE, Robert Smythson (plan), 1601–10

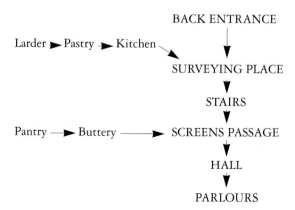

In planning Hardwick Hall, Robert Smythson turned the hall at right-angles to the façade, but his range of domestic offices remained very conventional, even though the kitchen–scullery–buttery access was much improved:

HARDWICK NEW HALL, DERBYSHIRE, Robert Smythson, 1590–7

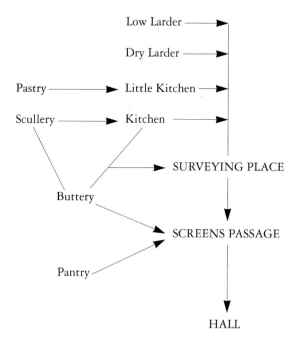

Alternatively the screens passage could be dispensed with entirely, Holland House being one of the first houses where the porch led directly into the body of the hall:

HOLLAND HOUSE, KENSINGTON, John Thorpe, 1605–6, and before 1614

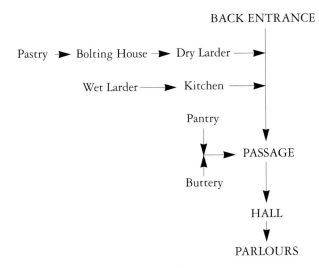

Over the following years, this old-established plan, in which the minimal range of domestic offices lay close to the hall on the ground floor of the house, began to be superceded by new arrangements. Even so its convenience meant that it took a long time to die out, as illustrated by the plans of Beddington Place, Surrey, of 1709; and Newbold Hall, Warwickshire, of 1716, which both have kitchens on the ground floors of one of their principal wings, and large two-storey halls only a short passage-length away towards the centre of the house:

NEWBOLD HALL, WARWICKSHIRE, Francis Smith, 1716

2. Early Basement Kitchens

Placing the domestic offices in the basement has a number of advantages, the main one being that of space, since it enables a house to be built on a much more compact area. It also provides a means of elevating the ground floor, making it drier, warmer, and more imposing. Thick foundation walls, supported by the surrounding soil, also enable the basement to be constructed with stone vaulted ceilings, thus reducing the risk of fire spreading up through the house, and enabling the principal appartments to be paved in stone or marble.

These advantages had already been appreciated by the Italian architect Palladio, who in 1570 had stated:

That the houses may be commodious for the use of the family . . . great care ought to be taken . . . that the most minute and least beautiful parts be accommodated to the service of the greatest and more worthy; for as in the human body there are some noble and beautiful parts, and some rather ignoble and disagreeable, and yet we see that those stand in very good need of these . . . as our Blessed Creator has ordered these our members in such a manner, that the most beautiful are in places most exposed to view, and the less comely more hidden, so in building also, we ought to put the principal and considerable parts in places most seen, and the less beautiful in places as much hidden from the eye as possible; that in them may be lodged all the foulness of the house. I approve, therefore, that in the lowest part of the fabric, which I make somewhat underground, may be disposed the cellars, the magazines for wood, pantries, kitchens, servants' halls, wash-houses, ovens, and such like things necessary for daily use. [This also makes] the said upper appartments wholesome to live in, the floor being distant from the damps of the ground.

(This translation was prepared by the architect Isaac Ware in 1738.)

Probably the first use of basement kitchens was in a group of tall square houses with small central courtyards which includes Barlborough, Derbyshire, of 1583–4; Heath Old Hall, Yorkshire, of *c.* 1585; Chastleton, Oxfordshire, of 1602; and Wootton Lodge, Staffordshire, *c.* 1607–11. Here, and at Gawthorpe, Lancashire, in 1600–5, and at the Little Castle at Bolsover, Derbyshire, the kitchens are not buried deep into the earth, but lay chiefly at ground level, a high external staircase

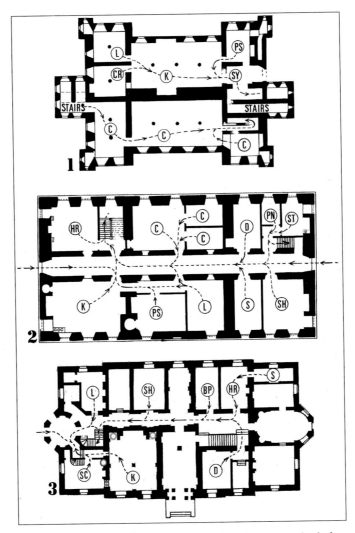

Early basement kitchens. The removal of the domestic quarters into the basement level of country houses first started in the late sixteenth century, establishing a tradition which continued for over two hundred years. These plans show this development, Sir Roger Pratt's highly original and efficient plan for Coleshill probably being the first to have a servants' hall at this level, leaving the hall above free for use as a major reception area and ceremonial route up to the first-floor dining-room (no. 2). Here too we see rooms for the housekeeper and her staff, following her introduction into the formerly male-dominated households. 1. Slingsby Castle, Yorkshire; 2. Coleshill, Berkshire; 3. Kirby Hall, Yorkshire. BP butler's pantry; C cellar; CR cook's room; D dairy; HR housekeeper's room; K kitchen; L larder; PN pantry; PS pastry; S store; SC scullery; SH servants' hall; ST stillroom; SY servery.

ascending to the principal rooms on the elevated 'ground' floor. The increased need for good access from one floor to another in these compact houses is well illustrated in the following chart:

THE LITTLE CASTLE, BOLSOVER, DERBYSHIRE, Robert/John Smythson, 1608–17 or 1612–21

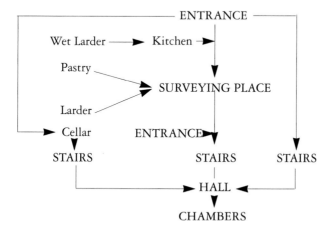

By the opening of the seventeenth century, houses with true half-height basements were being constructed, a plan of 'Mr Panton's' by John Thorpe placing 'all offices under ground'. Existing examples from this period include two Smythson buildings: Shireoaks Hall, Nottinghamshire, probably started after 1610; and Slingsby Castle, Yorkshire of *c.* 1630. Here again, the plan provides good access from the basement offices up to the rooms where food was to be served:

SLINGSBY CASTLE, YORKSHIRE, John Smythson, c. 1630

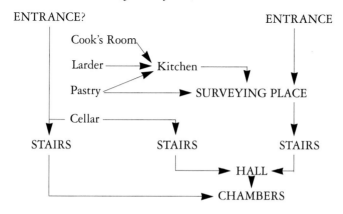

Within a few years, basement kitchens were to become quite common, but in the 1630s they were still extremely rare. Raynham Hall in Norfolk, one of the earliest classically inspired country houses in England, included this feature when it was built between 1621 and the 1630s. Here the kitchen lay in the wing to the left of the entrance front, occupying not only the basement level, but continuing up through the ground floor to provide welcome light and ventilation. The remainder of the preparation rooms were entirely within the basement, from which a staircase rose up to a ground-floor pantry, adjacent to the screens passage at one end of the centrally placed hall.

3. Spinal Corridor Basement Plans

From the opening of the seventeenth century the influence of Andrea Palladio had been gradually gaining strength in English architecture, partly as the result of informed visitors observing his buildings in Italy, and partly from the plates published in his *Quattro Libri di Architettura* of 1570. All his designs were based on classical architecture, including convenient symmetrical plan-forms with elegant classical proportions, pediments and detailing. Some of John Thorpe's drawings demonstrate a knowledge of Palladio's plans, as do the houses at Raynham, Wilton and Newmarket, but the most influential Palladian works of this period were produced by Roger Pratt, a gentleman amateur who had spent five years in France and Italy. At Coleshill, built for his brother about 1650, he adopted a simple rectangular plan, with the central door giving access directly into a great two-storey hall, which now contained a grand staircase, beyond lay a great parlour, with a great dining chamber above. Spinal corridors extending from the hall to backstairs at each end of the house on both floors gave access to eight almost identical suites of parlours and chambers, with accompanying closets and servants' rooms. The whole of the domestic offices were placed in the basement, doors at each end giving access to a long spinal corridor, as shown in the chart opposite. The use of the rooms shown here comes from *Vitruvius Britannicus* of 1771, but probably represents the original arrangement. A number of additional rooms have now appeared, one of the most important being the servants' hall, probably the first time that the servants had been purposely moved out of the main ground-floor hall into more distant domestic quarters, thus leaving the hall free to become a reception area. We can also see how female

COLESHILL, BERKSHIRE, Sir Roger Pratt, c. 1650

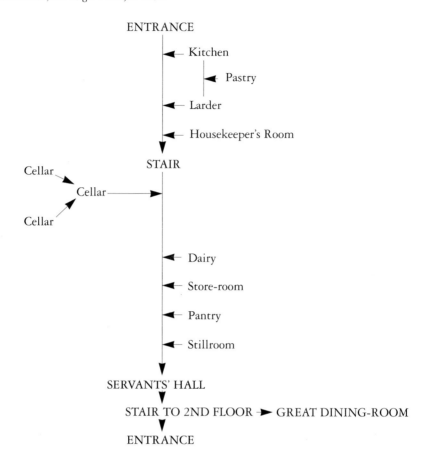

activities, such as housekeeping, dairying, preserving and distilling have been introduced into the domestic offices, reflecting the contemporary shift from the tradition of all-male kitchen staff.

After the Restoration, Pratt used the same elements in designing Kingston Lacy, Dorset, 1663–5; Horseheath, Cambridgeshire, 1663–5; and Clarendon House, Piccadilly, 1664–7. Since the latter was built for Charles II's chief minister, the Earl of Clarendon, it was particularly influential, being extensively copied throughout the rest of the country. In fact, it proved so successful with regard to the arrangement of the domestic offices, that architects were still building houses with spinal corridors through their basements over a century later. Examples include Henry Herbert and Robert Morris's Wimbledon, of 1732–3; John Wood's Prior Park, Bath, of 1737; Sanderson Miller's Hagley, Worcestershire, of 1747–8; Burlington and Robert Morris's Kirby Hall, Yorkshire, of *c.* 1750; Isaac Ware's Wrotham Park, Middlesex, of 1754; or John Wood the Younger's Buckland, Berkshire, of 1757. It is interesting to see how the kitchens at Wimbledon and Prior Park had a completely separate entrance, the food having to be carried out into the open air and brought into the main service entrance close by. This appears to have been purposely designed to stop the spread of kitchen odours:

WIMBLEDON, SURREY, H. Herbert and R. Morris, 1732–3

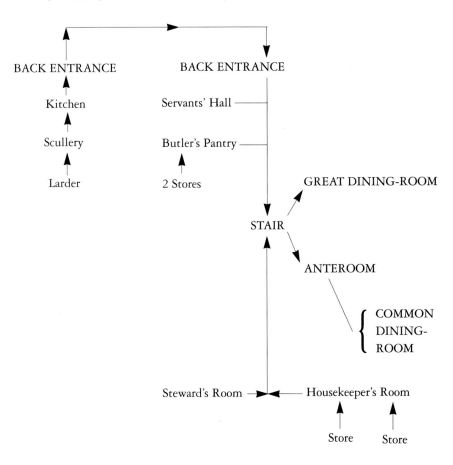

PRIOR PARK, BATH, John Wood, 1737

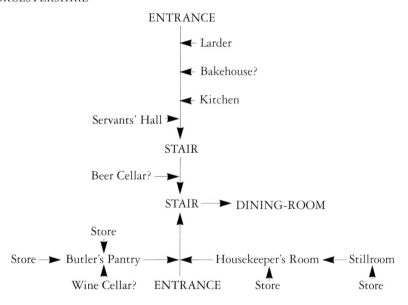

HAGLEY, WORCESTERSHIRE

KIRBY HALL, YORKSHIRE, Earl of Burlington and R. Morris, c. 1750

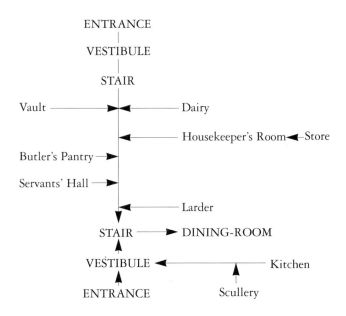

WROTHAM PARK, MIDDLESEX, Isaac Ware, 1754

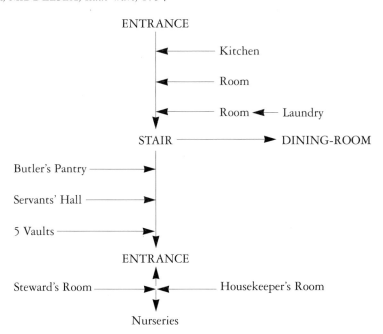

BUCKLAND, BERKSHIRE, John Wood the Younger, 1757

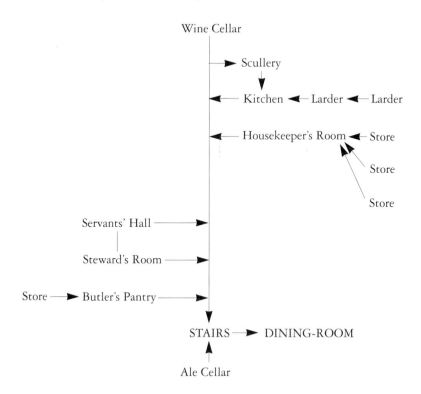

3a. Spinal Corridors Extending to Kitchen Pavilions

In a later development of this plan, the spinal corridor was extended beyond the walls of the main house by means of either an enclosed corridor, an open colonnade across an intervening yard, or a corridor through a link-block of ancillary rooms, to a separate kitchen pavilion. To maintain a symmetrical appearance, a stable or laundry block was usually built on the opposite side. This arrangement meant that the wetter, more odoriferous and inflammable female culinary activities were kept well away from the main house, while the basements could now offer more spacious predominantly male accommodation for cellars, the servants' hall, the steward, the butler or the housekeeper.

Roger Morris's 1733 Stanlynch (now Trafalgar House), Wiltshire, was modified in this way by John Wood the Younger in 1766, as shown below (p. 47):

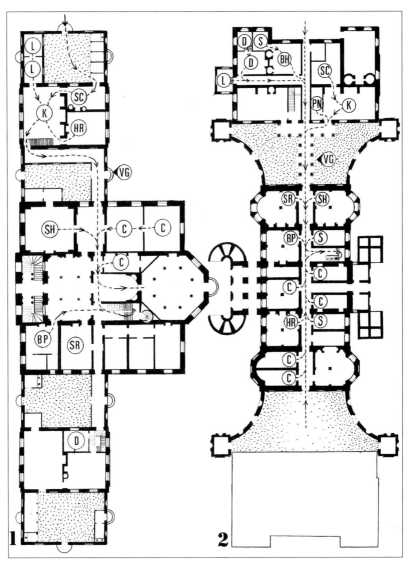

Spinal corridors extended to kitchen pavilions. From the mid-eighteenth century, the line of the spinal corridor through the basement began to be continued across open courts to flanking kitchen pavilions, thus removing all the accompanying noises and smells from the house itself. Any linking corridors were provided with opposed openings to give cross-ventilation to reduce the transmission of smells even further. 1. Basildon, Berkshire, 1776; 2. Foremark, Derbyshire, 1759–61. BH bakehouse; BP butler's pantry; C cellar; D dairy; HR housekeeper's room; K kitchen; L larder; PN pantry; S store; SC scullery; SH servants' hall; SR steward's room; VG ventilation gap.

STANLYNCH, WILTSHIRE, Roger Morris, 1733 extended by John Wood the Younger, 1766

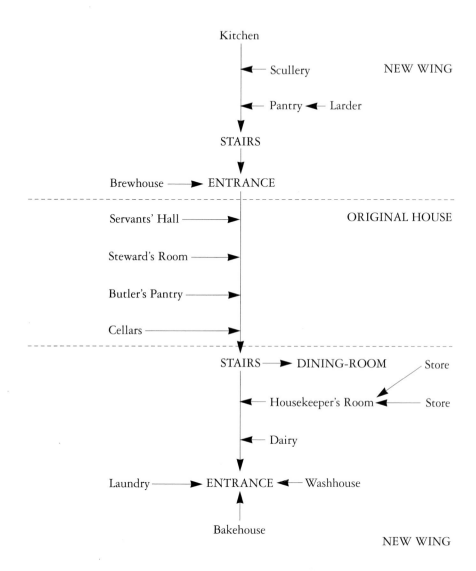

Other houses built in this manner date mainly from the 1770s. They include Foremark, Derbyshire, of 1759–61; Robert Adam's Witham, Somerset, of 1762; John Carr's Basildon, Berkshire, of 1776; and his Thornes House, Yorkshire, of 1779–81:

FOREMARK, DERBYSHIRE, 1759–61

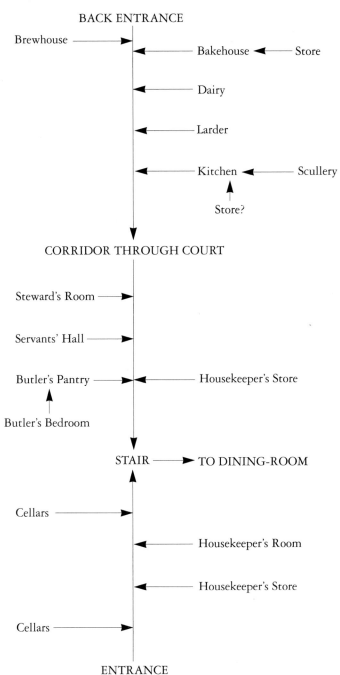

BACK ENTRANCE

Brewhouse ────────►

Bakehouse ◄──── Store

Dairy

Larger

Kitchen ◄──── Scullery

Store?

CORRIDOR THROUGH COURT

Steward's Room ────►

Servants' Hall ────►

Butler's Pantry ────►◄──── Housekeeper's Store

Butler's Bedroom

STAIR ────► TO DINING-ROOM

Cellars ────►

Housekeeper's Room

Housekeeper's Store

Cellars ────►

ENTRANCE

BASILDON, BERKSHIRE, John Carr, 1776

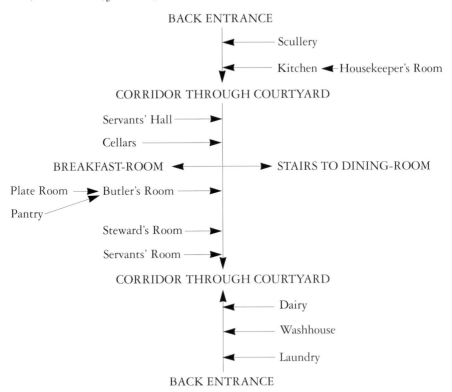

THORNES HOUSE, WAKEFIELD, John Carr, 1779–81

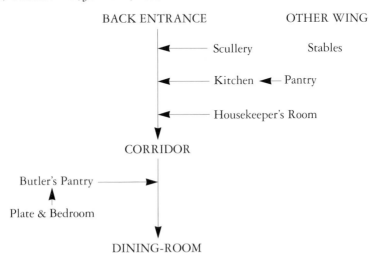

4. Linked Pavilions

In the medieval period, the major landowners had used domestic service as a means of publicly demonstrating their place at the head of an extensive feudal power base. Their chief household officers had been drawn from those of only slightly lower social status, these officers then maintaining servants from the next rank down the social scale. This traditional service-based hierarchy began to break up in the early/mid-seventeenth century, partly as a result of the growing influence of the new gentry who had flourished on the profits of trade and former monastic lands. They neither wished to enter the domestic service of greater men, nor to maintain

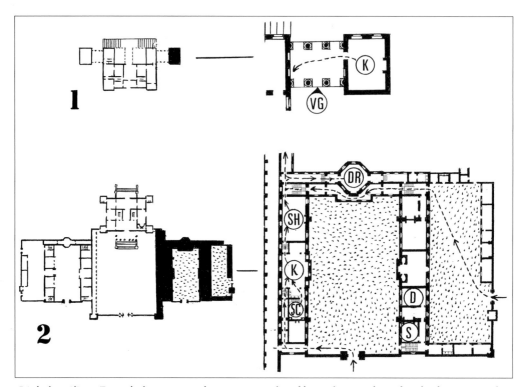

Linked pavilions. From the late seventeenth century a number of houses began to have their kitchens arranged in wings extending from the sides of their main façades. The earliest kitchens of this type tended to be quite simple, as seen in this example from Bramham Park, while those designed by Sir John Vanburgh were truly monumental, appropriate to the scale and quality of his vast creations, such as Eastbury. 1. Bramham Park, Yorkshire, c. 1703–10; 2. Eastbury, Dorset, c. 1715–38. D dairy; DR dining-room; K kitchen; S store; SC scullery; SH servants' hall; VG ventilation gap.

extensive households of their own, particularly since their money and time could be much more enjoyably and profitably spent in following their personal social and business interests. These changes, already apparent in the opening years of the seventeenth century, were greatly accelerated by the Civil War, which effectively saw the end of the medieval style of household management, with all its associated traditions and ceremonies.

In practice, this meant that the number of household servants was much smaller, they came from a much more uniform lower social group, and, in culinary areas in particular, women largely replaced the men. The purpose of household servants was no longer primarily a matter of demonstrating power and prestige, but was almost entirely concerned with the efficient running of the household in the most discreet and unobtrusive way. The lavish display of servants was now reserved only for grand occasions. Otherwise, the owner and his family much preferred to enjoy a greater degree of personal privacy. Their need to separate their living areas both from those of their servants and from the various domestic operations soon found concrete expression in the planning of their country houses. At Coleshill, Sir Roger Pratt had commenced this operation by removing the servants from the main hall down into the servants' hall in the basement, and by constructing back-stairs, to ensure that the family was not unnecessarily disturbed by the presence of servants going about their duties. By the end of the seventeenth century, this concept was being extended by placing many of the culinary and other domestic facilities in completely separate pavilions, their only connection to the main house being by corridor, colonnade, or simply the open air. In addition, this arrangement prevented the spread of odours, noise and potential fires from the kitchens to the main house, and also gave scope for the architects to adopt some of the elegant classically inspired pavilion and colonnade designs already plentifully illustrated by Palladio.

The first English houses to be built with linked pavilions appeared in the 1680s, and they became increasingly popular over the course of the following century. Their plans may be considered in the following approximately chronological sequence:

a) *Early Pavilion Kitchens*
   The earlier pavilions were relatively simple rectangular blocks projecting forward at each side of the entrance front, as at Nether Lypiatt Manor, Gloucestershire, of *c*. 1700–5, or flanking it, as at Robert Benson's Bramham Park, Yorkshire, of *c*. 1703–10.

b) *Vanburghian Pavilion Kitchens*

In the works of Sir John Vanburgh the pavilions were considerably extended forwards to line each side of massive rectangular forecourts, following Palladian precedent to enhance the majesty of the processional approach to the main house. The servants' routes between the house and the kitchen pavilion were suitably discreet, however, being channelled along a combination of internal passageways and covered colonnades. A further feature of the Vanburghian plan was the provision of a large rectangular courtyard behind each kitchen/pavilion, its outer wing providing accommodation for the brewhouses, bakehouses, washhouses, etc., necessary for the efficient operation of the house. The southern wings of these courts could also provide pleasant sunny greenhouses, chapels and eating rooms for the benefit of the principal inhabitants. These features can be seen in most of Vanburgh's great houses, including Castle Howard, Yorkshire, of 1699–1712; Blenheim Palace, Oxfordshire, of 1705–24; Eastbury, Dorset, of *c.* 1715–38; and Seaton Delaval, Northumberland, of 1720–8.

With regard to the sequence of rooms within these houses, the following charts show that they are very simple and straightforward, providing a relatively easy route from the back entrance in the kitchen court through to the dining-room:

CASTLE HOWARD, YORKSHIRE, Sir John Vanburgh, 1699–1712

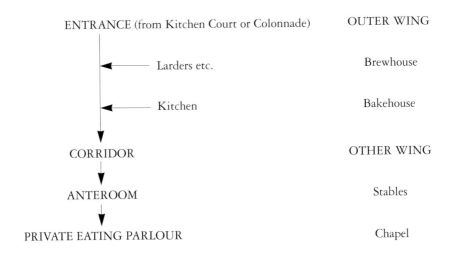

ENTRANCE (from Kitchen Court or Colonnade)	OUTER WING
Larders etc.	Brewhouse
Kitchen	Bakehouse
CORRIDOR	OTHER WING
ANTEROOM	Stables
PRIVATE EATING PARLOUR	Chapel

BLENHEIM PALACE, Sir John Vanburgh, 1705–24

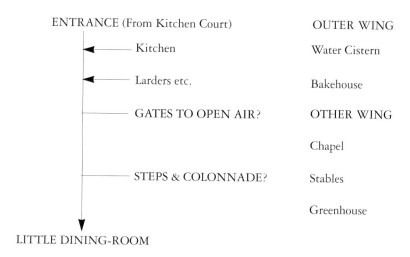

ENTRANCE (From Kitchen Court)   OUTER WING

   ← — Kitchen   Water Cistern

   ← — Larders etc.   Bakehouse

   — GATES TO OPEN AIR?   OTHER WING

        Chapel

   — STEPS & COLONNADE?   Stables

        Greenhouse

LITTLE DINING-ROOM

EASTBURY, DORSET, Sir John Vanburgh, c. 1715–38

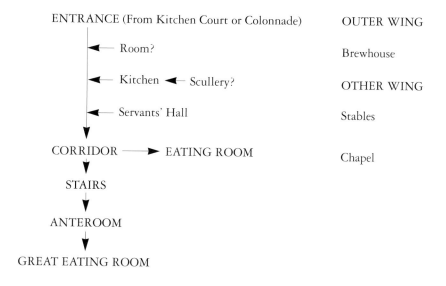

ENTRANCE (From Kitchen Court or Colonnade)   OUTER WING

   ← Room?   Brewhouse

   ← Kitchen ← Scullery?   OTHER WING

   ← Servants' Hall   Stables

CORRIDOR ⟶ EATING ROOM   Chapel

STAIRS

ANTEROOM

GREAT EATING ROOM

Although virtually no other English houses of this period approached this enormous scale and grandeur, the practice of placing pavilions at each side of a large rectangular courtyard was followed by a number of other architects,

such as Thomas Archer's Heythrop, Oxfordshire, of 1707–10; John James'
design for Wricklemarsh; Sir Gregory Page's house at Blackheath, Kent, of
1725.

c) *Linked Kitchen Pavilions*

Describing his design for Leonardo Mocenico's house, Palladio states that it
has 'Four loggias, which like arms tend to the circumference, seem to
receive those that come near the house. Near these loggias are the stables . . .
and on the part backwards, the kitchens, and the places for the steward,
and the farme . . .'. The large square house shown in his accompanying
plans has four quadrant-shaped loggias or colonnades extending the two
main façades out to kitchen and stable blocks. Other houses illustrated by
Palladio, such as those designed for Francesco Badoero and Counts
Francesco and Ludovico de Trissini show similar schemes, but with two
wings extending one frontage only. From the early eighteenth century,
both these forms were being adopted by a number of major English
architects. The four-pavilion plan was used by James Moyser and James
Paine at Nostell Priory, Yorkshire, between 1731 and the 1740s; by
William Kent at Holkham Hall, Norfolk in 1734; and by James Paine and
Robert Adam at Kedleston Hall, Derbyshire, 1757–9 and 1759–70
respectively. The two-pavilion plan was even more popular, especially with
James Paine, John Carr, James Gibbs, Samuel Saxon, Sir James Thornhill,
etc.

Usually the kitchen pavilion was of two storeys, with pastries, sculleries, larders,
etc. serving the kitchen on the ground floor, while the first floor was occupied by
servants' bedrooms and the upper part of the kitchen. The other domestic offices
devoted to food preparation, such as dairies, larders and brewhouses might be
contained within another wing, while those devoted to the service of food and the
administration of the household, including the steward's, butler's and housekeeper's
rooms, etc., were frequently arranged within the basement level of the main house.
These are only general trends, however, since the detailed arrangements differed
according to the size of the kitchen pavilion, the amount of servant accommodation
available in the main house, or in other pavilions, etc. This may be seen in the
following examples:

NOSTELL PRIORY, YORKSHIRE, James Moyser and James Paine, 1733–c. 1750

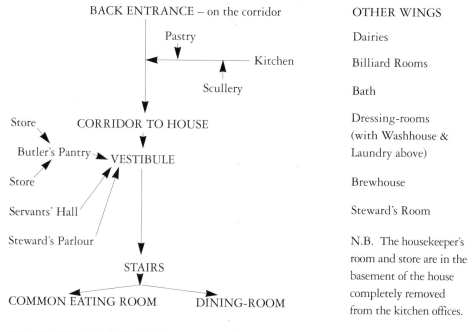

BACK ENTRANCE – on the corridor

Pastry

Kitchen

Scullery

CORRIDOR TO HOUSE

Store

Butler's Pantry → VESTIBULE

Store

Servants' Hall

Steward's Parlour

STAIRS

COMMON EATING ROOM   DINING-ROOM

OTHER WINGS

Dairies

Billiard Rooms

Bath

Dressing-rooms
(with Washhouse &
Laundry above)

Brewhouse

Steward's Room

N.B. The housekeeper's
room and store are in the
basement of the house
completely removed
from the kitchen offices.

HOLKHAM HALL, NORFOLK, W. Kent, 1734

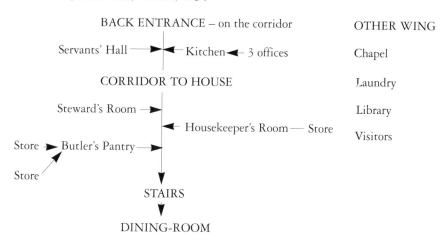

BACK ENTRANCE – on the corridor

Servants' Hall → ← Kitchen ← 3 offices

CORRIDOR TO HOUSE

Steward's Room →

← Housekeeper's Room — Store

Store → Butler's Pantry →

Store

STAIRS

DINING-ROOM

OTHER WING

Chapel

Laundry

Library

Visitors

During the late eighteenth century, a number of houses were built with much larger linked pavilions, which incorporated an improved range of domestic offices, and their own integral courtyards. Their design shows a far greater

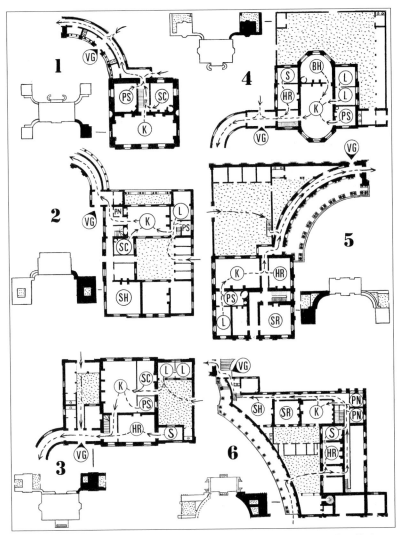

Linked kitchen pavilions. From the early eighteenth century the increasing influence of Palladian architecture and the growing number of separate rooms required in kitchen offices led to the construction of much more sophisticated pavilions either in pairs or in fours, linked to the corners of the main house by curving corridors. Some later examples filled in the triangular spaces behind their curving colonnades to produce larger kitchen wings, and broad, impressive façades to their garden fronts. 1. Nostell Priory, Yorkshire, 1733–c. 1750; 2. Buckminster Park, Leicestershire, 1795–8; 3. Denton Hall, Yorkshire, c. 1770; 4. Oakland Hall, Cheshire, 1760–7; 5. Fonthill House, Wiltshire, 1757–70; 6. Moor Park, Hertfordshire, c. 1720–8. BH bakehouse and back kitchen; HR housekeeper's room; K kitchen; L larder; PN pantry; PS pastry; S store; SC scullery; SH servants' hall; SR steward's room; VG ventilation gap.

appreciation of the kitchen processes, each functional room being arranged in logical order, to provide an efficient flow from the back entrance through to the dining-room:

OAKLAND, OR TABLEY HALL, CHESHIRE, John Carr, 1760–7

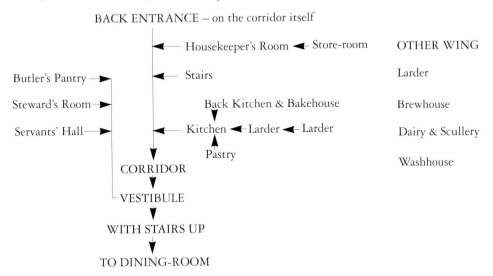

DENTON HALL, YORKSHIRE, John Carr, c. 1770

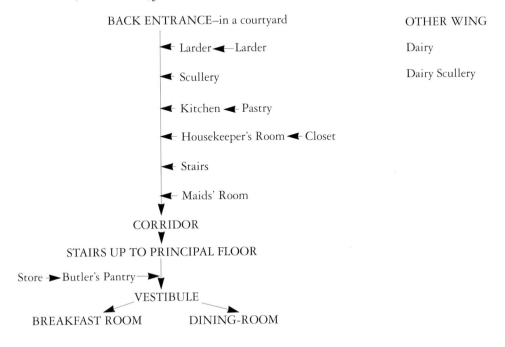

BUCKMINSTER PARK, LEICESTERSHIRE, Samuel Saxon, 1795–8

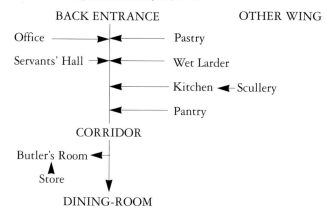

Some of Palladio's plans show quadrant-shaped linked ranges, with concave colonnades extending forward from each end of the entrance front, to mask a roughly triangular area of courtyards and domestic offices. This arrangement maintained the 'open arms' to welcome visitors to the entrance front, provided the garden front with a handsome flat façade, from which the main body of the house boldly projected, and gave useful additional space for kitchens, stables, etc. Houses such as Moor Park typify this plan ideally:

MOOR PARK, HERTFORDSHIRE, Sir James Thornhill, c. 1720–8

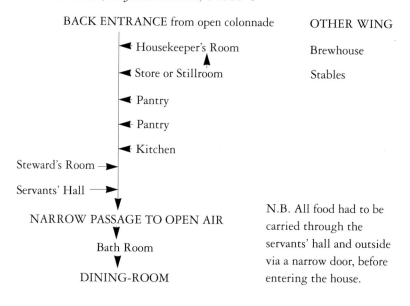

Other houses, such as Fonthill, Wiltshire and Crownest, Halifax are basically of the more usual linked pavilion plan, but have their two-storey pavilions linked to the main house by these 'triangular' single-storey areas of courtyards and minor outbuildings:

FONTHILL, WILTSHIRE, 1757–70

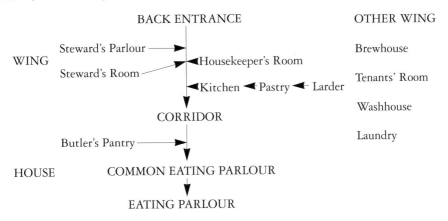

CROWNEST, HALIFAX, Thomas Bradley, 1788

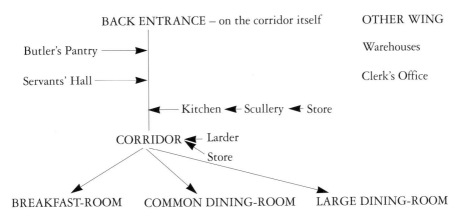

The actual linkages between the houses and their pavilions were designed in a great variety of forms to blend aesthetic considerations with such practical matters as good communications, sufficient ventilation to stop the spread of kitchen smells, the provision of convenient privies, etc. In brief, the following were the main types:

a) *Screen walls*: single walls which defined the forecourt area of the house, and restricted access through to the garden front, as at Heythrop, Oxfordshire.

b) *Square colonnades*: with columns to the forecourt side and walls on the garden side, as at Wricklemarsh, Kent; Eastbury, Dorset; and Seaton Delaval, Northumberland. These were most popular in the early eighteenth century.

c) *Quadrant colonnades*: with columns to the forecourt side and walls on the garden side, as at Moor Park, Hertfordshire, and Latham Hall, Lancashire.

d) *Square corridors*: with walls on both sides, as at Kertlington Park, Oxfordshire.

e) *Quadrant corridors*: with walls on both sides. This was the most widespread form, being used at Oaklands, Cheshire; Denton and Cusworth, Yorkshire; Sunbury, Surrey; and many other houses.

f) *Quadrant corridors*: with colonnades to the forecourt. These 'double' linkages had the advantage of presenting an impressive open colonnade towards the forecourt, which would not be encumbered by the passage of servants, since they could now pass unseen to and from the house through the corridor behind. This type was built at Fonthill, Wiltshire and Houghton, Norfolk, for example.

In the hands of an ingenious architect, the design of the linkages could greatly enhance the communication between the house and its kitchen pavilion. This is perhaps best seen at Kedleston, Derbyshire, in the work of James Paine, 1757–9, and Robert Adam, 1759–70. Here the ground floor of the link is a quadrant corridor with an open arcade towards the forecourt, but the first floor is a single wide and well-lit corridor, heated with its own fireplace, which provides access from the kitchen stairs directly into the dining-room. Presumably this area was used as a serving-room, greatly improving the ease with which hot food could be delivered promptly to the dining table:

KEDLESTON HALL, DERBYSHIRE, James Paine, 1757–9 and Robert Adam, 1759–70

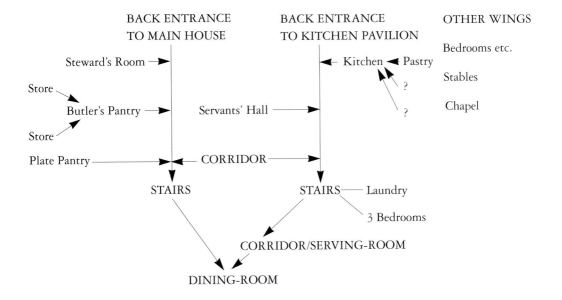

5. *'Northern' Kitchen Wings with Courtyards*

In his design for a large town house for Count Iseppo de Porti, Palladio had shown how a large atrium or courtyard at the back of the major house could be further extended by an additional wing for the use of visitors etc. Translated into the needs of the English country house, this formula could leave the main body of the house completely unencumbered by projecting wings etc., so that light could flood into it from the east, south and west throughout the course of the day. It also gave greater privacy, and provided uninterrupted views from all the major rooms. To the north of the house, the kitchen wing and other domestic offices could then be arranged around a courtyard, with a back entrance at the rear of the whole structure. Roger or William Hurlbutt used this arrangement at Maiden Bradley in Wiltshire, around 1683, which had a kitchen wing running down one side of the courtyard, to a stable-block at the rear. James Wyatt's Bowden Park, Wiltshire, built over a century later in 1796, has kitchen offices round two sides of his courtyard, with a greenhouse forming the third side, to produce a very efficient plan (p. 63):

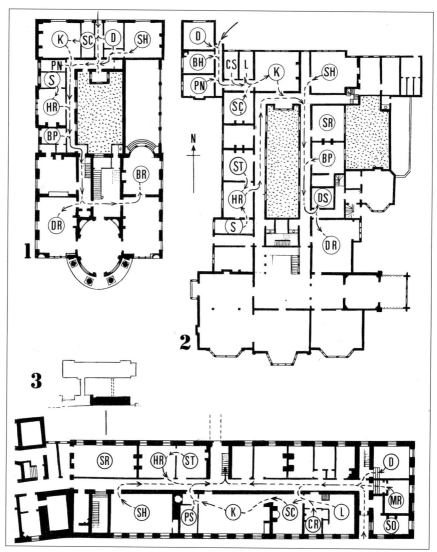

'Northern' kitchen wings and separate kitchen blocks. The efficient plan of putting the kitchens to the cool north side of the house, leaving the east, south and west sides open to the sunlight and good views, was first introduced in the late seventeenth century, and continued in popularity for two hundred years. 1. Bowden Park, Wiltshire, 1796; 2. Tortworth Court, Gloucestershire, 1849–52. Other kitchens were built as completely separate blocks. 3. Petworth House, Sussex, mid-eighteenth century. BH bakehouse; BP butler's pantry; BR breakfast-room; CR cook's room; CS china store; D dairy; DR dining-room; DS dinner service room; HR housekeeper's room; K kitchen; L larder; MR meat room; PN pantry; PS pastry; S store; SC scullery; SH servants' hall; SO steward's office; SR steward's room; ST stillroom.

BOWDEN PARK, WILTSHIRE, James Wyatt, 1796

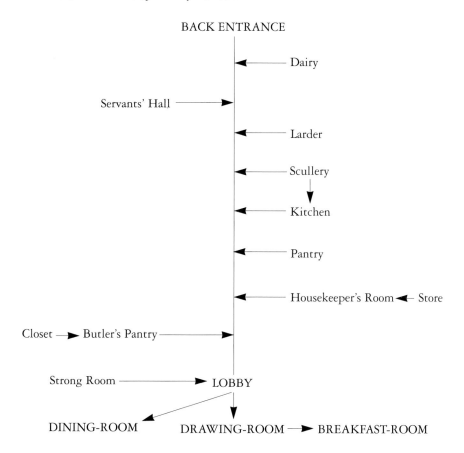

Robert Adam was familiar with it too, as may be seen in his unexecuted designs for Saltram of 1779.

This classical plan-form continued in use even when country houses began to be built in the Gothic revival style from the late eighteenth century onwards. Examples include William Railton's Beaumanor Park of 1845; and S.S. Teulon's Tortworth Court of 1849–52. In the latter, we can see how it has been adapted to keep the male and female sides divided by the courtyard:

TORTWORTH COURT, GLOUCESTERSHIRE, S.S. Teulon, 1849–52

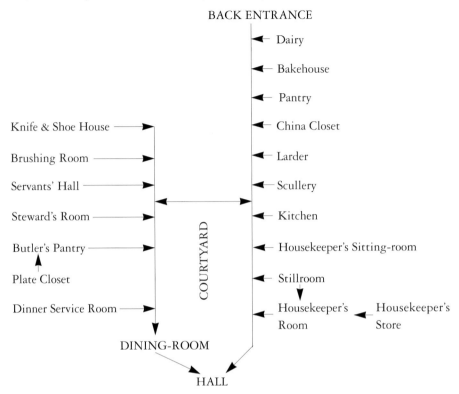

Even as late as 1876–8, Norman Shaw was using elements of the same general arrangement at Pierrepont, Surrey, although by this time it was heavily disguised beneath a pronounced 'Old English' asymmetry.

In a further group of houses, a single kitchen wing, almost identical to one of the kitchen pavilions discussed earlier, was built to the north of the main block, being joined to it by a short link-block of service rooms. This arrangement combined the advantages of the pavilion, since it effectively separated the kitchen and servant quarters from those occupied by the family, while still preserving the open aspects of the east, south and west façades. Winestead, or Red Hall, Yorkshire, probably built with the advice of Lord Burlington in the 1720s; and James Paine's St Ives, Bingley, Yorkshire of 1767, provide good examples of this type:

RED HALL, WINESTEAD, YORKSHIRE, Lord Burlington?, 1720s

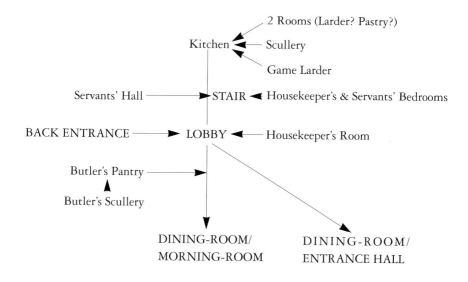

6. *Detached Kitchen Blocks*

Where the kitchen quarters needed to be so large that they could not be conveniently built on to the main house, or where there was a great desire to keep all evidence of domestic activity completely out of sight, they could be placed in a detached block some distance away. Communication to and from the house could be through the open air or a bridge over the moat as at Coughton Court, Warwickshire, but a subterranean tunnel ensured that the servants were never seen, and rarely heard, by the family and their guests. At Uppark, for example, food was carried from the eighteenth-century detached kitchen block to the house through an underground passage, along which charcoal-heated wooden trollies were trundled, the dishes then being carried up the back stairs to a service lobby adjoining the dining-room. In some of the larger houses, these blocks could grow to an enormous size, that at Petworth measuring some 200 by 50 feet, with long central corridors giving access to a full range of domestic offices on the ground floor, and staff bedrooms at first floor level. Here we can see the offices set out in an almost idealized manner, designed to process the food smoothly and efficiently from the larders and sculleries, through the kitchens etc., through the tunnel leading into the basement of the main house, and on into the dining-rooms:

PETWORTH, SUSSEX

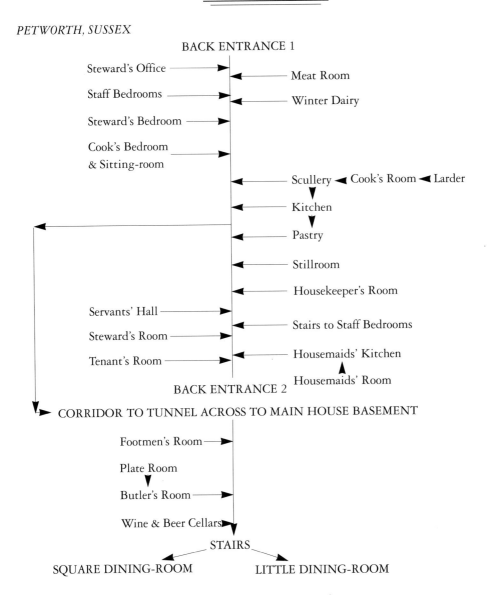

7. *Later Basement Kitchens*

Basement kitchens continued to be built through into the early nineteenth century. At best, they continued the spinal corridor plan first seen at Coleshill, or, in the case of larger houses, they had their offices arranged around corridors encircling courtyards, or rather large light-wells, in the flanking wings, as at John Carr's Harewood House (p. 68):

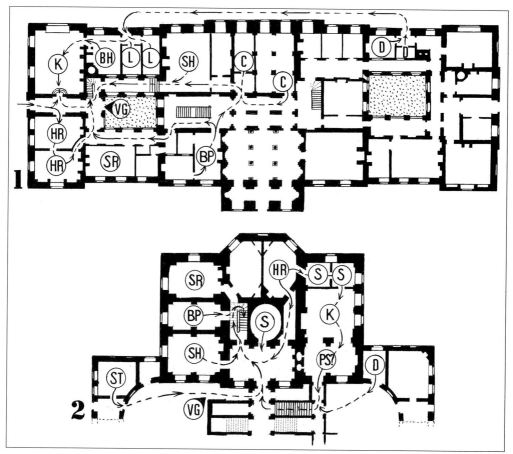

Later basement kitchens. As houses increased in size and the number of domestic offices increased, the basement kitchen of the later eighteenth century had to be skilfully designed. John Carr's Harewood House has a very efficient plan, while Leadbetter's Newnham must have been difficult to operate, with the kitchen two floors below the dining-room, the stillroom distant from the housekeeper's room, and relatively awkward routing for the reception and service of the food. 1. Harewood House, Yorkshire, 1759–71; 2. Newnham, Oxfordshire, 1756–64. BH bakehouse; BP butler's pantry; C cellars; D dairy; HR housekeeper's room; K kitchen; L larder; PS pastry; S store; SR steward's room; ST stillroom; VG ventilation gap.

HAREWOOD HOUSE, YORKSHIRE, John Carr, 1759–71

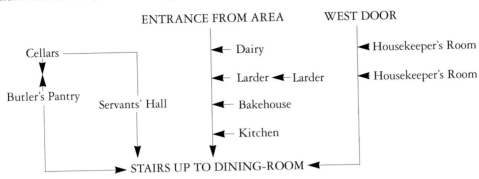

In other houses, however, the architects concentrated their efforts on providing elegant accommodation on the ground and first floors, then packing the domestic offices into the spaces left between the foundation walls at basement level. William Chambers' Castle Hill, Dorset of *c.* 1760 has long cul-de-sacs, and awkward passage-ways, which must have made it difficult to work in, while S. Leadbetter's Newnham, Oxfordshire, of 1756–64, is similarly congested, especially since the only entrance, and the sole way up to the ground floor, had to be contrived amid the convolutions of the external entrance staircase:

CASTLE HILL, DORSET, Sir William Chambers, c. 1760

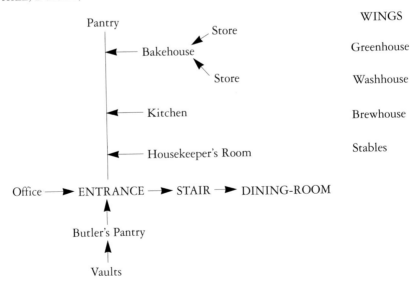

NEWNHAM, OXFORDSHIRE, Stiff Leadbetter, 1756–64

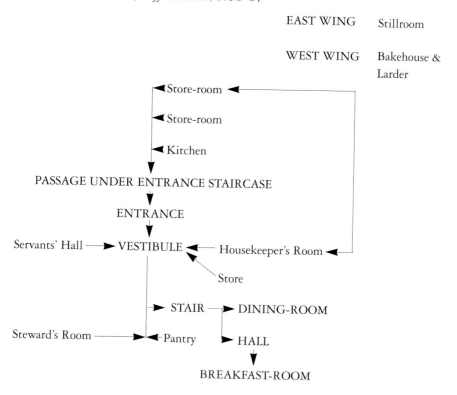

From the early nineteenth century, whatever the plan of the house itself, the kitchen quarters were largely designed in one of three ways.

8. *Courtyard Kitchens*

These kitchens, found only in the largest houses, were planned around a central courtyard, which served largely as a light-well. It was particularly suitable for houses in the Elizabethan and Jacobean styles, such as Barry's Canford Manor of 1848–53; Paxton and Stokes' Mentmore of 1857; D. Brandon's Hemstead House of 1862; or Hanbury Tracy's Toddington, Gloucestershire of 1820–35. This plan, popular in the greater houses built between the 1820s and mid–1860s, enabled a full range of service rooms to be linked in a logical and efficient order along good communication corridors, even though the distance between the kitchen and the dining-rooms could be considerable:

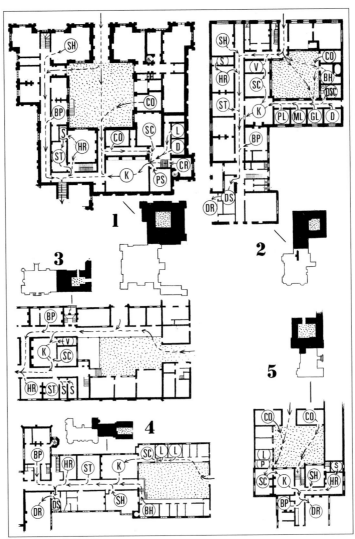

Courtyard kitchens. The kitchen wings of the great mid-Victorian 'Elizabethan' and 'Jacobean' mansions were so large that they had to be built around a large courtyard, which served mainly as a source of light and ventilation for the surrounding rooms. 1. Mentmore, Buckinghamshire, 1857; 2. Hemstead House, Kent, 1862. For smaller houses, an open courtyard with cart access to coal sheds, larders, bakehouses and similar preparation rooms were much more convenient; 3. Great Moreton Hall, Cheshire, 1841–3; 4. Batsford Park, Gloucestershire, 1887–93; 5. Crendle Court, Dorset, 1908–9. BP butler's pantry; CO coals; CR cook's room; D dairy; DR dining-room; DS dinner service room; DSC dairy scullery; GL game larder; HR housekeeper's room; K kitchen; L larder; ML meat larder; P pots; PL pastry larder; PS pastry; S store; SC scullery; SH servants' hall; ST stillroom; V vegetable store.

MENTMORE, BUCKINGHAMSHIRE, Paxton and Stokes, 1857

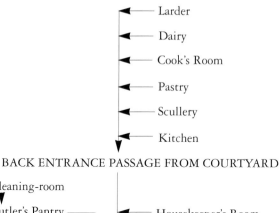

Larder

Dairy

Cook's Room

Pastry

Scullery

Kitchen

BACK ENTRANCE PASSAGE FROM COURTYARD

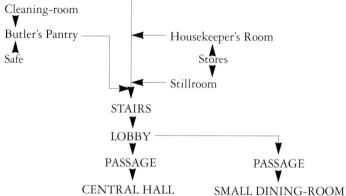

Cleaning-room

Butler's Pantry — Housekeeper's Room

Safe

Stores

Stillroom

STAIRS

LOBBY

PASSAGE   PASSAGE

CENTRAL HALL   SMALL DINING-ROOM

DINING-ROOM

HEMSTEAD HOUSE, KENT, D. Brandon, 1862

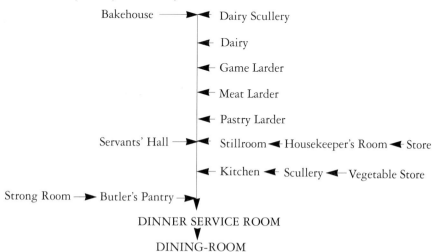

Bakehouse — Dairy Scullery

Dairy

Game Larder

Meat Larder

Pastry Larder

Servants' Hall — Stillroom ◄ Housekeeper's Room ◄ Store

Kitchen ◄ Scullery ◄ Vegetable Store

Strong Room — Butler's Pantry

DINNER SERVICE ROOM

DINING-ROOM

TODDINGTON MANOR, GLOUCESTERSHIRE, *Hanbury Tracy, 1820–35*

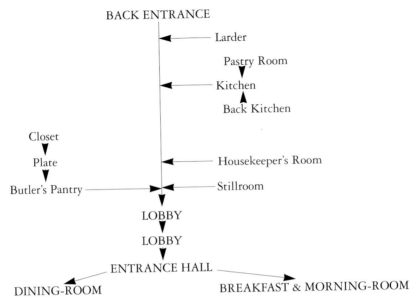

9. *Corridor and Open Courtyard Plan*

During the 1840s a very practical form of kitchen wing was developed in which the main domestic offices were contained within a rectangular block abutting one side of the main house. A central corridor running through its centre led to a long courtyard, its sides being lined with the minor offices of coals, laundry, brewhouse, etc., while its furthest end was open to provide good cart access. Edward Blore's Great Moreton Hall of 1841–3 was of this type, but, being an extremely large house, it had two parallel corridors running through from the house to the courtyard. Other examples include Ashwicke Hall, Somerset, of 1857–60; Dobroyd Castle, Yorkshire, of 1865–9; Cloverley, Shropshire, of 1864–70; Hassobury, Essex, of 1866–70; Clouds, Wiltshire, of 1881–6; and Batsford Park, Gloucestershire, of 1887–93. In smaller houses, especially those with Elizabethan or Jacobean E- or H-plans, the kitchens could even occupy one of the major cross-wings, almost returning to the medieval tradition, as at Avon Tyrell, Hampshire, of 1890–2; and Crendle Court, Dorset, of 1908–9. One of the great advantages of this plan, in addition to its compactness and practicality, was that the kitchen was very close to the dining-room, only twenty feet separating their doors at Ashwicke Hall, which ensured that the food could arrive on the table in prime, hot condition, and with a minimum of labour for carrying:

STANDEN, SUSSEX, Philip Webb, 1891–2

BACK ENTRANCE

Larder

Larder

Cook's Pantry

Scullery

Servants' Hall — Kitchen ◄—— Store

Butler's Pantry

CORRIDOR

DINING-ROOM

BATSFORD PARK, GLOUCESTERSHIRE, George and Peto, 1887–93

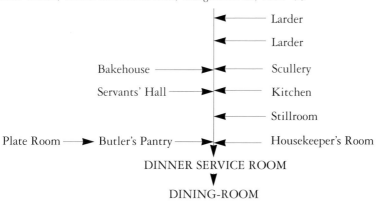

Larder

Larder

Bakehouse — Scullery

Servants' Hall — Kitchen

Stillroom

Plate Room → Butler's Pantry — Housekeeper's Room

DINNER SERVICE ROOM

DINING-ROOM

CRENDLE COURT, DORSET, Walter Brierley, 1908–9

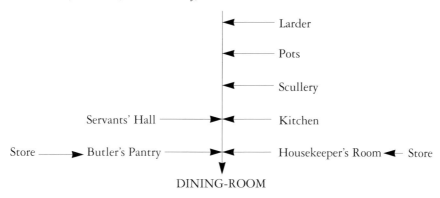

Larder

Pots

Scullery

Servants' Hall — Kitchen

Store → Butler's Pantry — Housekeeper's Room ◄— Store

DINING-ROOM

10.   *Corridor Kitchen Wings*

From the late eighteenth century the kitchen wings in an increasing number of smaller country houses began to adopt a very flexible plan, in which the various domestic offices were arranged along one or both sides of a corridor leading from the back entrance through to the dining-room. In the smallest of the symmetrically planned houses, the corridor could take a simple straight course along its route. However, in the more interesting free-planned houses, especially those in the popular Gothic or Old English styles, it could change direction every few yards, still retaining its efficiency as a means of communication, but giving the architect great scope to achieve an exciting massing of his buildings. At first it may appear strange that such an effective formula had not been adopted before, but this plan could only be implemented where only a limited number of domestic offices were necessary, for it certainly could never have coped with the requirements of the greater houses of the eighteenth and nineteenth centuries.

CONCLUSION

This study of the English country house kitchen and its plan has traced the developments from the sixteenth and seventeenth centuries, when there were relatively few rooms and an all-male staff, on to the mid-seventeenth century, when there was an increasing number of rooms; the introduction of a distinct female side to the domestic quarters, and a pronounced division between the polite and service areas of the house. The late seventeenth century saw the removal of the kitchens into separate, but linked, kitchen pavilions, to distance their noise, smells and traffic from the residential areas, while in the nineteenth century kitchens tended not only to move closer to the house, but also to expand in size in order to accommodate an ever-increasing number of separate rooms for each separate function. As the expense of maintaining large households then began to rise, and as transport facilities, food preservation and food production methods became much more efficient, the size of the kitchen quarters began to shrink, so that more compact and convenient plans could serve the needs of the country house. Finally, due to the social and economic changes of inter-war years, most country house kitchens ceased to function, their place usually being taken by well-equipped, compact modern kitchens placed as close as possible to the family's dining-room.

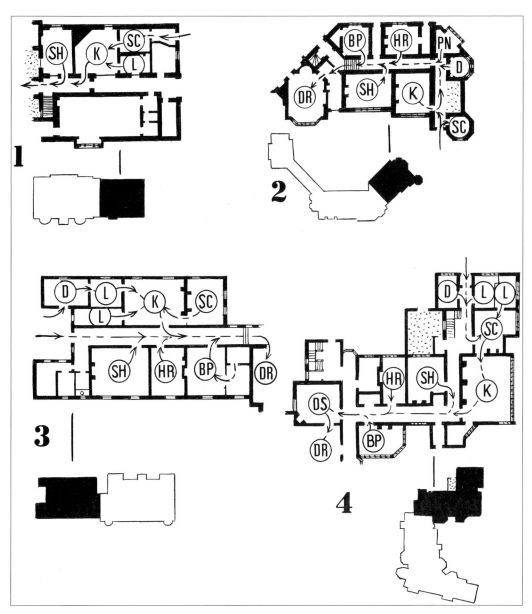

Corridor kitchen wings. In many of the smaller country houses, whether of classical symmetry or Gothic revival free-planning, one of the most convenient arrangements was to place the various kitchen offices at both sides of a long corridor which proceeded from the back entrance through to the dining-room. 1. Claverton Manor, Somerset, c. 1820 (classical); 2. Endsleigh, Devon, c. 1810 (Gothic); 3. Wittington, Buckinghamshire, 1898 (classical); 4. Bidston Court, Cheshire, 1891–2 (Gothic). BP butler's pantry; D dairy; DR dining-room; DS dinner service room; HR housekeeper's room; K kitchen; L larder; PN pantry; SC scullery; SH servants' hall.

It must be stressed, however, that these are only the major national trends, for, as with all aspects of human history, each particular household continued to modify its kitchen facilities, rebuilding, extending or re-planning them to accommodate its changing circumstances. Each individual kitchen therefore has its own particular story to tell, and its own particular contribution to offer to the understanding of the household it served, probably throughout many centuries of continuous production.

CHAPTER THREE

COOKS, KITCHEN-MAIDS AND KITCHEN HELPERS IN THE COUNTRY HOUSE

C. Anne Wilson

The commanding figure in the country house kitchen was, of course, the cook. Some people might think the cook was the most important member of the entire domestic staff, but in fact he or she had a very precise position in the hierarchy of the household. In the grandest houses the man-cook ranked not only below the house-steward, but also below the clerk of the kitchen.

The clerk held a post that went back to medieval times and continued in the greatest country houses of the eighteenth and nineteenth centuries. He was responsible for the purchase of all produce not supplied to the house either by the estate itself or through gifts – for the butcher's meat, fish, vegetables, fruit, dairy produce and eggs that were converted in the kitchen into meals for family, guests and servants. Either he or the house-steward, according to the arrangements within a particular household, ordered the grocer's goods such as sugar loaves, spices, dried fruits, oil, tea and coffee, from the nearest town and sometimes even from London. But it was the clerk who checked off all these foodstuffs when they were delivered, and entered their value in his account books. He also bought kitchen wares – pots, pans, cloth for pudding and jelly bags, tape for binding collars of meat, scrubbing brushes and pails and the many other items needed to maintain the work of the kitchen, and duly accounted for them in his books.

The clerk of the kitchen was responsible for seeing that foodstuffs were safely stored away. He kept the keys to the main cupboards in the store-room, and made sure they did not fall into the hands of any unauthorized person.[1] With several people at work in the kitchen and surrounding areas there was always the risk that one or two might take to pilfering, passing out food to relatives or friends who called at the back door, or selling it to pedlars.

Another task for the clerk was the distribution of the sugar, spices and other storegoods to the cook each morning to meet the needs for the meals immediately

A man-cook at work in his kitchen. (A. Chambers,
The Ladies Best Companion, c. *1800)*

in view. He was in a good position to judge what quantities should be taken out of store and transferred into kitchen containers, because he drew up the menus, showed them to the mistress of the house for her approval or amendment, and then instructed the cook accordingly.

The cook's main responsibility was the cooking of the more complicated dishes on the menu. Plain cookery for the family table and for the servants' meals was carried out by his assistants in the kitchen, as were such jobs as preparing vegetables and washing and scouring the utensils after use. The cook-maids or kitchen-maids and scullery-maid were lower servants who worked to the command of the cook. But the cook, although he was subordinate to the clerk of the kitchen, still counted as an upper servant, with privileges such as taking his breakfast, supper and the second course of dinner in the steward's room along with the other upper servants. The cook also had a room of his own where he slept at night. The room was usually on the same floor as the kitchen and not far away, making it a convenient spot for him to retire to during the day if, for instance, he wanted to sit down and work out the details of a recipe away from the noise and heat of the kitchen.

This was the arrangement in the large country houses of wealthy and noble families. In other larger houses the office of the clerk of the kitchen had already disappeared by the eighteenth century, with his former duties divided between the house-steward and the cook. This usually meant that the cook did a lot of his own marketing, and planned the menus himself.

But in medium sized and small houses, there was already a bigger female element in the kitchen staffing arrangements. Here it was the housekeeper who was responsible for buying provisions and recording them in her account book, for drawing up menus and discussing them with the mistress of the house, for issuing foods from store to the cook each morning, for making desserts and cakes in the still-room, and for preserving, jam-making and pickling when fruits and vegetables were in season. All this she did in addition to her duties connected with the maintenance of the rest of the house, that is to say, looking after the furniture and linen and organizing the work of the housemaids. (In the very large houses the housekeeper's whole time was taken up with these latter duties, but of course those houses had more furniture and linen to be looked after, and more housemaids to keep an eye on.)

A woman-cook and maids at work. (M. Bradley, The British Housewife, *vol. 1, 1756)*

The smaller houses with their busy housekeepers also tended to have women cooks. As in the great houses, the housekeeper and the cook were upper servants, but the wages of a woman-cook were lower than those of a man-cook. Both housekeeper and cook had bedrooms of their own. That of the woman-cook was usually on the attic floor not far from the rooms of the kitchen-maids, with the housekeeper's bedroom either on the same floor or on the floor below near the back staircase. But the housekeeper had in addition a sitting-room-cum-office near the kitchen, where the senior staff met to take most of their meals, and where both cook and housekeeper could retire during any off-duty time they were able to take during the day.

It was more economical to employ a woman-cook, not only because of the wage differential, but also because having a man-cook involved the further expense of the servants' tax. From 1777 onwards the employers of menservants had to pay a tax on each one (originally imposed to help meet the costs of the American War of Independence). By 1808 the tax had risen to a scale that began at £2 4s 0d for a single male servant (who almost certainly would not have been a cook), and increased according to the number of male servants kept, up to £7 1s 0d each for eleven or more.[2] Although it was gradually reduced through the nineteenth century, this tax remained in force until the 1930s, when it was 15s 0d a servant; and it was finally abolished in 1937. Those who employed the lower-cost women-cooks often preferred to engage one who had formerly been first kitchen-maid or cook-maid to a male cook. Several late eighteenth-century newspaper advertisements draw attention to this by requiring, or advertising, a woman-cook who has 'lived under a man-cook'.[3]

In 1745 Jonathan Swift made the distinction between 'the custom . . . among People of Quality to keep men-cooks and generally of the French Nation' and 'the general Run of Knights, Squires and Gentlemen', whose cooks were women.[4] French cooks were well established in England long before the French Revolution when their numbers were increased by refugee cooks who had lost their noble masters in France. The upsurge of interest in French cookery in Court circles was probably due to the influence of Henrietta Maria, Charles I's Queen, and it was reinforced through the years when Charles II and his close supporters were in exile before 1660, and were enjoying French cuisine in its native land. All the important French cookery books were soon translated and brought out in English versions. Examples are: La Varenne's *The French Cook*, first published in England in 1653; Massialot's *The Court and Country Cook* in 1702; La Chapelle's *The Modern Cook* in 1736; and Beauvillier's *The Art of French Cookery* in 1824. French cookery was more complex than English, requiring meat dishes to be partially cooked with one set of seasonings, and then finished off with a different, elaborate and highly flavoured sauce.

The Fortescues of Castle Hill in Devon paid £50 a year to their French cook in 1792, a large sum compared with the average of £10 or £12 paid to English women-cooks in the 1790s.[5] But he was no doubt one in a long series: in the family's library were a 1736 edition of La Chapelle's *The Modern Cook* and the original French first edition of Beauvillier's *L'Art du Cuisinier* of 1814.[6]

A French man-cook was complete master in his kitchen. He organized his own

Men at work at an oven and charcoal stove. (From the title-page of A. Beauvilliers, L'Art du Cuisinier, *vol. 2, 1814)*

marketing, and dictated the timetable of his many assistants. He dealt direct with his employers when it came to menu-planning. In the words of the anonymous author of *A Treatise on the Use and Abuse of the Second Table*, written about 1750, the French cook 'so soon as he has found how to please the palate of his master, he immediately becomes absolute, and a daily consultation with him is necessary'.[7] So we can imagine the Earls Fortescue and their French cooks poring over the French cookery books together in the library.

In the mid-nineteenth century Charles Pierce described the man-cook as 'this artist' and noted:

It is usual for the cook when he has to present himself for orders, to do so in his full kitchen costume, with his jacket, apron and cap, and not to remove his cap, even in the presence of royalty. His dress should be the pattern of neatness and cleanliness, and his manners agree with his dress.[8]

Eighteenth-century kitchen staff attired in clothes of their own choice. (E. Smith, The Compleat Housewife,
11th edn, 1742)

In the eighteenth century indoor servants, other than the liveried footmen, still normally wore clothes of their own choice (or, in some cases, cast-offs donated by their employers). The French cook, with his high wages, would have been able to appear attired in the fashionable clothing of his day. Eventually this freedom was to give way to the more uniform white jacket and cap and cook's apron, while female kitchen workers began to wear uniform print dresses, with white caps and aprons.

The French cook was undoubtedly a professed cook, but professed cooks could be Englishmen too, and also Englishwomen. The word simply implied that the cook had had some training under a more experienced cook, whether French or English, who could interpret menus, and if necessary draw them up, and who understood the preparation of 'fashionable foreign delicacies', and knew how to introduce 'certain seasonings and flavours to his dishes, which render them more inviting to the palate of his employer'.[9] Most substantial country houses would have had a professed cook at the head of their kitchen staff.

Working under the direction of that cook and assisting him or her was the first kitchen-maid, sometimes called the first cook-maid. She was expected to take charge of all the roasted and boiled meats, and she also did most of the plain cooking, including making simple puddings. She cooked the meals for the servants' hall, and the food for the nursery. In some households she prepared the sauces and gravies for the family's table. The second kitchen-maid cleaned and trimmed the vegetables, plucked, drew and trussed the poultry and game, trimmed joints and meat cutlets, and scaled and filleted fish, carrying out most of this work on a dresser in the scullery adjoining the kitchen. She laid the table for meals in the servants' hall; and in some establishments she baked the bread for the household in the bakehouse.[10] In the larger houses there was also a pastry-maid, with her own separate dresser or table in the kitchen well away from the fire for pastry-making. In the largest houses of all there was a completely separate pastry-room, usually off the kitchen, where the pastry-maid carried out her work.[11] Alternatively, pastry was both prepared and baked in the stillroom. At the busiest times all the maids were in the kitchen, most of them in close attendance on the cook, grinding and chopping, mixing and beating, and otherwise transforming raw ingredients to be incorporated at the right moment into the more elaborate dishes which he or she was preparing. Meanwhile, further down the long table, one junior maid gave similar assistance to the first cook-maid or kitchen-maid who was at work on her contributions to the meal.

Keele Hall kitchen, c. 1900. The principal French man-cook stands at the table with the second and third men-cooks behind him. At the back of the room are the family's butcher and their game and fish supplier, and their head gardener is in the doorway. One English cookmaid is at the front of the table, while two others stand at the side of the room. (Keele University Library)

The scullery-maid was the lowliest member of the kitchen staff, with the dreary task of washing and scouring all the kitchen pots, pans and other utensils after use, to the great detriment of the skin on her hands. Copper pans could be scoured with a brush and sand, and great stress was placed on making them totally clean, so that no trace of verdigris lurked in the angles. Tinned copper vessels could not be sanded inside for fear of scratching off the tin coating, but had to be soaked with water, gently cleaned with a cloth and, according to one authority, any specks remaining on the tin 'may be removed by scraping with the nails'.[12] The scullery was the source of hot water, for cleaning and other purposes: it was heated in a boiler over its own fire; and there was a cold water supply to the sinks, which were usually sited under the windows. The scullery-maid also assisted with the cleaning of vegetables, plucking of fowls and scaling of fish.

The lower servants, including most of the maids, took all their main meals in the servants' hall. At the end of the morning's work they were joined there for the first course of dinner by the upper servants. The butler carved the meat, the cook served out the vegetables, and the filled plates were passed to each person on the staff in strict order of precedence. Then the seniors rose and departed to the housekeeper's or steward's room where they took their second course, which often consisted of superior fare left over from the family's table, while the lower servants tucked into plain puddings back in the hall. The stillroom maid or the steward's boy was also obliged to leave after the first course in order to wait upon the upper servants.

Only the junior kitchen-maid and the scullery-maid had no part in the communal dinner in the servants' hall. They ate at a table in the kitchen, so they could keep an eye on the food cooking there. Doris Clarke, scullery-maid and afterwards third kitchen-maid at Shugborough Hall in Staffordshire during the 1920s, recalled the delicious food she ate in the kitchen as being much better than that in the servants' hall.[13] This tradition is likely to go back a long way, and was probably due to generous quantities of food cooked for the family's table, so that when it had all been dished and garnished, there was enough left over to supply the next dinner for the kitchen watchers.

There was of course considerable variation in staffing levels between large country seats of the nobility and the smaller homes of local squires of the manor. The largest establishments might have a second male cook to assist the principal one, as well as additional kitchen-maids. Again, the distribution of the lowlier tasks could vary slightly, shared out in different ways between the junior kitchen-maids and scullery-maid.

Sometimes there was a kitchen-boy or kitchen-man near the bottom of the hierarchy.[14] This was the case at Erddig in Clwyd in the later eighteenth century. Here the housekeeper, the cook and the other kitchen staff were all women. But Philip Yorke, owner of Erddig, thought highly enough of Jack Nicholas, the kitchen-man, to have his portrait painted, and to adorn it with his own verse in praise of:

. . . him that waited on the Cook
And many a walk to Wrexham took,
Whether the season cold or hot,
A constant Porter to the pot:
Then in the Kitchen corner stuck,
He pluck'd the fowl, and drew the duck,
Or with the basket on his knees,
Was sheller-general to the peas . . .[15]

Jack Nicholas, kitchen-man at Erddig, near Wrexham, painted in 1791 (detail). (National Trust and the Courtauld Institute of Art)

Several manuals were published during the eighteenth and nineteenth centuries advising on the duties of servants. They stress the importance of cleanliness: the personal cleanliness of the cook and the maids who prepared food in and around the kitchen; and the cleanliness of the kitchen, its scullery and larders. In spite of the higher value placed on male cooks, the following observation appeared in 1835 in the fourth edition of *The Servants' Guide and Family Manual*: 'Cleanliness is considered the first virtue of every cook; in this respect females are considered superior to those of the other sex.'[16] More than sixty years earlier Eliza Haywood had given advice to kitchen-maids: 'Be particularly careful to keep all the utensils in the kitchen free from any kind of dirt or rust, and your hands very well washed and your nails close pared before you touch the meat.'[17]

Country house owners today may sometimes have to discourage smoking among members of the kitchen staff.

During the eighteenth century the problem was snuff-taking. Eliza Haywood also pointed out, in 1771, that 'it is very odious for servants to use themselves to the taking of snuff. The most careful cannot answer, that what they are dressing may not be spiced with some of this powder, which is so finely ground . . . that in the very opening of the box that contains it, you may see the dust fly out.'[18]

Keeping the workplace clean meant that kitchen- and scullery-maids had to rise early, at six o'clock or before. In the kitchen the fire-grate was cleared out (if the ashes had not been removed the night before), the fire was re-laid, and the ironwork of the fireplace and range was wiped over daily and blackleaded every two or three days. The kitchen floor was swept each day and washed twice a week at least, and the fire was lit before the kitchen-maids began with preparations for breakfast. An additional task for the first kitchen-maid in Victorian times was to prepare and take a morning tea tray at about 7.00 a.m. to the professed woman-cook, who did not make an appearance downstairs until shortly before the upper servants' breakfast.[19] Meanwhile the scullery-maid washed the scullery floor and cleaned the floors of the larders, the passages and the servants' hall.

The stillroom maid rose equally early to clean the housekeeper's room, re-lay and light the fire and lay the upper servants' breakfast table. She also had to make ready the morning tea trays for the family and guests. Either she or a kitchen-maid baked the rolls for the family's breakfast (though the dough might be prepared and left to prove overnight).

During the day tables and dressers in the kitchen were scrubbed after use by the junior kitchen-maids, and used pudding cloths, tapes and jelly-bags were washed by the first kitchen-maid. The scullery-maid had to work hard to keep her scullery clean, clearing away the garbage from meat, fish and vegetables, scrubbing the dresser frequently, and swilling over the paved floor with water carried off by a drain which passed under an outer wall. 'The drainage is important,' wrote the Victorian architect Robert Kerr, 'for the vapours from a scullery drain are notably unpleasant.'[20]

The cook was entitled to certain perquisites: dripping, bones and fat trimmed from meat, rabbit skins, used tea-leaves (in the days when China tea was expensive, and Indian tea unknown); in some houses the cook could also claim worn tablecloths, rags and broken metal objects.[21] All these could be sold off. There were various ways of increasing the volume of dripping, by roasting joints very dry, by melting butter to oil and mixing it in, and even by melting down old candle ends.[22] Several authors refer to the candle ends; they were really the butler's perquisite, but some evidently came into the hands of the more unscrupulous cooks.

There were also gains to be made by the person who did the marketing, either cook or housekeeper or, in the greatest houses, the clerk of the kitchen. Tradespeople were happy to allow commission to the servant who placed the orders, in return for the custom of a large household. This did not, of course, show up in the household books where the full price for each item was set down. An example is Mary Webster, who worked as cook and cook-housekeeper at Erddig for over thirty years in the mid-nineteenth century, and who had more than £1,300 in her bank account when she died in 1875.[23] Her total earnings during her career at Erddig would have added up to a good deal less, and the inference must be that she had a good working relationship with the shopkeepers of Wrexham.

The country house family often transferred itself to a house in London, or Edinburgh in the case of the Scottish family, for the 'season' each year. This made a welcome change for those servants chosen to accompany their employers: the cook, and as many maids and menservants as were needed to maintain the lifestyle of the capital.[24] Many dinner parties were given in the town house, but there were also frequent evenings when the family dined out with friends, allowing the kitchen and other servants time for social life of their own, either entertaining fellow servants from other houses belowstairs, or going out to alehouses, tea-gardens or clubs.[25] Marketing could provide both social and financial opportunities, for in some families very little food was sent up from the country estate, and most if not all of the provisions for the household had to be purchased from city shops, where tradespeople vied in offering perks to the cook so as to win the chance to supply the family – at high prices – throughout the season.[26]

But once the season was over, family and servants returned to their country house and its familiar routines. There, in the kitchen, with a small team working so close together for long hours, life must sometimes have been fraught with personal tensions. But it was a life involving much cooperation too, and where the team was a happy one, the cook's best perk of all may well have been job satisfaction. Cooks who were backed up by helpful assistants and were able to rely on fine quality

Daguerrotype of servants outside Erddig in 1852. Mary Webster, holding a fowl, is second from left in the front row. (National Trust)

ingredients for their dishes, many of them produced locally on or near the estate, and whose culinary creations won appreciation and praise from the family and their guests, must have enjoyed a great sense of achievement. For such a cook the kitchen was a miniature kingdom of which he or she was monarch. But even the lowlier maids and kitchen helpers, in a well-run house, shared shelter, security, companionship and enough to eat, as well as the hard work of the kitchen;[27] and they could count themselves well off in comparison with many of their friends and relatives in the world outside.

NOTES

1. J.J. Hecht, *The Domestic Servant Class in Eighteenth-century England* (London, 1956), pp. 42–3.

2. P. Horn, *The Rise and Fall of the Victorian Servant* (Dublin, 1975), p. 9.

3. Hecht, *Domestic Servant Class*, p. 65.

4. J. Swift, *Directions to Servants* (London, 1745), p. 17.

5. T. Jaine, 'Castle Hill, Devon', in C.A. Wilson (ed.), *Traditional Country House Cooking* (London, 1993), p. 22; Hecht, *Domestic Servant Class*, p. 147 for several examples of wages paid to women cooks during the 1790s.

6. Jaine, 'Castle Hill', p. 22.

7. 'A Coachman', *A Treatise on the Use and Abuse of the Second . . . Table* (London, *c.* 1750), p. 61.

8. C. Pierce, *The Household Manager* (London, 1857), pp. 274 and 358, note 2.

9. S. and S. Adams, *The Complete Servant* (London, 1825), p. 368.

10. *The Servants' Practical Guide* (London, 1880), pp. 156–7; T. Webster, *An Encyclopaedia of Domestic Economy* (London, 1844), p. 336.

11. As early as the sixteenth century there was a pastry-room at Hengrave Hall in Suffolk, according to a contemporary inventory; see R. Kerr, *The Gentleman's House*, 3rd edn, revised (London, 1871), p. 39. Very large nineteenth-century houses also had this additional room, see, as an example, the plan of Mentmore in Kerr, facing p. 448, reproduced here on p. 70.

12. J. Armstrong, *The Young Woman's Guide to Virtue, Economy and Happiness* (London, 1817), p. 84.

13. I am indebted to Dr P. Sambrook for this information from the transcript, now at Shugborough Hall, of an interview given in 1986 by Mrs Doris Henshaw (née Clarke). See also *The Servants' Practical Guide*, p. 157.

14. During the seventeenth century at Woburn Abbey, home of the Dukes of Bedford, the male cook was assisted by little boys who acted as turnspits, scullions, etc., and were obviously

continuing to perform the traditional jobs of the 'children of the kitchen' in medieval households; see G. Scott Thomson, *Life in a Noble Household, 1641–1700* (London, 1937), p. 121. Male scullions were still found in old-fashioned noble households in the first half of the eighteenth century; see Hecht, *Domestic Servant Class*, p. 68.

15.   M. Waterson, *The Servants' Hall* (London, 1980), p. 101.

16.   *The Servants' Guide and Family Manual*, 4th edn (London, 1835), p. 69.

17.   E. Haywood, *A New Present for a Servant Maid* (London, 1771), p. 3.

18.   Ibid., p. 3.

19.   Horn, *Rise and Fall*, p. 63.

20.   Kerr, *Gentleman's House*, p. 214.

21.   Haywood, *A New Present*, p. 31; Horn, *Rise and Fall*, p. 60.

22.   Swift, *Directions to Servants*, p. 6; J. Trusler, *London Adviser* (London, 1786), p. 49, quoted by Hecht, *Domestic Servant Class*, p. 157.

23.   Waterson, *Servants' Hall*, p. 82. Isabella Beeton, *The Book of Household Management* (London, 1861) gives from £14 to £30 as average earnings for a woman cook and from £20 to £45 for a housekeeper, but the Yorkes at Erddig paid their servants well below the average.

24.   The housekeeper sometimes came too, to help with marketing in London or Edinburgh; but she very often remained behind to organize spring cleaning and other tasks to keep the home-based staff occupied.

25.   By the late nineteenth century clubs had become 'an immense institution and a great resort of servants', Lady Violet Greville, 'Men-servants in England', *National Review*, Feb. 1892, quoted by Horn, *Rise and Fall*, p. 99.

26.   During the eighteenth century mutton and game were occasionally sent by coach from the home estate to the family staying in the capital. With the coming of the railways, a few families had their gardeners pack and dispatch fruit and vegetables to them on a regular basis. Jaine, 'Castle Hill', p. 25, notes that game, butter and clotted cream were sent regularly from Filleigh in Devon to London when the Earls Fortescue and their families were in residence there. The gardener of the Marquess of Bath, after the coming of the railway 'had a graded set of purpose-made boxes' in which he sent peaches, nectarines, soft fruit, asparagus, beans and other produce to his employer in London during the season.

27.   Servants were usually well fed, but a few cases are known where the cook connived with the other upper servants to ensure that those at the Second Table were well provided for and could entertain their friends there, while the lower servants went short. *Treatise on the Use and Abuse . . .*, pp. 15–17; and Hecht, *Domestic Servant Class*, pp. 110–11, quoting Nancy Woodforde.

CHAPTER FOUR

KITCHEN FIREPLACES AND STOVES

Peter Brears

E ven though the larders of the country house might be richly stocked, and its sculleries and kitchens equipped with every convenience, good cookery could not be undertaken unless the kitchen fireplaces and stoves were all in prime condition. Here every aspect of roasting, boiling, stewing, broiling, baking and toasting had to be completed in the most efficient manner if disaster was to be avoided, and the whole meal was to emerge perfectly cooked and on time in the dining-room. It was for this reason that fireplaces and stoves have always represented the largest financial investment in the kitchens, and why they remain the most substantial artefacts in numerous country house kitchens today.

Most surviving fireplaces are filled with enormous blackleaded cast-iron ranges, which incorporate roasting fires, ovens and boiling rings within their overall design. These mark the culmination of centuries of development, the first period of relatively slow progress terminating in the late eighteenth century, when scientists and manufacturers began to review the whole process of cooking and the production of culinary hardware. For this reason, we will start by looking at the basic individual pieces of equipment used in the earlier kitchens, and then take an overall view of the emergence of the all-purpose range.

THE ROASTING RANGE

Roasting meat by slowly rotating it in front of an open fire is probably the oldest, simplest and best method of preparing it for the table. The combination of the richly browned surface of the joint with the succulent and tender meat within, and the lighter, fresher flavour achieved by the free evaporation of the coarse fats and juices, all combine to give roast meat its well-deserved reputation for excellence.

Up to the eighteenth century many country houses, and even palaces, carried on the medieval methods of roasting, using a huge fire of logs raised slightly above the hearth on iron firedogs or andirons, within a vast open fireplace measuring perhaps

This fireplace in Wolsey's kitchen at Hampton Court Palace was in regular use up to the 1730s and still has its original cob-irons on which the spits rotated. Here they are supported on walls which also helped to contain the fierce heat radiating from the great log fires.

fifteen feet or more in width. At each side stood a cob-iron, a stand fitted with a number of hooks which supported the spits as they were turned before the fire. These came in a variety of forms. In the larger establishments, such as Hampton Court, Plas Mawr in Conway, or Cotehele in Cornwall, they were simply long bars of iron with inverted T- or U-shaped feet, which were propped up at an angle against the back wall of the fireplace, the spits then being placed in the row of hooks or racks which projected from their front faces. The second variety of cob-irons had hinged back legs, so that they could open into self-supporting A-frames at each side of the fire, and then collapse flat for hanging against a wall when not in use. The third variety, meanwhile, was permanently fixed on three legs, one of which might extend backwards to serve as an andiron for the fire.

In some establishments, such as large households and commercial cookshops, where meat was roasted in quantity, the roasting fire, together with all its appropriate equipment, was raised on a table-height masonry hearth built within a large fireplace. These are clearly shown in Joris Hoefnagel's late sixteenth-century painting of the *Marriage Feast at Bermondsey*, where the spits hang on cob-irons, and also in the 1641 broadside entitled *The Lamentable Complaints of Nick Froth the*

Tapster and Rulerost the Cooke.[1] It is not known, however, if any of these raised hearths still exist today.

In those areas where coal, rather than timber, was the most convenient fuel for roasting, raised iron firebaskets called ranges had already come into existence by the sixteenth century. This is illustrated by references such as to 'le Rostyng-range' in Durham in 1525–6.[2] By the early eighteenth century roasting ranges had developed into a relatively standard form. The front was made up of a series of horizontal wrought iron bars mounted between two vertical iron posts, each topped by an ornamental knob or finial. Iron stays connected these posts to the masonry of the back wall of the fireplace, the actual fireback being built in brick with a sloping profile, narrowing towards the bottom of the firebars to accommodate the shrinkage of the coals as they settled and burnt. These ranges produced a good radiant heat for roasting, but their efficiency was further increased by a number of additional features. In many examples, the sides or 'cheeks' of the range were made of iron plates which could be wound in and out using a rack-and-pinion mechanism, so that the length of the fire could be adjusted to suit the size of the roasts. Sometimes these sliding cheeks had iron rings or trivets mounted above them to hold cooking vessels over the fire. On the range itself, the top bar could fold down forwards to accommodate further pans, while the lower bars might lift out to make it easier to rake out the fire and ashes when they were no longer needed. Some ranges even had each end of every firebar forged in the shape of a hook which fitted into an appropriate loop on each of the posts, this arrangement permitting the easy replacement of burnt-out firebars. One further refinement was the inclusion of integral spit-racks, which extended from each side of the range, thus leaving the hearth completely free of cob-irons, and thus much easier to keep clean.

Once the fire had burnt up to give a clear, bright heat, the meat could be trussed and mounted on the spit or broach, a series of tapes, skewers, sliding spikes, or the hinged bars of the basket spits, all ensuring that the meat and the spit both turned as one. If this process was not completed effectively the meat remained stationary in front of the fire, quickly burning on one side, while the spit continued to rotate within it.

For centuries the task of turning the spit was performed manually, a handle forged at one end of the spit having to be turned continuously for hour after hour, in very unpleasant conditions. Sitting by the fire meant being roasted on one side, and chilled on the other as the flames sucked cold draughts up the chimney. It was also thirsty work, a ready supply of ale being required to slake the thirst caused by the combination of heat and exercise. Given these working conditions, it is not surprising that turnspits had a well deserved reputation for unsavoury habits, the very word 'turnspit' becoming a term of contempt. They continued to be employed in fairly large numbers up to the early eighteenth century, twelve serving in the kitchens of William and Mary in 1689, for example, but by this time they were being replaced by cheaper and more convenient devices.[3]

In 1536 Dr Caius described 'A certain dog in kitchen service excellent. For when any meat is to be roasted they go into a wheel, they turning about with the weight of their bodies so diligently look to their business that no drudge or scullion can do the feat more cunningly'.[4] The wheel was in fact a simple wooden tread-mill some three feet in diameter and up to a foot wide, mounted on an iron axle usually in an elevated position to one side of the fireplace. Once the long-bodied, short-legged turnspit dog had started to run inside the wheel, a small pulley fixed on to the end of the axle provided a direct drive to a pulley at one end of the spit by means of a continuous loop of strong cord or chain. The use of these wheels tended to be restricted to the West Country and South Wales, where they continued in use up to the early nineteenth century.[5]

Mechanical spit-turning devices, called 'jacks' since they effectively replaced the work of a man, were in use in England before 1587, when 'the jacke which turneth the broche' is referred to in the will of William Hyde of Urmston in Lancashire.[6] These weight-driven clockwork mechanisms were fixed to the upper part of the chimney breast, usually on the left-hand side of the fireplace. Once the long cord bearing the weight had been wound up on to its ratcheted drum, a task which only took a few seconds to complete, a simple flywheel escapement on top of the jack slowed its descent down to some fifteen to twenty minutes, during which time it turned a pulley wheel, which then drove the spit by means of an endless cord. These jacks proved to be extremely efficient, being used throughout the country in virtually every sizeable household as long as open-fire roasting continued to be practised, as can be seen from their prevalence in the illustrations from manuals of domestic economy.

From at least the late fifteenth century a second variety of mechanical jack had been used in England, one which took its power from the rush of smoke and air up the chimney by means of a circular fan or propeller called a fly. The upright shaft of

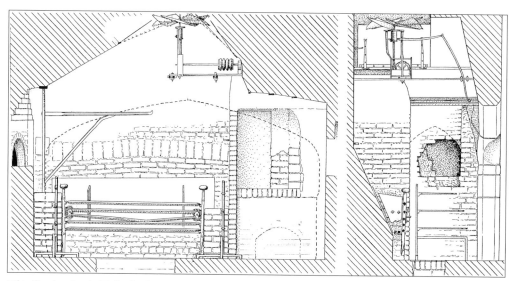

This fireplace in the Tudor kitchens at Cowdray, Sussex, was last used in 1793. It still retains its contemporary wrought-iron range with sliding cheeks, its chimney crane, and the smoke jack which turned its spits.

one of these jacks has been found in a fifteenth-century context in Pottergate, Norwich, its size making it suitable for use on one of the raised cooking hearths of that period.[7] However, smoke jacks do not appear to have been widely used here until the early eighteenth century, but from that time they enjoyed great popularity. In order to install a smoke jack, the wide chimney rising up above the fireplace arch had to be funnelled into an opening around two feet in diameter. The fly was then inserted into this space, its rotating motion being transferred through an oil-filled gear box to a shaft which usually projected through the chimney breast. In the simpler and earlier examples, the shaft terminated in a series of wooden pulleys, which drove the spits by means of continous ropes or chains. In later examples the shaft was fitted with a bevelled gear which then turned one or two horizontal bars mounted across the front of the chimney breast. These not only turned the ordinary spits by means of wooden pulleys mounted at their outer ends, but also powered a series of dangling hooks, from which joints could be rotated on a vertical axis in front of the fire.

Whenever the spits were being turned by jacks and pulleys, special kinds of cob-

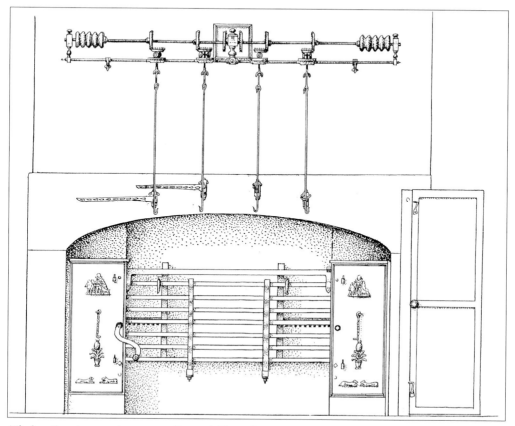

The late Georgian roasting range at Petworth House, Sussex, incorporates massive sliding cheeks, cast-iron face-plates to the hobs, an iron door on the right which linked it to a roasting screen, and a totally enclosed smoke jack which powered four dangling and up to eight horizontal spits.

irons or spit dogs had to be used. That at the pulley end always had a series of vertical pegs which ensured that the spit remained at a constant distance from the fire, but provided no vertical support, thus ensuring that the weight of the spit was taken by the rope or chain from the jack pulley above. The spit dog at the other end was far more conventional in design, supporting the pointed end of the spit in a hook or rack in the normal way. For dangling hooks the distance from the fire was controlled by means of a series of hooks mounted on a horizontal arm which swung out from the chimney breast, the cook simply placing the dangler in the appropriate hook to adjust the rate of roasting.

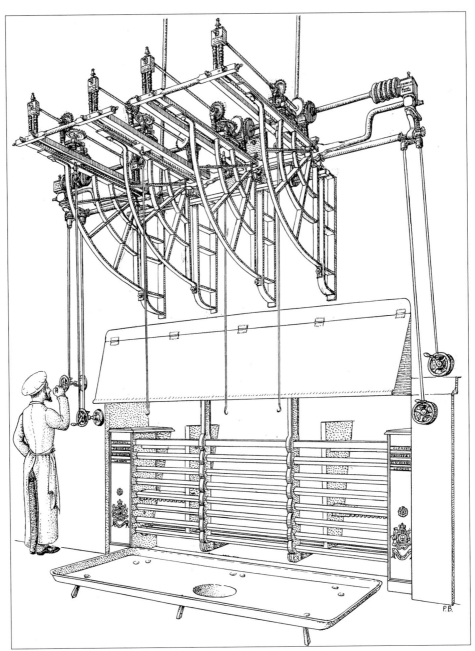

By the mid-nineteenth century, country house roasting ranges were being constructed on the most enormous scale. For the Earl of Lonsdale's Lowther Castle near Penrith, Clement Jeakes made this huge range, some twelve feet wide by fourteen feet high. Its smoke jack could power up to eight horizontal and four vertical spits, the latter being adjusted by the handles to each side. It is probably the finest roasting range ever to have been made in this country.

As the meat began to cook, its juices and fat, together with any additional fats, olive oil or butter used for basting, were caught in the large rectangular dripping pan of tinned copper or sheet iron which stood beneath the spits. Earlier examples appear to have been simple trays with a pouring lip either at each end, or at each corner, from which the dripping could be poured off into an appropriate vessel. From the mid-eighteenth century at least dripping pans were being provided with a sunken well into which all the dripping drained, ready for basting back over the joint. Later examples had raised rims around their wells with piercing to strain out any lumps of cinder or coagulated juices which might have fallen into the pan, as well as a lid to ensure that the fat remained as clean as possible. The actual basting was carried out with a ladle, its brass or tinned copper bowl perhaps having a strainer incorporated in its design, and an iron handle measuring anything up to four feet in length, so that the cook would not be scorched when working so close to the fire.

Spit roasting was not the only way in which the radiant heat of the ranges could be utilized for cooking. Small pieces of meat could be spiked on standing toasters, for example, or on broiling irons, these being described by Gervase Markham in 1615 as 'a plate Iron made with hooks and pricks, on which you may hang the meat and set it close before the fire, and so the Plate heating the meate behinde, as the fire doth before, it will both the sooner and with more neatnesse be readie'.[8] Roasters were also made of tinplate or of coarse glazed earthenware, half-round examples of the latter dated to the early eighteenth century being recorded from Somerset, Staffordshire, Sussex and Yorkshire. Food placed within them, and stood either on the dripping pan or on a separate iron stand would have cooked quite quickly in front of the fire.[9] By the mid-eighteenth century at least much larger roasting screens were being constructed in the form of tinplate-lined open-backed wooden cupboards. When trundled up before the fire, separated from it only by the dripping pan, they fulfilled the dual function of a hot-cupboard for warming plates and keeping food hot ready for the table, while also acting as an effective fire-screen, shielding the kitchen from the fierce heat. Some fireplaces even had folding iron screens attached to their jambs, so that the gaps between the fireplace and the screen could be sealed off to contain the heat even further. This was a very necessary precaution, for the heat of a fully-charged roasting range was tremendous, quite beyond anything which can be experienced in any working kitchen today.

The Stove

Because of its very size and fierce heat, the range was unsuitable for undertaking the more delicate cooking operations, especially those which involved gentle stewing, making sauces, preserves, or confectionery. For small-scale operations of this kind, the most convenient source of heat was an iron, bronze or pottery charcoal burner called a chafing dish or chafer.[10] These had been introduced by the fourteenth century, and were still in use in parts of rural England in the late Victorian period. They had an open bowl-shaped container about six inches in diameter for the burning charcoal, with firebars or a pierced base to provide sufficient draught, and a number of projecting knobs around the rim, on which a plate, frying pan or bowl of food could rest while being heated. Where a large quantity of fine cookery had to be undertaken, a number of iron chafing dishes were set into a table-height masonry base to form a permanent stove.

It is probable that stoves of this type were already in use in the late medieval kitchens of English royal palaces, but to date there is apparently no positive archaeological or documentary evidence for this. By the sixteenth century, illustrations of fully developed charcoal stoves are found in a number of European sources, and they would most certainly have been in use in the major English households at this time.[11] Among the earliest stoves which still survive today are those built within Henry VIII's kitchens at Hampton Court in the seventeenth century.[12] Made entirely of red brick, with iron firebars, their six grates, each some fifteen inches in diameter by four inches deep, are served by three arched openings which act as combined air ducts and ash pits, two further arches being provided for supplies of fresh charcoal.[13] The output of heat of stoves of this size would be very considerable, and it is probable that they would have heated great tinned copper cooking pots of perhaps ten to fifteen gallons or more. Catering on this scale would certainly have been required when Patrick Lamb was working here for the later Stuarts.[14] Stoves of this scale could have wooden cranes with blocks and tackle mounted at their sides, to enable the cooks to manœuvre their pots into position, one of these being shown in J. Stephanoff's 1817–20 watercolour of the kitchens at Windsor Castle.[15] Most country house stoves tended to be of appropriately modest proportions, those fitted at Skipton Castle in the 1680s having just three iron-sheathed grates some six inches in diameter.[16]

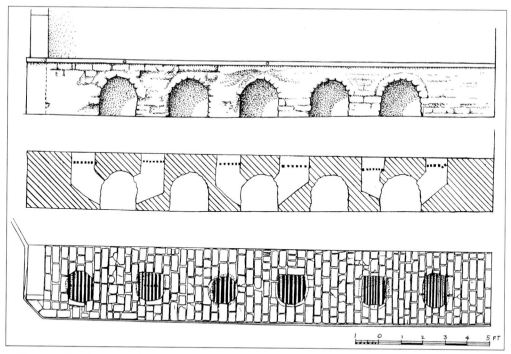

Hampton Court's seventeenth-century stove was built on a series of five brick arches, three acting as combined draught holes and ash pits, while the other two held supplies of fresh charcoal.

Since the burning charcoal produced quantities of carbon dioxide, and since good lighting was always of great advantage, the best position for a stove was directly beneath a window, this location being adopted at houses such as Kenwood, Harewood or Astley Hall, near Chorley, where a wooden hood was fitted to carry the fumes towards the topmost window openings. Another favoured location was in one of the arches at the side of a roasting range, as at Sir Gregory Page's house at Blackheath, for example, or as may be seen in various early eighteenth century baby-house kitchens, such as those at Nostell Priory, or at York Castle Museum. Where Tudor kitchens were being up-dated, stoves could be built within existing fireplaces, as at Hampton Court and Cowdray Park, while fireplaces specifically designed to receive stoves were incorporated in the kitchens of many country houses built from around 1700.[17] Where this was not possible, large smoke-hoods with ventilation ducts leading to the open air

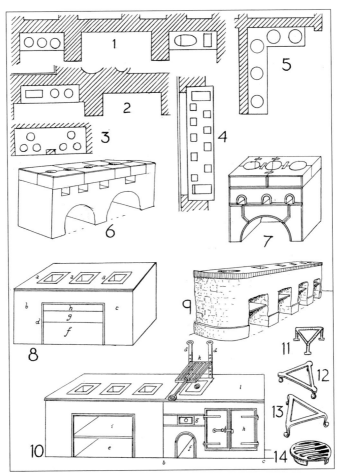

Stewing stoves. Plans of the stoves at: 1. Sir Gregory Page's house at Blackheath; 2. Earl Spencer's Wimbledon of 1732–3; 3. Buckland, of 1757; 4. Harewood House of 1756–64; 5. Eastbury of 1715–38. 6. a seventeenth-century stove at Skipton Castle, Yorkshire; 7. an early eighteenth-century stove, also at Skipton Castle; 8. this stewing stove from Thomas Webster, An Encyclopedia of Domestic Economy, *has a lower drawer for charcoal, an upper one to catch the ashes, and a space above which provided the draught required by the fires burning in the grates; 9. the stove at Buckland Abbey, Devon, has iron plates across its arches to catch the ashes, the space below probably holding fresh charcoal; 10. Mr W. Jeakes of Great Russell Street, London, designed this stove, which incorporates a standard three-grate stove on the left, and a boiling stove on the right, where a single fire heats the hot-plate, the oven beneath, and the broiling or grilling stove above. 11. stove trivet illustrated in Randle Holme's* Academy of Armory *of 1688; 12. stove trivet in J. Stephanoff's painting of the kitchens at Windsor Castle of c. 1817; 13. an example at Beamish, County Durham; 14. and at Cowdray House, Sussex, of pre-1793.*

were fitted directly over the stoves, as at the Royal Pavilion at Brighton, where a row of lamps had to be installed so that the cooks could see what they were doing. In spite of these precautions, the fumes from the charcoal remained a problem in the kitchen, for a sudden draught could easily direct a strong yet invisible stream of hot carbon dioxide up the cook's nostrils, completely taking his breath away and making his eyes water.

One solution, introduced by the renowned Mrs Elizabeth Raffald of Manchester in the later editions of her *Experienced English House-Keeper* of 1769, was to use 'stove-fires for the kitchen, that will burn coals or embers instead of charcoal [which] have always been found expensive, as well as pernicious to the cooks . . . .'. As her foldout frontispiece engraving shows, her stove had ducts from the sides of the grates leading to flues beneath the top of the stove, and behind its back wall up into a chimney. This convenient arrangement enabled cooking pots to entirely seal the tops of the grates, ensuring that no fumes entered the kitchen, a principle which was used in many later stoves.

On the traditional stoves, low iron trivets supported the cooking vessels about an inch or two above the top of the grate. These were often triangular in shape, probably continuing the form of 'treipedi' illustrated in 1570 by Bartolomeo Scappi, in 1688 by Randle Holme, and *c.* 1817 in Windsor Castle and St James' Palace by J. Stephanoff.[18] At Cowdray, the eighteenth-century trivets are circular, enclosing narrow parallel bars, and standing on two curved strips of iron,

Stove built into the scullery at Shugborough, Staffordshire. The worktop has a grid for charcoal and an ash pit beneath, but is unusual in that it is built into a chimney which leads into the main kitchen flue. The stove was probably built with the kitchen in the mid-eighteenth century and later bricked up.

which make them particularly stable. Grid irons were also used for broiling fish, steaks, and chops over the stoves, some stoves having special rectangular grates specifically for this purpose.

BOILERS

In the late sixteen century the boiling house, with its large copper boiler set in a masonry 'furnace', was still one of the major features of any large kitchen. Here meat would either be boiled ready for the table, or parboiled before being roasted or baked, the resulting stock forming the basis of the ubiquitous pottage which appeared at most meals. Their construction was fairly straightforward: the boilers were supported by iron bars secured in the masonry, and heated by faggot-burning fireplaces which conducted the flames into flues which encircled the boiler before passing into the chimney; lead flashing gave a practical waterproof seal between the boiler and its surrounding walls. The recently restored seventy-six gallon example at Hampton Court gives an excellent impression of a boiler of this period.

Similar boilers were still being installed in the nineteenth century, although by this time they tended to be rather smaller in size, and made of cast iron. Some were even oval in plan and divided vertically so that two separate boiling operations could be carried out at the same time, wooden doors and ventilation ducts above effectively carrying away the steam.[19] They were useful for boiling puddings and net bags of vegetables, etc., but now these were mostly boiled in separate pans over the fire or the stove.

OVENS

Beehive-shaped baking ovens, their masonry domes heated from within by faggots of burning wood, produced excellent loaves and other bakery in the hands of a skilled baker. They were very troublesome and dirty to operate, however, bringing unwelcome smoke and mud into the kitchen, and demanding a great deal of time and attention which could be better employed elsewhere. As early as 1635 John Sibthorpe had taken out a patent for an oven which could 'be used with sea coles or any other coles digged out of the earth, and therewith may bake as soone and as fayre and for less charge than they now doe in heating with wood'.[20] On 23 June the following year Robert Lindsay and John Hobarte patented 'a new way whereby soe great expence of wood may be saved by use of sea coales, peate, turfe, or any other fewell with much less expense thereof than hath been used, noe fire nor smoake coming into the oven, and yet theire baking, roasting and boyling shal-be sweete and att farre lesse charges than they nowe are att.'[21] However, it was not until the mid-eighteenth century that sheet iron ovens heated by separate wood or coal-burning grates began to be installed in any quantity. At Shibden Hall near Halifax, for example, the Revd John Lister paid for a 'Perpetual Oven and setting up £4 4s 0d [£4.20]' with a further 16s 5d [82p] builders' expenses in 1750, showing how expensive these could be.[22]

NEW DEVELOPMENTS c. 1770–1820

The last quarter of the eighteenth century was a period of great progress in the British manufacturing industry. As far as cookery equipment was concerned, it saw a great increase in the use of cast iron, both in the production of entire ovens and stoves, etc., and in the provision of face-plates which sheathed their masonry supports, making them easier to keep clean, and appear more elegant with their classically inspired decoration.

Roasting ranges of enormous size were now provided with cast-iron face-plates etc., and also with wrought-iron back-boilers to produce both hot water and steam for the kitchens. Their basic form then remained virtually unchanged up to the end of the nineteenth century, and even though smoke jacks continued to provide the most popular means of turning spits on the larger ranges, they were now supplemented by a number of mechanical spring-driven jacks which provided either vertical or horizontal movements.

As far as stoves were concerned, they could now be fitted with cast-iron grates and with cast-iron work-tops, as at Astley Hall near Chorley, or be made entirely in cast iron, as at Brighton Pavilion. The arched recesses in their bases could also be improved by inserting a cast-iron shelf halfway up, making space for ashes above and for fresh charcoal below, as at Buckland Abbey in Devon. Later examples might also have separate iron drawers, which meant that ash and charcoal dust were no longer left free to blow around the kitchen.[23]

Although these changes were significant, other more important developments were taking place. In 1780 Thomas Robinson, a London ironmonger, patented a new form of range which, apparently for the first time, incorporated an oven into a roasting range.[24] Although it claimed 'every Advantage and [was] calculated for universal Benefit, being capable of every Use and Purpose that can possibly be required, without the least Expence or Trouble', it had numerous imperfections. The oven was simply an iron box built into the solid masonry of one of the hobs, the heat of the fire only coming into contact with one side. This meant that its heat was very uneven, some later models even having a rotating oven shelf to enable the food to be cooked on each side in turn. Boilers working on the same principle were added to the range's other hob following the 1783 patent of Joseph Langmead, a London ironfounder. 'Poker' ovens were also developed, these having a large bar of iron projecting into the fire to improve the conduction of heat into the oven, but these too were far from ideal.

Probably the first real scientific approach to culinary technology was that undertaken by Benjamin, Count Rumford, who published his researches in his *Essays, Political, Economical and Philosophical* in London in 1802. His tenth essay is devoted to 'the Construction of Kitchen Fire-Places and Kitchen Utensils'. After reviewing the imperfections of the existing equipment, he set out the following proposed improvements for stoves:

1. Each cooking vessel should have its own separate closed fireplace, the door to its grate and ashpit being fitted with a draught-controlling register, and its flue with a damper.
2. Fireplaces over 8 to 10 in diameter should be fuelled from openings just above the level of the grate, smaller ones being fed from the top.
3. Portable boilers and stewpans should be circular and suspended deep inside the fireplaces by the rim, fixed ones being rectangular and shallow.
4. All boilers or stewpans should have well insulated lids, preferably of double tinplate construction.

Using these principles, it was possible to effect great improvements in the efficiency of stewing. By controlling the fires, food could be cooked at just under boiling point, giving it increased tenderness, juiciness and flavour. There were also great economies in fuel consumption particularly since the boilers and stewpans were completely sunk within their fireplaces, and there were no more noxious charcoal fumes to poison the cooks. Despite these advantages, the complexity of these stoves, which might burden the cook with the individual control of fourteen cooking vessels, fourteen fires, fourteen draught controls, and fourteen dampers, meant that their initial popularity was not sustained. Within thirty years virtually all these stoves had disappeared, although some of their features were adopted in later ranges.

In his search for efficiency, Count Rumford also developed very effective steamers, the smaller ones being of double-walled and double-lidded tinplate construction which fitted on top of the boilers on his stove, while the larger were big wooden boxes lined with tinplate, fed by a steampipe from a separate boiler. Both of these had flanges around their lids which fitted into water-filled troughs around the tops of the steamers, thus forming an efficient steam-tight seal. However, as one writer commented in the 1840s 'this excellent contrivance appears to be forgotten already'.[25]

The open roasting range brought the Count's bitterest criticism, since 'more fuel is frequently consumed in a kitchen-range to boil a tea-kettle, than, with proper management, would be sufficient to cook a good dinner for fifty men. To complete the machinery (which in every part and detail of it seems to have been calculated for the express purpose of *devouring fuel*) a smoke-jack is placed in the chimney!' If a steam engine was used for this purpose only one-thousandth of the fuel would be needed, besides which they were 'troublesome', noisy, expensive, frequently out of order and couldn't perform as well as a weight or spring-driven jack.

To solve these problems he devised the Rumford roasting oven which gave the cook full control of the heat, dryness or moisture of the meat. This had a horizontal cylindrical iron oven, with an insulated door and a shelf three inches below the centre to hold a dripping pan, on which the meat was placed on a raised grid. Two iron blow-pipes entered the bottom of the oven, their outer ends being sealed by removable stoppers, while a single steam tube left the oven at the top. About twelve to fifteen minutes before roasting was completed a clear fire was formed using bundles of dry wood, so that the blow-pipes were made red-hot. The stoppers were then removed, sending a current of superheated air through the oven, to brown the meat and complete its cooking.

In tests, joints emerged 6 per cent heavier than identical spit-roast examples, besides being '*decidedly better*, that is to say more delicate, more juicy, more savory, and higher flavoured than when roasted in the common way'. In 1799 Mr Sumner,

Although Count Rumford's stoves and fireplaces incorporated all the best scientific principles, they enjoyed only a relative brief period of popularity during the first quarter of the nineteenth century. Here we see: 1. an early Count Rumford stove in Munich, its brick base incorporating thirteen separate fireplaces to heat its thirteen separate cooking vessels; 2. a section of Rumford's roasting oven, as set in its masonry support; 3. the Rumford roasting oven, with its insulating double door (a), the iron oven (b), the blow-pipes which provided blasts of hot air (c) and the vent pipe which carried off the vapours (d); 4. the cross-section of the roasting dish, with a grid above to hold the meat, and a dish beneath which held water to prevent the dripping from burning.

ironmonger of New Bond Street, installed one of these ovens in his kitchen where it could be seen by his customers, then going on to sell 260 Rumford roasting ovens, similar successes being achieved by other London, Edinburgh and provincial ironmongers. After this burst of popularity, they gradually went out of fashion, a writer in the 1840s stating that they were no longer manufactured, and that capable manufacturers and installers were not to be found.

In reviewing Count Rumford's achievements, it should be emphasized that some of the principles he promoted had already been put into practice by other less well known improvers. Mrs Raffald's coal fired stoves had been around for decades, and Mr Strutt of Derby had invented a very effective double-walled roasting oven in 1797. However, as a direct result of his analytical scientific approach to the processes of cookery, the widespread influence of his *Essays*, and the practicality of the equipment he installed at the Royal Institution etc., he completely revolutionized the design and manufacture of cooking stoves and ovens. Although most of his own designs rapidly went out of fashion, the principles he had established continued to be very influential throughout the nineteenth century.

In the same year that Count Rumford published his *Essays* other less celebrated, but more user-friendly cooking equipment was already being developed. On 27 February 1802 George Bodley of Exeter patented the first practical closed-fire cooking range. From a central fire grate, the hot air and flames passed underneath a hotplate, around the top, side, and bottom of an oven, under the ash pit, past the bottom and side of a boiler at the other side of the fire and then up the chimney. This arrangement provided almost everything that the cook required in one relatively simple, compact and convenient unit. The fire could be opened at the front for roasting, the oven provided an even heat for baking, there was a constant source of hot water from the boiler, and pans could boil and stew on the hotplate. Over the course of the following decades various improvements were made to the Bodley range, one being much more efficient boilers, and another the introduction of roasting ovens, in which the blow-pipes of Rumford's roaster were replaced by a double bottom to the oven, from which, by opening a register, a blast of very hot air could be directed through the oven, and on up the chimney.

The popularity of closed ranges for country house, villa, hotel and institutional use ensured that they were manufactured in large numbers both in London, South Yorkshire, the West Midlands, as well as in other provincial centres. The best

The oven of Thomas Robinson's patent range of 1780 (1) drew its heat from the fire burning against one of its side walls, which gave a very uneven distribution of heat. In the second quarter of the nineteenth century ranges were developed into extremely efficient units, one example (2) from Thomas Webster's Encyclopedia of Domestic Economy, *incorporating a practical roasting range, a large boiler, and an oven heated by its own separate fireplace. The closed stove or 'Leamington' enabled a single fire to perform a number of functions, both Wright's (3) and Black and Green's ranges (4) having their fires enclosed behind mica doors, from where they heated ovens, water boilers and steam raising boilers.*

The Gold Medal Eagle range, shown in the Foundry's catalogue of 1908, was an extremely efficient piece of cooking equipment. Its facilities included a roasting oven, a baking oven, eight boiling rings, a powerful grill, a series of hot closets, and a fire which could be rapidly converted from open to closed (or vice versa) at will.

known maker was William Flavel of Leamington Spa, whose 'Patent Kitcheners' of the 1820s provided the nationally recognized term of 'Leamingtons' for all ranges of this type. By 1900 most country house kitchens were equipped with one or more Leamingtons, along with additional roasting ranges, stoves, boilers and hot cupboards, etc., to meet their particular requirements. Made by such firms as Barnard, Bishop and Barnard of Norwich, the Coalbrookdale Company, the Rotherham Foundry Company, Hattersley Brothers of Sheffield and many others, they all offered very similar facilities. A study of the Eagle Range made by the Eagle Range and Foundry Company of London, Bristol and Birmingham, clearly demonstrates the advantages of the fully developed closed range.

The range itself occupied the lower half of the wide fireplace, the recessed area above being lined with cast-iron plates for cleanliness, and having a rack on which plates etc. could be kept warm. The firebox was located in the centre of the range, its sides having patent smoke consuming fire cheeks, its front having a grating, its back being a boiler, and its bottom a movable grating hinged at the back, so that it could be raised when only a small fire was required, or dropped when a large fire was required, or roasting was to be carried out. The top of the firebox was usually closed by a flat iron lid, but this could be lifted and doors opened at the back of the range to produce an ideal open fire for grilling on a grid iron. A roasting oven usually occupied one side of the range, with a pastry oven at the other, the latter having dampers which could direct the flames under its base, to produce the bottom heat essential for good bakery. By manipulating the dampers, the flames could also be conducted all around the oven for an equal heat, or just to the top of the oven, so that it could be converted into a roaster. The hot iron top of the range made an ideal clean and smoke-free stewing stove, which could also boil efficiently by placing the pans on lift-out boiling rings.

It is not surprising that the Eagle became one of the greatest of all Victorian ranges, being installed in the kitchens of the dukes of Wellington, Northumberland and Buccleuch, numerous peers, baronets and knights, together with institutions as diverse as the Beefsteak Club, Mrs Marshall's School of Cookery and the MCC.

In the largest kitchens, central or 'Continental' ranges were built in the centre of the room, away from the walls so that the cooks could enjoy much better access to their ovens, hot cupboards and hotplates. The smoke and fumes were carried off by flues which either rose above these ranges, or sank under the floor and across to a distant chimney. A good example of this type can be seen at Saltram in Devon, this being made by Flavel & Co. of Leamington in 1885. Similar ranges, heated by steam rather than by solid fuel, were also popular, one at Burghley House in Lincolnshire being cast in an appropriate Elizabethan design, with fine brasswork.

The advantages of steam for cooking had become clearly recognized during the late eighteenth century, both for domestic and for agricultural purposes. To cook in boiling water, the steam was fed into a pierced pipe which ran around the interior of the bottom of the copper, while food could also be cooked in kettles fed with steam from boilers within the firebox of the range. By the 1830s pressurized steam was being generated by purpose-made boilers, lagged pipes then conducting it to

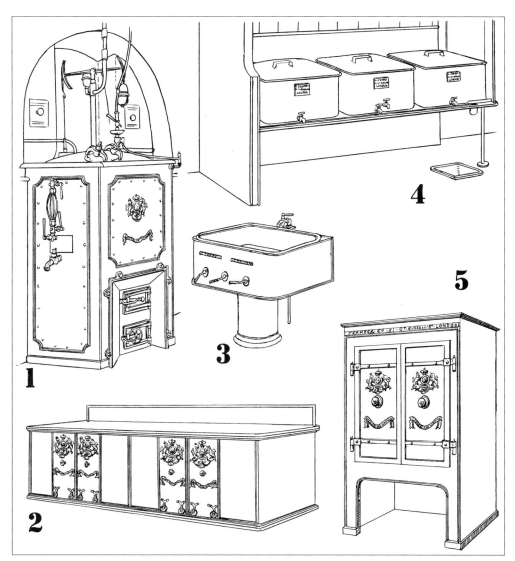

Steam cooking apparatus made by Clement Jeakes, of 51 Great Russell Street, London, in the 1870s. The boiler (1), hot-plate and hot cupboard (2), bain-marie (3), and steam kettles (4), were all installed in the Petworth House kitchens in 1875, while the hot closet (5) was erected in the dinner service room at Lanhydrock, where it kept food and tableware really hot ready for the table.

113

double-walled hot cupboards, hotplates and steaming kettles in the kitchens, as well as to hot closets in the dinner service rooms, so that food could now be served really hot, on hot dishes and plates. Two of the major developers, manufacturers and installers of this steam equipment were Robert Hicks and Clement Jeakes, the latter becoming one of the most successful suppliers of country house kitchen plant of the Victorian period.[26]

The introduction of steam for cooking clearly demonstrates how country house kitchens led the way in culinary technology. Gas plants for lighting and then for cooking were installed in many houses from the 1840s, these being followed by electricity generating plant from the 1880s. In the case of new houses, the best equipment of the day would always be fitted throughout the kitchens, but in the older houses the introduction of new ranges and ovens tended to take place on a much more piecemeal basis, and even in the early twentieth century it was not unusual to find cooks working on Georgian roasting ranges and charcoal stoves, Victorian ovens and gas stoves, and modern electrical cookers and insulated closed ranges, perhaps all set within the stack of a great medieval fireplace. The age of the equipment was of no real concern, however, for, as in previous centuries, its true value lay in its ability to enable the cook to produce food of the finest quality, both efficiently and on time.

NOTES

1. These are reproduced in P. Brears and others, *A Taste of History* (London, 1993), pp. 136 and 180.

2. Durham Account Rolls, *Surtees Society,* p. 107.

3. *A Collection of Ordinances and Regulations for the Government of the Royal Household,* The Society of Antiquaries (London, 1790), p. 404.

4. J. Caius, *Of Englishe Dogges: The Diversities and the Properties* (1579), trans. A. Fleming, *Caius' Dogs* (1880), p. 35.

5. For a good general account of jacks and ranges see D. Eveleigh, 'Put Down to a Clear Bright Fire', *Folklife,* 29 (Leeds, 1991), pp. 5–18.

6. *Lancashire and Cheshire Wills* (Chetham Society, 1860), p. 190.

7. M. Atkin, A. Carter and D.H. Evans, *Excavations in Norwich, 1971–78* (Norwich, 1985), part 2, p. 61, fig. 43, no. 62.

8. G. Markham, *The English Hus-wife* (London, 1615), pp. 63–4.

9. P. Brears, *The Collector's Book of English Country Pottery* (Newton Abbot, 1974), pp. 147–50.

10. P. Brears, *A Catalogue of English Country Pottery Housed in the Yorkshire Museum, York* (York, 1968), pp. 27–8; and P. Brears, *Traditional Food in Yorkshire* (Edinburgh, 1987), pp. 79–80.

11. For example, see Hans Burgkmair's woodcut of 1542 and the 1570 engraving in Bartolomeo Scappi's *Opera*, both of which are reproduced in S. Thurley, *The Royal Palaces of Tudor England* (New Haven and London, 1993), p. 153.

12. S. Thurley, 'The Sixteenth-century Kitchens at Hampton Court', *Journal of the British Archaeological Association,* 143 (London, 1990), p. 9.

13. These are illustrated in S. Thurley, *The Tudor Kitchens, Hampton Court Palace* (London, 1990), p. 15.

14. See P. Lamb, *Royal Cookery* (London, 1710); and F. Sandford, *The History of the Coronation of . . . James II* (London, 1687).

15. D. Watkin, *The Royal Interiors of Regency England* (London and Melbourne, 1984), p. 17.

16. P. Brears, *The Gentlewoman's Kitchen* (Wakefield, 1984), pp. 11–12.

17. For examples see C. Campbell, *Vitruvius Britannicus* (London, 1715–25).

18. E. David, *Italian Food* (London, 1987), p. 110; R. Holme, *Academy of Armory* (Chester, 1688), lib 3, chap. 14, nos 30–1; and Watkin, *Royal Interiors*, pp. 17 and 58.

19. See P. Brears, 'A North Yorkshire Recipe Book', in C.A. Wilson (ed.), *Traditional Food East and West of the Pennines* (Edinburgh, 1991), p. 193.

20. M. Harrison, *The Kitchen in History* (Reading, 1972), p. 64.

21. Anon., *The History of the Coal Devouring Cooking Range and its Progeny Smoke and Fog* (n.d), p. 11.

22. Calderdale Archives, Halifax, Lister Papers, accounts of the Revd John Lister, January 1750.

23. T. Webster, *An Encyclopaedia of Domestic Economy* (London, 1844), p. 830.

24. The original advertisement for this range is reproduced in C. Davidson, *A Woman's Work is Never Done* (London, 1982), p. 58.

25. T. Webster, *Encyclopaedia*, p. 835.

26. For information on cooking by steam see J.C. Loudon, *An Encyclopedia of Cottage, Farm and Villa Architecture and Furniture* (London, 1833), pp. 724–5 and 1020; A. Rees, 'Steaming', *The Cyclopedia*, 34 (1819); and T. Webster, *Encyclopaedia*, pp. 832–3 and 850–1.

CHAPTER FIVE

THE BATTERIE DE CUISINE

Peter Brears

'*B*atterie de Cuisine comprehend all utensils for the service of the kitchen, whether of iron, brass, copper or of other matters' stated Rees' *Cyclopedia* of 1819. Although 'battery' originally referred specifically to copper and brassware raised by hammering, ever since the early nineteenth century the French term *batterie de cuisine* has provided the English language with a very convenient collective noun for the entire contents of the kitchen. The extent of the *batterie* could vary considerably from household to household and from generation to generation, depending on their particular circumstances. In order to explore the major development of country house kitchen equipment, it is necessary to find an example which has enjoyed a continuously high level of prosperity, has a good quality of documentation, and has retained the bulk of its kitchen wares intact through to the present day. All of these requirements are amply satisfied by Petworth House in Sussex, one of England's greatest country houses, and one which has descended through the same family ever since 1150.

For this study, four main sources of information have been used, the first of these being the inventory taken in 1632 following the death of Henry Percy, 9th Earl of Northumberland. Known as the Wizard Earl from his scientific and alchemical experiments, he had been suspected of involvement in the Gunpowder Plot, and for this reason passed sixteen years in the Tower of London before returning to spend the rest of his days at Petworth.[1] The second source is the 1764 inventory of Charles Wyndham, 2nd Earl of Egremont, who had died on 21 August 1763. He was responsible for establishing Petworth's great collections of Old Masters and antique sculpture, and was also an active politician, participating in many official banquets, which led him to claim 'Well, I have but three turtle dinners to come, and if I survive them I shall be immortal.'[2] Finally there are two inventories of the *batterie de cuisine* currently at Petworth: one taken in 1869 after the death of George Wyndham, 1st Lord Leconfield; and another apparently dating from the last quarter of the nineteenth century, from the time of Henry Wyndham, 2nd Lord

Leconfield.[3] These documents list every single movable item which was used in the kitchens at Petworth at approximately 130-year intervals during the post-medieval period, and present a very useful body of information. Their contents have now been extracted and prepared as a single comprehensive list at the end of this chapter in order that their evidence can be made readily accessible for discussion.

THE STUART KITCHENS

From the early seventeenth century list, the presence of both a fire fork and a coal rake suggest that both logs on the open hearth and coal in an iron range provided heat for cooking. With twenty-one spits, two pairs of spit racks, six dripping pans and three basting ladles, it is obvious that roast meat made up a very important part of the diet. The absence of a mechanical jack is particularly noticeable, showing that, as in many other great households up to the Civil War, the spits were turned by men known as turnbroaches. This is confirmed by payments to John Bradshaw, 'turnbreach' at Petworth in the household accounts of 1626–30.[4] It is similarly interesting to find that a large fixed boiling copper and nine brass and three iron pots, either hanging over the fire from the pot hooks or standing over it on the iron trivets were available for boiling meat. The scummers, shallow brass ladles with pierced bowls, enabled the scum to be effectively scooped off the boiling stock, while the beef fork was used to lift out the cooked joints, showing that the medieval tradition of serving boiled meats and pottages based on their stocks still continued here in the 1630s. Presumably both local freshwater fish and seafish and cockles from the coast some fifteen miles to the south were cooked in the nine brass fish kettles and the iron cockle pan.

Since the Percys employed Robert Jaggard or Jacket as French cook, as well as a number of English cooks, it is probable that a charcoal stove was installed at Petworth, but, being a fixture, it would not appear in the inventories.[5] For this reason it is not possible to confirm its existence, and the trivets, frying pans, grid irons and wafer irons could equally well have been used over the open fire. Certainly there were neither saucepans nor stewing pans at this time, the only utensils suitable for more refined cookery or sauce making being five small three-legged brass skillets which stood in the embers on the hearth, and a pair of querns for grinding mustard seed.[6]

For baking, only the most basic equipment was provided, just four wooden and one iron peel for inserting and removing the food, and two iron doors to seal each oven. All the pies, pasties and other pastries were simply moulded by hand, so no baking tins were needed.

THE GEORGIAN KITCHENS

By the 1760s the domestic organization of great houses had undergone a period of considerable change, due to the dispersal of the great medieval-style male-dominated households, and the introduction of new 'female sides', including the housekeeper's department. Now French cookery techniques were increasingly prevalent, and developments in industrial technology were introducing new kinds of cooking vessel into the kitchen.

As far as roasting was concerned, just a single coal fire was now in use with nine spits. There were a number of very significant improvements however, including both a mechanical jack and a smoke jack which automatically turned the spits in front of the fire, and a tin-lined open-fronted roasting screen, which reflected the radiant heat of the fire on to the meat, helped to keep the kitchen cool, and acted as a hot-cupboard for dishes of food waiting delivery up into the dining-room. In addition, a Dutch oven and a toasting iron were available to hold small cuts of meat, small birds, etc. in front of the fire, and there were salamanders too, these poker-like instruments with large thick flat heads being made red hot in the fire before being held over foods to brown or toast their surfaces.

For boiling, two large fixed coppers, eleven copper boilers, two scummers and a beef fork provided ample capacity for cooking meats, preparing stocks and soups, and boiling puddings. Fish kettles were still in regular use, but now two large kite-shaped fish kettles enabled turbots to be cooked whole to make a very impressive addition to any dinner. The requirements of French cookery, with its numerous rich sauces, made a large charcoal stove absolutely essential in any great English country house such as Petworth. Eleven triangular trivets were specifically provided for the stove, together with thirty-six large and small stewpans and nine saucepans.

All these vessels, coppers, boilers, kettles, stewpans and saucepans were made of copper, an absolute contrast to their predecessors of 1634 which (with the sole exception of the copper itself) were all made of brass. Brass, latten and bell-metal had been the major non-ferrous materials for cooking vessels in England from the medieval period, particularly since the combined effects of a restrictive royal monopoly on copper mining and poor copper-working technology meant that supplies of this highly malleable and highly conductive metal had to be imported from Sweden, and so was extremely expensive. Following the cancellation of the monopoly in 1689, and the imposition of a heavy duty on Swedish copper in the same year, the English copper industry began to flourish, especially in Bristol.[7] From the early eighteenth century copper cooking vessels began to replace those of brass, except for preserving pans. The only problem with copper was that it gave the food a bad taste and its verdegris was extremely poisonous, but these effects were prevented by tinning the interiors of the vessels, and perhaps the top inch of their exteriors too. Contemporary writers such as John Farley were fully aware of the dangers involved in using copper with badly worn or damaged tinning, and mistresses of large houses, such as Susanna Whatman of Turkey Court, Kent, made sure that their cooks were instructed to 'see that every saucepan etc. is well cleaned within, but that they should not be scowered bright without, except the upper rim'.[8] This practice appears to have been continued up to recent times in most kitchens.

By 1764 the use of metal baking ware was already well established, the kitchens now having copper and brass baking pans for puddings, pies and cakes, patty pans for individual tarts or cakes, biscuit moulds, and copper baking sheets, four square and two round, on which bakery was arranged before being put into the oven.[9] Further metalwork was kept in the housekeeper's room and her nearby stillroom. Here she and her stillroom maid distilled liquors, toilet and medicinal waters through two stills, used preserving pans for making jams, jellies and similar sweet preparations, saucepans and numerous moulds for making ice-creams, and a coffee mill, a boiler, and coffee and chocolate pots for hot drinks. Most of these foods, together with their related equipment, had been quite unknown in the 1630s, but now formed an essential part of country house catering.

THE VICTORIAN KITCHENS

The food produced in the Georgian kitchens had been truly excellent, the quality and quantity of the *batterie de cuisine* being quite sufficient to meet the requirements of the most demanding of chefs. However, by the late Victorian period it would have been considered to be totally inadequate, since the elaboration of presentation and garnishing had advanced to the most amazing levels of complexity.[10] Now

Kitchen at Lanhydrock House in Cornwall, showing part of the batterie de cuisine *and the roasting range with elaborate smoke jack. (By courtesy of* Country Life)

decoration was carried to extreme lengths, with all major made dishes combining a great variety of separate elements which had to be separately carved, turned, modelled or moulded into shape before being assembled, glazed, sauced and garnished into their final forms. There were also significant developments in cooking technology.

Fortunately the English tradition of excellent plain roasting managed to survive this onslaught relatively unscathed, since nothing could really improve the appearance of a beautifully roasted joint, with its fine frothing or crisp crackling. For this reason the roasting equipment remained virtually unchanged in its eighteenth-century scale and techniques. Similarly plain boiling remained popular, although its quality was considerably improved by the introduction of steamers, which produced more delicate results.

The real differences with the earlier periods are clearly seen in areas such as stewing and sauce making. The trivets and charcoal stoves formerly used for these purposes were now replaced by gas stoves and steam-heated hotplates and bain-marie, these hot water baths keeping their tinned copper pots just below the boiling point to cook delicate sauces gently, and keep others at the correct temperature, ready for use. It is also significant that the total number of stewpans and saucepans had increased from forty-five to ninety-six, reflecting the increasing diversity of sauces and glazes.

A similar change is to be seen in the baking equipment. Twice the number of baking sheets were needed to serve the new cast-iron pastry ovens, and corrugated tinplate stands were introduced to protect the finer items of bakery from the direct heat of the oven shelf. There were even greater increases in bakery ware, tinplate now having largely replaced brass and copper for this purpose. Baking pans and hoops increased in number from four to thirty-one, with a proportionate diversity of shapes, but individual patty pans and bun tins actually increased from 20 to over 264, including the round patties, fluted patties, boat patties, queen cake tins, and tins moulded to a variety of ornamental shapes, which were necessary to produce all the cakes, tarts, etc. for elegant teas or desserts.

There had been only three copper moulds in the kitchens in 1764, but now there were over two hundred, with cylinder and ornamental moulds for desserts and puddings, ring moulds to provide foundations for major dishes, both sweet and savoury, quenelle and mousseline moulds for richly moulded forcemeat dumplings and highly decorated garnishings, and dariole moulds both plain and decorative, for hors-d'œuvres, savouries, entrées and hot and cold sweets. There were also fine moulds for making game pies in the form of medieval bastions, and moulds for round, shallow hot pies, both of these being supplied by French manufacturers.

In the housekeeper's room and stillroom, the degree of change was not quite so noticeable, but here ice-cream continued to be important, with a machine producing delectable ices of various rich flavours which could be moulded as *bombes*, steeples, Neapolitan bricks, fluted columns, or as individual fruits, vegetables, nuts and flowers, realistically coloured, and served amid real leaves to form the most impressive and luxurious of desserts.

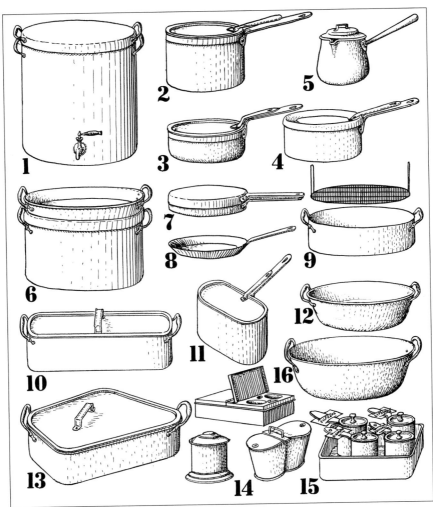

By the mid-nineteenth century most cooking vessels were being manufactured in a reasonably standard range of shapes, as may be seen in this illustration. All are made of copper sheet, tinned on the interior, with cast brass loop handles, or long iron handles for lifting. The only exception is no. 14, for seasoning boxes were usually made of brass. 1. stockpot; 2. stewpan; 3. vegetable stewpan, rounded between the walls and the base; 4. glazing stewpan, with its lid recessed to hold hot embers to achieve a good top heat; 5. bellied stewpan; 6. braising pan, with a tall rim around its lid to hold a deep bed of embers; 7. sauté pan; 8. omelet pan; 9. fish frier or frying kettle with its wire drainer; 10. fish kettle, which, like nos 11 and 13, has a flat pierced draining plate inside its base, with upright handles, to enable the fish to be removed without breaking; 11. mackerel pan; 12. preserving pan; 13. turbot kettle; 14. seasoning boxes, for salt, pepper, flour, sugar, herbs, etc.; 15. bain-marie, or hot water bath, with bain-marie, pots for sauces etc.; 16. basin.

Part of the Petworth House batterie de cuisine *on the shelves of the dresser,* c. 1930. *Note the moulds on the top shelf, the stewpans beneath and the row of bain-marie pans on the bottom shelf. A fine series of seasoning boxes stands on the table, in front of the two kitchen-maids. This photograph was provided by Mrs Dot Digby, who worked here in the late 1930s.*

At Petworth, as in the majority of country houses throughout the first half of the twentieth century, the *batterie de cuisine* built up during the late Victorian and Edwardian periods continued in regular use, with relatively few additions. By the 1940s and '50s, changing social and economic conditions, particularly in the areas of taxation and crippling death duties, meant that the lavish entertainment enjoyed by previous generations, and the army of servants required to provide it, had come to an end. In many cases, these changes were followed by massive sales of contents, and all too often the demolition of the country houses, leaving much of the rural landscape bereft of its major economic and cultural centre. Even in those houses which survived in the hands of their private owners or preservation societies, elitist attitudes have usually meant that the domestic quarters and their contents have not received the respect that they deserve, their original equipment, fixtures and even buildings being dispersed to make room for cafés, shops, toilets and stores. Fortunately this has not happened at Petworth, where visitors can still see a totally original country house kitchen, with every item of its own *batterie de cuisine* lining the great dressers, exactly as when it was in everyday use. Only in kitchens of this integrity is it possible to appreciate fully the quality and quantity of the tools and equipment which were required to maintain one of the world's finest culinary traditions.

KITCHEN EQUIPMENT AT PETWORTH HOUSE

This information has been collated from the inventories listed in notes 1, 2 and 3 below

Weighing	1632	1764	1869	*c.* 1900
beam scales	1	1	1	1
other scales	1		2	2
weights	8+ 'a pile'	?	13+	5+
The Range				
range	1	?	1	1
fire shovel	4	1	1	2
fire fork	1			
poker	1	1	1	2
coal rake	1			1
cinder sifter				1
Roasting				
jack		2	1	1
spits	21	9	9	9
pairs of spit racks	2	2	1	1
dripping pans	6	1	1	1
basting ladles	3	1	1	2

	1632	1764	1869	c. 1900
meat screens		1	1	1
Dutch ovens		1	2	
salamanders		2	2	5
toasting irons		1		
grid irons	5	3	5	?
Boiling				
large fixed coppers	1	2	1	1
beef forks	2	1	3	
pot hooks	2			1
pots/boilers/stock pots	9	11	11	3
steamers			3	3
skimmers/scummers	2	2	8	1
Fish				
large fish kettles	4	5	5	5
turbot kettles		2	2	1
small fish kettles/mackerel pans	5			6
cockle pans	1			
Stewing				
chafing dishes		2		
trivets	5	11	14	
large stewpans		24		18
small stewpans		12		34
glazing stewpans			68	6
vegetable stewpans				12
bain-marie & saucepans		9	5	26
skillets	5			
Frying				
frying pans	4	2	4	6
sauté pans/omelette pans			7	7

	1632	1764	1869	c. 1900
Baking				
egg whisks			10	
baking pans/hoops		4	48	31
patty pans		20	183	264
long biscuit moulds		24		
rolling pins			3	1
baking sheets		6	26	12
baking stands				10
peels	5	1	2	
wafer irons	2	1		
wire cooling trays				3+
Moulds				
'flowerpot'		3		
cylinders				27
borders				5
ornamental			49	41
darioles etc.				100
quenelles				76
game pie				3
hot pie				1
cutlet pans				25
unspecified			12	
Grinding				
chopping/mincing knives	1	2	8	?
marble mortars	1	1		2
mincers				1+
mustard querns/spice mills	2		1	
Spice and Seasoning Boxes				
spice boxes	2			
seasoning boxes & pots				11

Hand Tools	1632	1764	1869	c. 1900
bread graters	1	1	3	?
broth ladles		4	5	3
cleavers	3	2	2	1
collanders		1	2	1
knives			3	
potato ricers				2
saws			3	
slices		2		?
soup spoons		4		1+
spring tongs		1	2	?
vegetable scoops			8	4

HOUSEKEEPER'S ROOM AND STILLROOM

	1632	1764	1869	c. 1900
stills		2		
trivets		2		
jelly bags			7	
preserving pans		6	7	6
skimmers, ladles & strainers		4	2	
sugar boiling pans				1
sauce pans		4	7	
ice moulds		44		55
ice chests			1	1
freezing pots				4
ice spatulas		4		5
ice-making machine				1
boilers		1		1
tea kettles			3	7
tea pots			8	
coffee pots		5	9	4
chocolate pots		1	1	
coffee mill		1		?
mortar & pestle		2		1

NOTES

1. 'Inventory of the Goods of Henry Percy, 6th December 1632' (Syon MS. H II 1b) printed in 'The Household Papers of Henry Percy 1564–1632', *Camden Society,* 3rd series, 93 (1962).

2. 'An Inventory of Furniture Belonging to the Rt Hon. the Earl of Egremont at Petworth in Sussex 31st August 1764', Petworth House Archives.

3. The first is in the Petworth House Archives, while the second inventory is held by the National Trust, Petworth House.

4. *Inventory of Henry Percy,* p. 149.

5. Ibid.

6. For the development of skillets, see D. Eveleigh, 'Cooking Pots and Old Curios: The Posnet and the Skillet', *Folk Life,* 32 (1994) pp. 7–32.

7. R. Gentle and R. Feild, *English Domestic Brass 1680–1810* (London, 1975), pp. 29–36.

8. J. Farley, *The London Art of Cookery* (London, 1783, reprinted Lewes, Sussex, 1988), pp. 374–9 and S. Whatman, *The Housekeeping Book of Susanna Whatman 1766–1800* (London, 1987 edn), p. 44.

9. For references to baking pans see H. Glasse, *The Art of Cookery made Plain and Easy* (London, 1747): Oxford puddings, p. 77; mince pies, p. 74; and pound cake and Portugal cake, pp. 138–9.

10. See D. Attar, 'Keeping up Appearances', in C.A. Wilson (ed.), *The Appetite and the Eye* (Edinburgh, 1991), pp. 123–40 and contemporary sources such as A.B. Marshall, *Mrs Marshall's Larger Book of Extra Recipes* (London, 1891).

The writer wishes to record his thanks to Lord Egremont for access to the *batterie de cuisine* at Petworth, and for permission to quote from the Petworth House Archives. Sincere thanks are also due to Dr Diana Owen, administrator for the National Trust at Petworth, for her great help when working in the kitchens at Petworth.

CHAPTER SIX

STILLHOUSES AND STILLROOMS

C. Anne Wilson

The stillhouse is a building that has virtually disappeared. A single example of a complete stillhouse has recently been identified at Ham House by Peter Brears, but so far no others have been recognized, even in a ruined state.[1] Yet from Elizabethan to Georgian times the home-distilling of medicines, of flower waters for culinary and cosmetic use, and of spicy alcoholic waters for social drinking, was a regular practice; and there are plenty of inventories to prove that stillhouses existed in considerable numbers among the domestic offices of sixteenth- and seventeenth-century country houses, and that they contained stills, and glass bottles filled with distilled waters and other relevant objects.

The stillhouse underwent more radical changes than did any of the other domestic working areas: a change of location, from being an outbuilding to being a room within the house itself; a consequent change of name from stillhouse to stillroom; and, finally, a change of usage as its secondary use for preparing and storing conserves and sugar-based confections gradually displaced its primary purpose. The disused stillhouse was either taken down or reconstructed for some other activity, and was lost from view.

The object of distilling when it was first introduced into Britain was to extract the virtues from herbs, flowers, seeds and roots so as to make them available as ingredients for medicines. In the later Middle Ages medicinal distilling was carried out mainly by monks in monasteries and by apothecaries in the towns. But by the beginning of the sixteenth century it was also taking place in the largest domestic households. The *Northumberland Household Book* of 1512, which records the arrangements in the Percy family's two castles in Yorkshire, states: 'It is ordained to provide yearly for 30 sacks of charcoal for stilling of bottles of waters for my lord'; and it lists 'the Names of the said waters', comprising twenty-eight simple herbal waters, plus 'water for the stone' which was probably compounded from several different herbs, 'that his Lordship is accustomed to cause to be stilled yearly'.[2]

On the list are water of borage, water of walnut leaves, water of primroses, water

A seventeenth-century stillhouse interior. (Part of the engraved title-page to H. Wolley, The Accomplisht Ladys Delight, *6th edn, 1686)*

of scabious, and many more. But the first item of all is 'water of roses'. All through the sixteenth and seventeenth centuries rosewater was the distilled water most in demand, as it came to be used extensively for flavouring cooked dishes and sweet foodstuffs, as well as being valued for its medicinal virtues – it stengthened the heart, and was a cooling ingredient added to potions for patients with fevers and 'hot' diseases.[3]

Huge quantities of flowers were gathered in the rose season for making rosewater. An entry in the Rutland family accounts for 1593 shows a payment of 20s 'to James Nicholson of Southewell, for twentyfour thousand of red roses for stilling for her Ladyship, taken by Thomas Paynter, the gardener, at sundry times at xd. *le* thousand'.[4]

To accommodate roses in their thousands as well as the many other plants gathered each season for distillation required a stillhouse with one or more tables where the flowers could be stripped down and packed into still-bases, and where the stillheads and other equipment could be assembled; and of course a furnace to heat the stills. The early stillhouse was constructed as an outbuilding, well away from the main part of the house because of fire risk. Some stillhouses may have been wholly or partly freestanding: 'One Styllehouse in the passage leading to the garden' is mentioned in a document of 1558.[5] But others formed part of a range of outbuildings. At Ingatestone Hall in Essex, home of Sir William Petre, the outbuildings occupied two and a half sides of the outer court, and among them was the stillhouse, according to an inventory of 1600; but its exact location is not stated.[6] A stillhouse was inserted under the water cistern in the conduit house in the garden at Holmby House near Northampton.[7] William Lawson's *A New Orchard and Garden* (1626 edition) even has a diagram showing two little structures identified as stillhouses standing on mounts at the two corners of the main garden

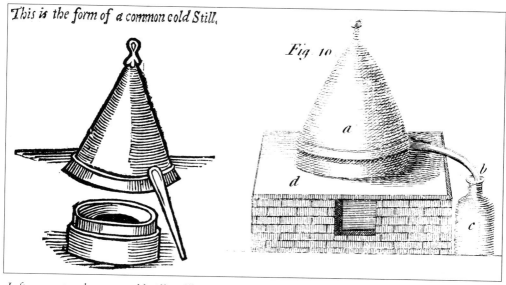

Left: a seventeenth-century cold still: stillhead and base (J. French, The Art of Distillation, 1653*); right: a cold still resting on a furnace. (A. Cooper,* The Complete Distiller, 1757*)*

nearest the façade of a country house. They look much more like banquet houses, but it is interesting that it was thought appropriate to label these structures, standing well away from the main building, as 'stillhouses'.[8]

Within the stillhouse the most important item was the furnace (or furnaces: they were sometimes joined in pairs or fours). The furnace was brick-built, and Gervase Markham described it as having two bottoms, the lower, at or near floor level, to receive ashes, while the upper 'must be made in the fashion of a Gridyron' to allow the ashes to fall through 'and not stay behind to choake up the fire that should heat the still'. At the upper level was a single opening, through which the fire was fed with charcoal; at the lower level there could be either one or several openings to allow ashes to be raked out and an updraught to enter.[9]

The brick furnace had a flat top with a circular aperture over the fire where a metal still could be placed to receive direct heat, or a waterbath could stand and gently warm a glass or pottery still. The ingredients were placed in the still-base, with added water or wine as required, and were often left to infuse overnight. Next day the stillhead and its receiver were attached and firmly sealed. Stillheads were of different types, according to the nature of the process by which the distillate was cooled. The simplest was that belonging to the so-called cold still or common still. This was a high, conical stillhead, with an outlet tube near the bottom. As the herbs or flowers in the base were heated, the steam rose and condensed on the inner surface of the stillhead, which could be cooled outside by applying a wet cloth, and the liquid trickled down to pass out through the tube into the receiving vessel.[10] The cold still was suitable for distilling simple flower or herb waters; the scented oils, which had boiling points well above that of water, came over with the steam and passed into the distilled water.

With alcohol it was a different matter. Alcohol boils just below 78°C and begins to vaporize a long way below that temperature. The water content of wine also begins to give off steam at a relatively low temperature, and the critical point in distilling is that when a little steam and a lot of alcohol vapour are coming off together, provided they can be recondensed as a liquid they will turn into strong alcoholic spirits. The two key factors are slow heating and speedy cooling, and it was to achieve the latter that the long serpentine cooling tube was invented far back in history. By the time it reached the stillhouses of Britain it had acquired the name of 'worm', and the tub of cold water through which it passed was known as the 'worm tub'.

The worm itself was a substantial piece of copper alloy, tin or lead tube, attached and firmly sealed to the outlet tube of the stillhead at one end, and to the receiver outside the water tub at the other end. The inventory of household furnishings made for Sir Patrick Murray of Ochtertyre House in Perthshire in 1763 refers to '1 lead worm for a staill weighted 83 pounds English weight' – so large that it had to be stored in the slaughterhouse. No doubt this hefty tube was used with the copper still kept in the guile house (brewhouse) for distilling whisky.[11] In country houses in England from the sixteenth to the eighteenth century the worm and worm tub were employed for the production of cordial waters – wine distilled over many herbs and spices – named 'cordial' because they quickened the action of the heart. The stillhead used with the worm was often curved and relatively small: most of the vapour passed straight through it to be cooled in the tube.

The third type of stillhead was known as the alembick or limbeck (a name of Arab origin) or as the bucket-head. This stillhead took the form of a fairly small cone with an inturned rim joined to an outlet tube. But around the outside of the cone was a bucket-shaped container, open at the top, into which cold water was poured. 'Take care', wrote Martha Bradley, 'that the head in the Bucket-still be

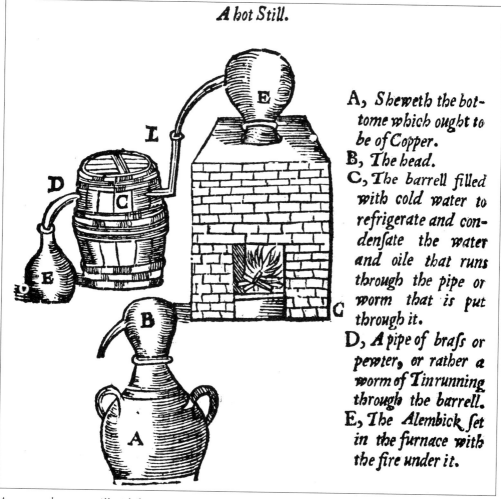

A hot Still.

A, Sheweth the bot-
tome which ought to
be of Copper.
B, The head.
C, The barrell filled
with cold water to
refrigerate and con-
densate the water
and oile that runs
through the pipe or
worm that is put
through it.
D, A pipe of brass or
pewter, or rather a
worm of Tin running
through the barrell.
E, The Alembick set
in the furnace with
the fire under it.

A seventeenth-century still with furnace and worm tub. The drawing is not quite accurate, as the pipe would actually
have spiralled down inside the tub, to emerge at a lower point (J. French, The Art of Distillation, *1653)*

always kept cool by drawing off the water in the bucket as fast as it grows all hot,
and putting cold water in the place.'[12]

Sometimes the bucket-head was called rather grandly a 'refrigeratory', as it was
in a recipe of 1710 for 'Strawberry Water'. Here the strawberries were first allowed
to ferment for a few days 'till the matter has acquired a vinous smell'. It was
distilled slowly in a tinned copper base, 'having its Head on with the

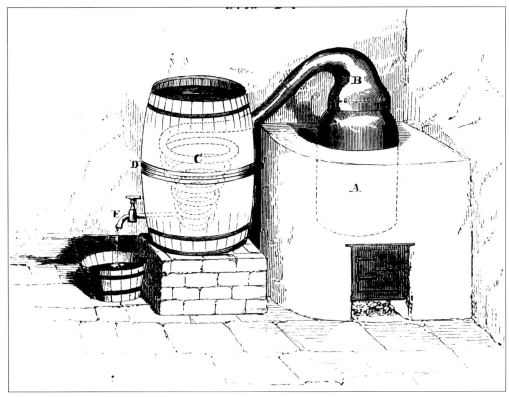

A nineteenth-century worm tub, with still and furnace. (J.H. Walsh, British Housekeeper's Book, *c. 1860)*

'Refrigeratory', which was placed in a water-bath, and yielded 'a Strawberry Water which is very spirituous, and good to corroborate the Heart and Brain; as also to purifye the Blood; being taken from half a spoonful to two. It is also made use of to clear and beautify the skin.'[13]

The biggest problem people encountered when they were distilling was the overheating of the still. This could happen even when simple waters were distilled, because the plant matter could burn on to the bottom of a tinned copper still-base, and the burnt flavour then came over with the plant oils – described by one writer as resembling 'the smell of burnt Tobacco'.[14] Another mistake was to let the contents of the still boil too violently so they 'boil over and run thick and foul into the vessel that is set to receive the water'. When that happened, 'the whole must be put back, and distilled over again'.[15] It was even worse if an alcoholic preparation

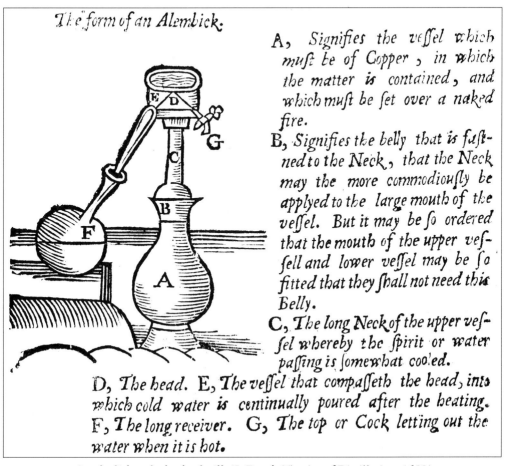

The form of an Alembick.

A, Signifies the veſſel which muſt be of Copper, in which the matter is contained, and which muſt be ſet over a naked fire.

B, Signifies the belly that is faſt-ned to the Neck, that the Neck may the more commodiouſly be applyed to the large mouth of the veſſel. But it may be ſo ordered that the mouth of the upper vef-ſell and lower veſſel may be ſo fitted that they ſhall not need this Belly.

C, The long Neck of the upper vef-ſel whereby the ſpirit or water paſſing is ſomewhat cooled.

D, The head. E, The veſſel that compaſſeth the head, into which cold water is centinually poured after the heating. F, The long receiver. G, The top or Cock letting out the water when it is hot.

An alembick, or bucket-head still. (J. French, The Art of Distillation, *1653)*

boiled up. It might break the seals, so that the alcohol escaped outside the still and caught fire; or it might boil over into the glass receiving vessel and burst it. Martha Bradley warned that it was 'the waters that have powdered ingredients that are most liable to these Accidents. Cinnamon Water is the most apt to boil over of all others, and care must therefore be taken accordingly.'[16]

When distillation had been successfully achieved, the glass receivers, suitably sealed, were generally used as containers for storing the distilled waters. Inventories show that they were kept thereafter in the stillhouse until needed. The contents of the stillhouse of Sir Thomas Fairfax at Walton in Yorkshire in 1624 were listed as:

'Fower stills, a seller for glasses, two shelves & thre(e) in the wall all full of glasses with distilled waters'.[17]

Another inventory made in the same year at Gilling Castle, also in Yorkshire, refers to the contents of the stillroom chamber, comprising a bedstead with items of bedding, a stool and a cupboard table.[18] This chamber probably adjoined the room where distilling took place, though it could have been above it under the roof; and its contents are a reminder that in the sixteenth century and the first part of the seventeenth, menservants often slept scattered through various rooms attached to domestic offices.

Quite early on, the stillhouse acquired an additional function. At Hengrave Hall, near Bury St Edmunds, in 1603 the stillhouse was used for 'preparing and keeping biskett cakes, marchpanes, herbs, spicebreads, fruits, conserves, etc.'[19] There were two main reasons for this development. One was that home distilling in the country house, and the preparation there of fruit preserves and other sweetmeats for the Tudor and Stuart banquet or dessert course, both came into fashion about the same time. Both activities were carried out under the direct supervision of the lady of the house. She was responsible for caring for members of her household who became ill, and often extended her care to poor sick neighbours, too; so the distilled herbal waters were part of her medicine chest, as were the dried herbs she stored in the still-room. But some of the spicy cordial waters were also produced for consumption at the banquet, alongside traditional spiced hippocras, which had been served as a digestive at the end of meals since medieval times. And they were accompanied by the preserved fruits, 'biskett cakes', and other banqueting fare.[20] So it made sense to have both the liquid and the solid components of the banquet made in the same place, well away from the hurly-burly of the kitchen.

It also made sense to store them in the stillroom. Damp was seen as a great cause of decay; and damp, unheated areas as places unsuitable for long-term storage of food. The stillhouse was a dry area because its furnace was in operation many times during the year, not only in summer. Dried herbs were distilled in winter to make simple waters such as mint water; and spiced cordials could often be prepared then, too. There were even ways to preserve fresh-picked rose petals, so that rosewater could be made again long after the rose season was over.

The stillhouse with its dry atmosphere thus became the place not only to dry out herbs, but also to store the 'biskett cakes', dry sweetmeats and preserves in boxes,

Stillhouse with stills and furnaces in the doorway, and herbs strung up to dry.
(N. Bailey, Dictionarium Domesticum, *1736)*

alongside the wet sweetmeats in their jars and the distilled waters in their glasses. It was important that the various solid sugary confections should be properly dried out when they were first made. This was often done by putting them in the bread oven when it had cooled for a while after the bread was drawn. But during the seventeenth century a new drying device was adopted from France and given the English name of 'stove'. It resembled a cupboard without doors, and had shelves of metal-wire mesh to allow maximum circulation of air around the things dried in it. Books of recipes for conserving and candying began to refer to the stove. A recipe for 'The best way to dry plums' has them resting at first in sugar syrup, but ends with the instruction: 'Set them to dry in a stove; for if you dry them in an oven they will be tough.'[21] The dry air of the stillhouse and later of the stillroom made them ideal places for the stove to stand.

The stillhouse at Ham House was identified by Peter Brears because it includes a number of features typical of such buildings. It may not have been the first stillhouse there, for architecturally it seems to belong to the late seventeenth or early eighteenth century, and it is hard to believe that no provision was made for distilling through most of the seventeenth century. The present stillhouse is not on the plan of Ham House of c. 1671–2 attributed to John Slezer and Jan Wyck; but two unidentified free-standing rectangular buildings are shown in the yard behind the kitchen, and one of them could have been used for distilling at an earlier period.

The inventory of 1677 certainly records a very well-equipped stillhouse, with three stills, nine glass heads for stills, four preserving pans, a pair of scales and weights, a copper oven, a skillet, three chafing dishes, a marble mortar and wooden pestle, '12 wooden boxes for sweetmeats' and several other items, making it clear that preserved fruits and 'biskett cakes' were prepared there as well as distilled waters. The 1683 inventory is even longer. The stills now comprise 'three stills with pewter heads', suggesting that the glass heads had not survived; and new additions are 'one copper thing for distilling' (probably a 'worm'), and a 'balneo Maria', that is a water-bath to stand over the furnace and provide a source of gentle heat for the still placed within it. Two iron stoves for drying sweetmeats are also listed here; and these continued in use along with the four preserving pans, marble mortar and wooden pestle, and a chafing dish in 1723 when a shorter inventory was drawn up.

At Ham House the kitchen has a semi-basement position at the west side of the house, with a flight of steps leading down to its door from the yard. The present rectangular stillhouse stands a few feet higher in a corner of the yard with one short side abutting the stack of the kitchen chimney. The air within was thus kept warm and dry throughout the year, guarding the sweetmeats and distilled waters stored there from damp and cold. Inside the building one brick-built furnace stands against the west wall, with another probably on the north wall, both having a window high above them. On the long south side is the entrance, with its original wooden door which contains an opening panel in the upper section to provide ventilation and a through draught across the upper part of the interior to carry off charcoal fumes. The flat roof extends beyond the doorway on this side to cover a pillared portico, a useful area in which herbs could have been strung up to dry.

A final clue as to the usage of the building emerges from the black and white

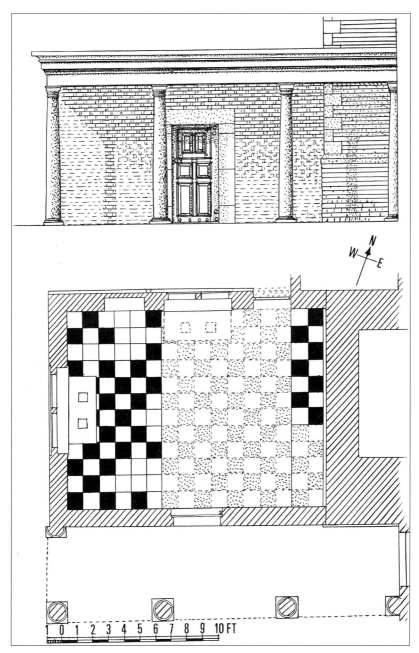

The stillhouse, Ham House, Surrey. Built in the late seventeenth century against the kitchen chimney stack at the north-west corner of Ham House, this stillhouse, with its fashionable black and white chequered marble floor and brick-built stoves, provided warm, dry and very convenient facilities where Elizabeth Murray, Countess of Dysart and Duchess of Lauderdale, could prepare and store her distilled waters and sugar confectionery.

chequerboard marble paving which extends from the furnaces, a floor suitably grand for the lady of the house when she carried out or supervised distilling operations. The doorway of the stillhouse is situated close to the exit from the western staircase of Ham House, so that she and her associates could have reached it without passing through the servants' quarters.

The domestic stillhouse met its end when the new fashion came in, during the later seventeenth century, for constructing country houses with the kitchen and service offices at garden level, below the family dining parlour and the saloon. Here the housekeeper (whose post was also relatively new) had her room, and here too was sited the stillroom, successor to the stillhouse, often nextdoor to the housekeeper's room. She became directly involved in both distilling and preserving activities, assisted by the stillroom maid. The stillroom was used for preparing desserts, and for making and storing fruit marmalades and jams. The furnace now stood below a chimney flue set in the wall; and a small wall oven was installed next to it, thus making it possible to bake pastry and biscuits in the room. This equipment was later superseded by a cast-iron cooking range with a fire-basket.

For another hundred years or so home distilling continued, but the need for it decreased as it became easier to purchase distilled waters from the ever-growing number of professional distillers and from the apothecaries. Families where distilling was practised often bought in molasses spirit or brandy, and redistilled them with their own ingredients, thus producing some very alcoholic spirits. Flavoured brandies were also made by infusing fruits, herbs and spices in brandy for a prescribed number of days or weeks, then straining off the liquid and bottling it. From about the 1830s onwards, brandies of this type were the only form of spirits for which recipes were published in cookery books, and home distilling died out altogether.

Well before that time the stillroom maid had acquired further duties. She acted as personal servant to the housekeeper, and rose early to clean the housekeeper's room and re-lay and light the fire there, before laying the table for the upper servants' breakfast. In the largest houses the upper servants ate their meals (apart from the first course of dinner, taken in the servants' hall) in the house-steward's room where the steward's boy laid the table, acted as waiter and cleared away afterwards. But in the many smaller establishments where the housekeeper supervised the running of the household the upper servants ate in her room, at what was known as the 'second table'; and it was the stillroom maid who laid out the crockery and cutlery, waited at mealtimes, and cleared away and washed up afterwards.

Other new duties came her way in the eighteenth century in connection with the growing popularity of tea and coffee, not only among the owners of country houses. Well before 1750 female servants were demanding either tea money or tea to be supplied ready to drink twice a day as part of their annual wages.[22] They drank it at breakfast, and two or three hours after their dinner; and from this second tea-drinking, which took place about 4.00 p.m., developed a tea meal with scones and plain cakes, served to the female staff in the housekeeper's room, and organized and cleared away by the stillroom maid.

She also looked after most of the tea and coffee requirements of the family and their guests, no small matter by Victorian times in view of the size of some of the house-parties held in country houses. At that period the stillroom maid had to get ready the trays for 'the eight o'clock bedroom teas', to give out 'the china and cake for the drawingroom five o'clock tea', and finally to prepare 'the tray with the tea cups and coffee cups for the after-dinner tea and coffee'.[23] These would be carried to the drawing-room later by the butler. The trays were set out and the tea and coffee were made in the stillroom.

Home distilling dwindled and died out, but the stillroom survived because of the many other functions it had acquired. Thomas Webster's *Encyclopaedia of Domestic Economy* of 1844 states that the housekeeper's 'care of the table is confined chiefly to pickling and preserving; and in preparing confectionery, arranging the desserts, and making the ice-creams. These preparations are all performed in the stillroom, and with the assistance of the stillroom maid.'[24]

During the nineteenth century new, smaller country houses often did not include a stillroom at all. As early as 1825, Mrs Parkes' book *Domestic Duties*

The store-room, successor to the stillroom. (Engraved title-page to A. Cobbett, The English Housekeeper, *6th edn, 1851)*

defines the housekeeper's province as 'to have charge of the store-room, with the preserves, pickles and confectionery', showing that the store-room was already well on the way to taking over the storage function of the stillroom.[25] Where there was no stillroom the active preparation of desserts, jellies and confectionery took place in the housekeeper's room, where a cast-iron range was installed in the fireplace.

But terminology can outlast reality. In some of the largest and longest established country houses, the title of the stillroom and of the stillroom maid survived to the beginning of the Second World War.

NOTES

1. The National Buildings Record computerized data-base did not in 1992 hold any record of a stillhouse.

2. T. Percy (ed.), *The Regulations and Establishment of the Household of Henry Algernon Percy, Fifth Earl of Northumberland* (London, 1905), p. 371.

3. J. Gerard, *Herball* (London, 1597), p. 1082.

4. *Manuscripts of the Duke of Rutland Preserved at Belvoir Castle* (Historic Manuscripts Commission, 24), 4 vols (London, 1888–1905), vol. 4, p. 406. 'Her Ladyship' was Elizabeth, Dowager Countess of Rutland.

5. A. Feuillerat (ed.), *Documents Relating to the Office of the Revels in the Time of Queen Elizabeth* (1905), quoted in *Oxford English Dictionary*.

6. F.G. Emmison, *Tudor Secretary* (London, 1961), p. 54. The outbuildings appear in a drawing of 1605 by Walker.

7. M. Girouard, *Life in the English Country House* (New Haven and London, 1978), p. 208, quoting Hartshorne, *History of Holdenby* [Holmby], with references to a Parliamentary survey of 1650.

8. W. Lawson, *A New Orchard and Garden* (3rd edn, 1626, reprinted London, 1927), f. 12.

9. C. Estienne and J. Liebault, *Maison rustique, Or the Countrey Farme*, revised, corrected and augmented by G. Markham (1616), pp. 447–8.

10. H. Glasse, *The Art of Cookery Made Plain and Easy* (London, 1747), p. 158, 'How to use this ordinary still'.

11. J. Colville (ed.), *Ochtertyre House: Book of Accounts*, Scottish History Society, 55 (1907), pp. 247–52.

12. M. Bradley, *The British Housewife* (London, *c.* 1760), p. 208.

13. *A Queen's Delight* (new edn, London, 1710), p. 220.

14. A. Cooper, *The Complete Distiller* (London, 1757), p. 33.

15. Bradley, *British Housewife*, p. 208.

16. Ibid.

17. E. Peacock (ed.), 'Inventories Made for Sir William and Sir Thomas Fairfax, Knights, of Walton and of Gilling Castle, Yorkshire . . .', *Archaeologia,* 48 (1885), p. 139.

18. Ibid., p. 151.

19. J. Gage, *History and Antiquities of Hengrave* (1822), pp. 36–7, quoted by Girouard, *English Country House*, p. 208, n. 37.

20. See C.A. Wilson (ed.), *'Banquetting Stuffe': The Fare and Social Background of the Tudor and Stuart Banquet* (Edinburgh, 1991), especially chapters 2 and 4 for the types of sweetmeat consumed at the banquet.

21. *The Ladies' Cabinet Enlarded and Opened* (1654), p. 18.

22. T. Alcock, *Observations on the Defects of the Poor Laws* (1752), p. 48, quoted by J.J. Hecht, *The Domestic Servant Class in Eighteenth-century England* (London, 1956), p. 223.

23. *The Servants' Practical Guide* (London, 1880), pp. 158–9.

24. T. Webster, *An Encyclopaedia of Domestic Economy* (London, 1844), p. 334.

25. Mrs W. Parkes, *Domestic Duties* (2nd edn, London, 1826), p. 125.

CHAPTER SEVEN

THE PASTRY

Peter Brears

Our *English Hus-wife* must be skilfull in the pastrie, and know how and in what manner to bake all sorts of meate, and what paste is fit for every meate, and how to handle and compound such pastes.[1]

From the sixteenth century at least, the main function of the pastry was to produce the numerous meat pies and pastries which formed such a substantial part of the diet in all great households. However, over the succeeding centuries more sweet pastries began to be introduced, the pastry now becoming a specialized confectionery department within major suites of kitchen offices. In the wealthiest establishments its operation lay in the skilled hands of a pastry-cook or chef, while in most others, including Calke Abbey in Derbyshire, it was occupied by the cook.

Since the best pastries were always produced in the coolest conditions, the pastry was usually located in a north-facing room, quite separate from the heat of fires or ovens if at all possible. White marble slabs set on solid masonry bases provided the ideal clean and cool working surface, one alternative being to set marble pastry squares into the wooden benches which lined the walls of the pastry. The space beneath could be filled with sliding flour bins, racks for pastry boards and baking trays, and drawers for utensils, while the wall-space above was furnished with shelves, cupboards and pin-rails to provide additional storage.

Once the pastry had been mixed in wooden or pottery bowls, it was worked either on the marble slabs, or on portable wooden pastry boards, these usually being of sycamore or quarter-cut beech, with their ends rebated into sturdy cross-pieces to prevent splitting and warping. Having been dusted with flour from a copper, brass or tinplate dredger, the pastry was rolled out with rolling pins of sycamore, beech, ash, various fruitwoods, or even lignum vitae, cylindrical forms being by far the most common, although some had a convex profile, so that the cook could readily roll out the pastry in any chosen direction.[2]

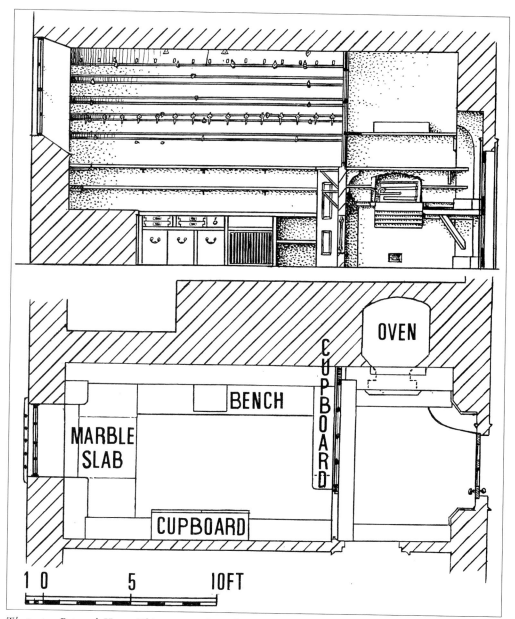

The pastry, Petworth House. This room was last refitted in the mid-1870s. Note the cool marble slab where the pastry was rolled out, the wooden benches with their deep flour bins, racks for pastry boards and baking trays, and drawers for equipment, and the shelves and pin-rails which provide extra storage around the walls above.

For trimming the pastry, any small knife could be used, but by the sixteenth century special pastry-jaggers or jagging-irons were being manufactured by the brassfounders. Florio's *Speronelle* of 1598 describes one of these as 'a brazen toole with a spoone at one end and a rowell or little spur at the other, that cookes use to cut out or marke their paste meates, called a jagging iron'. A mid-sixteenth century example was excavated from a former fishpond at St Neots, Huntingdonshire, in 1961.[3] It has a fig-shaped spoon-bowl at one end while at the other a copper rivet holds a brass wheel in place, its perimeter being filed into a zig-zag cutting edge. Cookery books such as Elizabeth Smith's *Complete Housewife, or Accomplish'd Gentlewoman's Companion* of 1727 describes how to use a 'spur [to] cut out little slips of paste the breadth of a little finger, and lay them over cross and cross in large diamonds', or 'with a jagging iron cut them out in little strips neither so broad or long as your little finger'.[4] Rather surprisingly, they were still being made in the opening years of the twentieth century, their overall design, including the cutting wheel, remaining virtually unchanged for around four hundred years. The only major difference to be found on the later examples was the replacement of the spoon-bowl with a variety of paste-pincers and cutters. The first were two broad grooved jaws, with which the pastry could be nipped into ornamental patterns, while the latter were sharp-edged frames mounted at right-angles to the shaft with which straight edges, crescents, leaves, stars, hearts, acorns, etc. were stamped out to decorate pies and other ornamental pastry-work. Harrod's catalogue of 1895 advertised these for sale at $6\frac{1}{2}d$, $8d$ and $10d$ each (i.e. $2\frac{1}{2}$p, 3p & 4p respectively), showing just how readily available they were at this period.

Wooden jiggers were also produced, their wheels being shaped by hand using a V-tool and a triangular file up to the 1860s, when James Howard of Chesham, Buckinghamshire, invented a machine for this purpose. His rapidly made, regularly toothed and extra sharp wheels were a great improvement on their predecessors, and were still being made by the Howard family in the late 1960s.[5]

If a number of regular shapes, such as round biscuits, were to be cut out of the pastry, any conveniently sized object could be called into service. Elizabeth Smith recommended her readers to use the top of a tin canister for cutting out small cakes in 1727, for example, Eliza Moxon cut out her cracknells with Queen Cake tins in 1741, while Hannah Glasse advised that gingerbread cakes should be cut out with either a tea-cup or a small glass in 1747.[6] Times were changing, however, Charles Carter stating in 1730 that if you wanted all your cracknells to be of the same size,

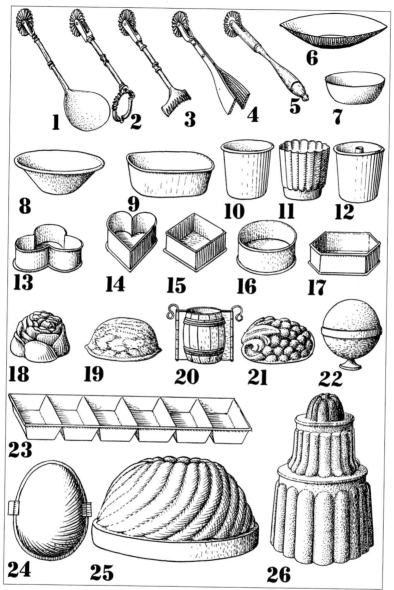

Equipment for the pastry: confectionery. Pastry jiggers, for cutting out the pastry: 1. brass, sixteenth century; 2–4. also brass, late nineteenth century; 5. an early twentieth-century wooden example. The late nineteenth-century baking tins include: 6. a boat cup; 7. a bouche cup; 8. a patty-pan; 9. a corbeille; 10. a dariole; 11. a fluted dariole; 12. a Monte Carlo mould; 13–17. Queen cake tins; 18. a rose mould; 19. a walnut mould; 20. a barrel mould; 21. a grape mould; 22. a bombe mould; 23. a sponge cake tin; 24. an ostrich egg mould; 25. a trois frères, turban or Turk's cap mould; and 26. a Savoy cake mould.

'You should have a Tin Mould on purpose to cut them'.[7] Furthermore, when making a French pie, some of the pastry should be rolled out thinly and then cut 'into vine-leaves, or the figures of any moulds you have'. From the second quarter of the eighteenth century, for the next two hundred years, 'moulds' or ornamental pastry cutters were made in vast numbers for use both in country house pastries and in commercial catering establishments. In their simplest form, they were sharp-edged rings of tinplate, probably neatly nesting one inside another in a circular box. They might have scalloped edges too, a design described by the author of *The Complete Confectioner* as being in the 'general fashion' in 1790.[8] Large oval cutters with scalloped edges were particularly favoured for vol-au-vents in the late nineteenth century. The most ornate pastry cutters took the form of miniature oak, holly, elm and ivy leaves, hearts, daisies, cherries, sprigs, ornamental borders, etc., each made of narrow strips of tinplate soldered on to small backing-plates and fitted with a handle. These were specifically for decorating the crusts of pies, enabling the cook to produce very attractive results with the minimum of additional trouble.

The practice of baking meat within a free-standing crust had become well-established in the medieval period, the method of hand-raising the crust apparently remaining virtually unchanged up to the present day.[9] Variously entitled pies, pasties or coffins, they might be round, oval or square in shape, usually with vertical or somewhat convex sides, and a shallow-domed inset lid.[10] From the nineteenth century at least, solid cylindrical blocks of sycamore or beech called pie-moulds or rammers were used to form the base and walls of the pies into their required shape, after which the filling could be inserted, the lid sealed down, and the decoration applied.[11] For game pies, chicken pies, etc., which were to be served cold on the table, elaborate moulds were introduced early in the nineteenth century. They had the double advantage of supporting the pastry throughout the period of baking, thus enabling a thinner crust to be used, while also moulding the pastry into elegant designs, without the need for further decoration. In their simplest forms, these raised pie moulds bore a band of vertical convex flutes around their oval walls, but grander versions might have garlands of laurel, or rich foliate patterns.[12] Finest of all, however, were those which transformed the pie into a massive-walled and stoutly battlemented medieval bastion which could effectively fortify the centre of the supper-table.

Finally, before the pies, along with other items of bakery, were placed in the

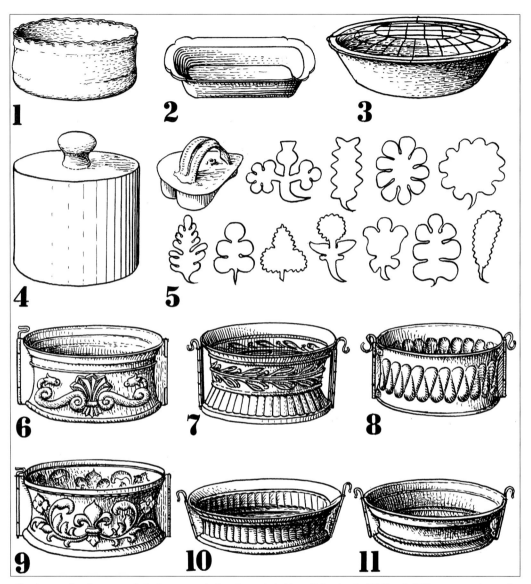

Equipment for the pastry: baked meats and pies. Ceramic baking dishes in: 1. Midlands Yellow-ware, sixteenth century; 2. creamware, from the Don Pottery, 1808; and 3. salt-glazed stoneware, with a wire grid to support the pastry lid, c. 1860. The pie-making equipment includes: 4. a wooden pie-block around which the pastry was raised, nineteenth century; 5. a tinplate cutter and further cutter designs used to decorate pie crusts etc., late nineteenth century; 6–9. tinplate raised pie moulds, mid-nineteenth century; and 10–11. hot pie moulds, late nineteenth century.

oven, they might have their upper surfaces coated with an appropriate glaze. Feathers were traditionally used for this purpose, but from the early eighteenth century, authors such as Hannah Glasse mention the adoption of the pastry-brush we use today, her orange tarts, for example, being buttered with either 'a Feather, or Brush'.[13]

OVENWARE

Although the traditional 'beehive' ovens were very practical for the baking of bread, they were rather less suitable for the production of fine pastries. One of the major problems was the fine ash and ember which always remained on the floor of the freshly heated oven, ready to become embedded in the cakes, pies, etc. placed upon it. Furthermore, the manipulation of small items of bakery within a hot, dark and probably rough-floored cavernous oven required considerable dexterity. It was for this reason that Ann Blencow recommended in 1694 that it was best to set small biscuits etc. 'on something that they may not touch the bottoms of the Oven'.[14] From this period, through to the present century, baking plates, or baking sheets, were made of tinplate, wrought iron, or copper, their use being quoted in numerous recipes. The traditional 11–18 in (28–46 cm) oblong and 10–14 in (25–35 cm) round shapes were still being offered for sale in Harrod's catalogue in 1895.

Some items, such as shortcakes, ginger nuts, and certain varieties of cake, were baked directly on the surface of these plates, but to prevent the bakery absorbing the heat too quickly, or sticking to the plates, a layer of some kind of insulating material was required. From the late medieval period, layers of wafers had served this purpose when making marchpanes, a practice which continued into the eighteenth century, as when Charles Carter baked his almond cakes on 'Wafers . . . on tin Plates' in 1730.[15] By this time, however, a commercially-produced alternative was available. Known as wafer-paper, it was a preparation of paste made in very thin sheets, Mrs Eales' recipe for bean'd breads published in 1718 stating that they should be laid 'in Lumps on Wafer-Paper, and set them on Papers in an Oven'.[16] Robert Wells' *Bread & Biscuit Baker* of 1889 was still covering tins or wires with wafer-paper when making biscuits, but from around this period the modern term 'rice-paper' came into general use.[17] The main advantage of this material was that it was edible, and therefore could be left in place beneath the macaroons etc. which had been baked on it.

For more general use, the kitchens of the larger households always carried a considerable stock of white writing paper. At Kiveton Park in South Yorkshire, for example, Mary Peel, the Duke of Leeds' housekeeper, had thirteen quires, of 312 sheets, in her charge in 1718.[18] This could be used simply as a clean, insulating layer on the baking plate, on which biscuit-mixtures could be dropped or placed, or buns set, above a sprinkling of flour. It could also be made into baking cases, as in this 1790 recipe for Naples biscuit: 'then put two sheets of paper on the copper plate you bake on, then take one sheet of paper, and make the edges of it stand up about an inch and a half high, and pour your batter in . . .'.[19] It also appears to have formed the original material from which hoops were made. These shallow vertical cylinders were used to surround cakes in the oven, causing the mixture to rise vertically, rather than spreading out in a flattish mass. Ann Blencowe's great cake of around 1694 is baked in 'a large strong paper, and butter it, & lett it be doubled with a paper hoope'.[20] Tinplate hoops were much more usual, however, the paper being used as a clean, insulating lining, Elizabeth Smith's great cake recipe of 1727 typically instructing that 'you must bake it in a deep hoop; butter the sides; put two papers at the bottom, flour it, and put in your cake'.[21] By the time Mrs Glasse published her *Art of Cookery . . .* in 1747, it was possible to suggest using 'a pan', in other words a modern cake-tin, as an alternative to the hoop, both utensils remaining in use until quite recently, Harrod's catalogue of 1895 listing hoops from 5½ to 11 in (14–28 cm), and pans from 4 to 11 in (10–28 cm) in diameter.[22]

The use of metal pans had already become well-established by the early seventeenth century at the latest, Sir Ralph Verney instructing that his new cook should be shown 'what brass baking pans there are in my house and also latten pans for puddings or tarts' in 1653.[23] Even pewter, with its low melting point, was made into bake-ware, Mary Chafin baking her orange pudding 'in a pewter Dish with Crust under and over it . . .' in 1698.[24] Probably the most common metals used in the making of pans were thin sheet iron and tinplate. Round, oval or rounded oblong shaped pans, with flat bases, walls flaring outwards from their bases, and perhaps handles too, were in constant use from this period through to the middle of the twentieth century. They were ideal for the general run of puddings and pies, but the inventive mid-Victorians designed a number of interesting variations. One, illustrated by Mrs Beeton, had a slightly domed wire framework which clipped on top of the rim once the contents were in place.[25] This supported the pastry cover during baking, preventing it from sagging into the fruit or meat, etc. in the dish below. One further mid-Victorian development of much more widespread and practical value, was the use of vitreous white enamel to coat pressed steel baking dishes. Ornamented with royal blue edges, this ware was bright and attractive, very hard-wearing and economical. It was still to be found in use in many households up to around the 1960s, when it was largely replaced by new oven-to-table wares in enamelled iron, heat-resistant glass, and stonewares copying the contemporary studio pottery.

Ceramic baking dishes had already been in use from the sixteenth century, and by the seventeenth these took the form of round dishes with flaring walls and broad rims, with vertical walls fluted around the rim like a pie-crust, or large round shallow bowls made from rolled-out sheets of clay pressed over a mould, all being suitable to contain food in the oven.[26] The 'Halfpenny Welch Dish' used by Hannah Glasse was of the latter variety, probably being made in the Buckley pottery in Flintshire.[27] During the later eighteenth century the new factory potteries also provided baking dishes in fine creamware, their materials and design following that of the elegant new Queens Ware dinner services made by Wedgwood, Leeds, and other leading companies. A glance through their pattern-books soon provides detailed illustrations of their 'Bakers round, or oval, 6 to 16 Inches', 'Octagonal Baker, 6 to 14 Inches' or even 'Cassarole, 6 to 12 Inches'.[28] Soon afterwards they were being produced with transfer-printed decoration to match every popular dinner-service design, those made in Spode's Blue Italian, for example, having been in continuous production from the early nineteenth century through to the present day. Bakers were also made in brown salt-glazed stoneware, one of the most robust and practical forms of ceramic ovenware ever devised. The main centres of production were in Derbyshire, where they were produced in a useful range of shapes and sizes by firms such as Pearson & Co. of Whittingham Moor, or James Pearson of Oldfield Pottery, Brampton, for much of the nineteenth and twentieth centuries.[29]

For smaller items of bakery, such as individual cakes, custards, savouries or puddings, small pans appropriately called patty-pans were used. William Howitt wrote enthusiastically about them in his book on the *Rural Life of England* of 1837: 'O! such cheesecakes, and such patties, and such little cakes of various names and natures, for tea, and *entremets* and dessert. I see the oven door open and shut, as the iron tray of nicely laden patty-pans goes into the oven, or comes out with a rich perfection, and with odours most delicious, most mouth-melting, most in-expressible!'[30]

Patty-pans were round, with shallow flaring sides rising from a flat bottom, their usual size being around three inches in diameter by up to an inch and a half in depth. They were made in a variety of materials, Hannah Glasse instructing that 'If you bake in tin Patties, butter them. . . . If in China, or Glass, no Crust but the top one . . .' when making tarts.[31] They were also made in large numbers in salt-glazed stoneware, but tinplate patty-pans have always been the most common, and are still available today under the name of tart-tins. Over the past three hundred years these small individual-sized baking tins have been made in a variety of shapes. Heart-pans became popular for Shrewsbury cakes, Portugal cakes, Queen cakes or best heart cakes in the early eighteenth century, while both fluted patty-pans and darioles, with their much deeper profiles, were in widespread use by the mid-nineteenth century.[32] From this time, however, the Victorian love of decoration brought a whole range of new tinplate moulds for sweets, savouries and biscuits on to the market, a fashionable kitchen now having access to:[33]

Patty-pans	plain or fluted, from 2½ in (6.5 cm) to 5 in (13 cm) diameter
Oval Patties	6½ in (16.5 cm) to 12½ in (32 cm) long
Cutlet Patties	3⅜ in (8.5 cm) long
Boat Patties	2½ in (6.5 cm) to 4 in (10 cm) long
Quenelle Patties	2¾ in (7 cm) long
Stamped Tins	in the form of halved walnuts, pears, pineapples, bunches of grapes, etc.
Darioles	plain or fluted, from 1⅝ in (4 cm) to 2½ in (6.5 cm) diameter
Bouche Cups	plain or fluted, 1¼ in (3 cm) to 2 in (5 cm) diameter
Queen's Cake Moulds	with vertical sides, in the shape of hearts, clubs, crescents, rounds, ovals, diamonds and squares
Cornet Tins	(for cornucopias, wafers, etc.)
Sponge Cake Tins	with compartments for six cakes, either oblong ('square') or finger-shaped
Syringe Moulds or Biscuit Forcers	devices introduced by the late eighteenth century by which soft biscuit doughs were extruded in decorative forms[34]

Barrel, Rose, Artichoke, Basket, Swan and Egg Moulds[35]

A similarly rich variety of moulds were also introduced for larger cakes, the traditional hoops now being supplemented by cake moulds of great complexity.[36] Most of them were used for the lighter, spongier mixtures, probably the most esteemed being the Savoy mould. This had a very tall fluted body, which was extended with a broad band of paper in order to enable an even taller cake to be baked within it.[37] Other moulds closely resembled the jelly-moulds of the period, with fluted tapering sides leading up to a flattish top of tinplate or copper deeply embossed with a geometric or naturalistic design, while the *trois freres* mould with its spiral flutes radiating from a central hole, now known as a kugelhupf, continued the eighteenth-century form of the turk's cap or turban mould.[38]

The period extending from the 1880s to the First World War, when moulds such as these were in regular use, represented the peak of the country house pastry's achievements. The unique combination of generations of accumulated skill, masses of specialized equipment and the finest of raw materials, all financed from the vast profits of industrial and commercial expansion in Britain and her Empire, now enabled the aristocracy and gentry to demonstrate their fashionable sophistication through the medium of lavish confectionery. By the 1920s this position had already begun to decline, as financial economies had to be implemented, and the High Victorian and Edwardian taste for richness and over-elaboration in every aspect of life was rejected in favour of lighter and more informal styles. As a result, pastry chefs disappeared, and the pastry, along with the great kitchen, fell out of use in most houses in the 1930s and '40s, its equipment being either scrapped or consigned to the attic, except for a few basic items which could still be used in the new compact kitchens which now fulfilled all the family's needs.

NOTES

1. G. Markham, *The English Hus-wife* (London, 1615), p. 64.

2. E.H. Pinto, *Treen and Other Wooden Bygones* (London, 1969), p. 141.

3. P.V. Addyman and J. Marjoram, 'An 18th-century Mansion, a Fishpond . . . at St Neots, Huntingdonshire', *Post Medieval Archaeology*, 6 (1972), pp. 91–2.

4. E. Smith, *Complete Housewife, or Accomplish'd Gentlewoman's Companion* (London, 1727), p. 138.

5. Pinto, *Treen*, p. 140.

6. Smith, *Complete Housewife*, p. 180; E. Moxon, *English Housewifry Exemplified* (Leeds, 1741),

p. 128; H. Glasse, *The Art of Cookery Made Plain and Easy* (London, 1747), p. 139.

7. C. Carter, *The Complete Practical Cook* (London, 1730), p. 173.

8. 'A Person', *The Complete Confectioner* (London, 1790), p. 25.

9. P. Brears, 'Pots for Potting', in C.A. Wilson (ed.), *Waste Not, Want Not* (Edinburgh, 1991), pp. 33–7.

10. For example G. Saintsbury (ed.), *The Receipt Book of Ann Blencowe AD 1694* (London, 1925), p. 131, and Carter, *Complete Practical Cook*, p. 160.

11. Pinto, *Treen*, p. 141.

12. For example I. Beeton, *Beeton's Book of Household Management* (London, 1859–61), p. 609, and J. Gouffe, *The Royal Cookery Book* (London, 1869), pp. 140–2.

13. Glasse, *Art of Cookery*, p. 75.

14. Saintsbury, *Receipt Book*, p. 7.

15. Carter, *Complete Practical Cook*, p. 115.

16. M. Eales, *Mrs Mary Eales's Receipts* (London, 1733 edn), p. 70.

17. R. Wells, *Bread and Biscuit Baker* (London, 1889), p. 46.

18. P. Brears, *The Gentlewoman's Kitchen* (Wakefield, 1984), p. 153.

19. 'A Person', *Complete Confectioner*, p. 6.

20. Saintsbury, *Receipt Book*, p. 3.

21. Smith, *Complete Housewife*, p. 169.

22. Glasse, *Art of Cookery*, p. 138.

23. M. Girouard, *A Country House Companion* (New Haven and London, 1987), p. 130.

24. M. Chafin, *Original Country Recipes* (London, 1979), p. 48.

25. Beeton, *Household Management*, p. 260.

26. E.g. P. Brears, 'Post Medieval Pottery', in P. Mayes and L.A.S. Butler, *Sandal Castle Excavations 1964–73* (Wakefield, 1983), pp. 215–20, figs 66, 68 and 70 for sixteenth-century baking vessels.

27. Glasse, *Art of Cookery*, p. 101.

28. Anon., *Don Pottery Pattern Book* (Doncaster, 1807), nos 38 and 153.

29. For a range of similar wares see *Silber and Fleming Glass and China Book* (reprinted Ware, Herts, 1990), p. 70.

30. W. Howitt, *Rural Life of England* (London, 1837), p. 93.

31. Glasse, *Art of Cookery*, p. 75.

32. Carter, *Complete Practical Cook*, pp. 169 and 170.

33. See *Harrod's Catalogue* (London, 1895).

34. Anon., *Take 6 Eggs* (Stafford, 1991), p. 8. 'To make Almond Puffs [*c.* 1655] . . . when tis paste put it through your Squirt Upon White [Sugar'd] papers and bake them in an oven That will not brown them.'

35. A.B. Marshall, *Mrs A.B. Marshall's Large Cookery Book of Extra Recipes,* (London, 1894 edn), pp. 539, 570, 525, 487, 483 and 490.

36. Beeton, *Household Management*, pp. 856, 859, 862 and 867.

37. T.P. Lewis and A.G. Bromley, *The Victorian Book of Cakes* (reprinted London, 1991), pp. 155–6.

38. Marshall, *Large Cookery Book*, p. 474 and F.S. Cooper, *Ironmonger's Catalogue* (London, 1859), p. 178.

CHAPTER EIGHT

THE BAKEHOUSE

Peter Brears

The Office of the Yeoman Baker [1605]

Hee is to receave his cornne from the yeoman of the garner, by tallie, and that deliver to the miller, and to see it bee sweete and well grounde, and to make thereof such proportion of manchett, cheat and ranchett, as the officers of the hosehoulde in theire discretion shall apointe . . .[1]

From the medieval period through to the opening decades of the twentieth century, most of the bakers who worked in the major country houses would have clearly recognized these duties, even if the names of their loaves might have changed over the years. In the smaller households, where no separate baker was employed, the same tasks were undertaken by the cook, or by a female member of the domestic staff. Susanna Whatman instructed her cook at Turkey Court in Kent to 'bake her bread in the morning in time enough for breakfast. She should bake Wednesdays and Saturdays', while at Bank Hall, Liverpool, it was the dairymaid who had 'once every week [to] make the house bread and [the servant men] shall help her to knead'.[2]

Wherever possible, the bakehouse was located in an outbuilding, where there was space for its stores of flour, meal and fuel and where its flour dust and smoking ovens would not contaminate the main house. Frequently it adjoined the brewhouse, as at Calke Abbey in Derbyshire, since their physical requirements were very similar, and the duties of baker and brewer might be combined in a single servant who understood the qualities of grain and the management of yeast.

In this most conservative of crafts, the basic methods and range of equipment remained unchanged for generations. One of the best descriptions of the baker's tools and equipment used at the start of this period comes from Randle Holme's *Academy of Armory*, published in Chester in 1688.[3] This encyclopaedic book on heraldry illustrates and defines every conceivable device which could ever appear on a coat of arms.

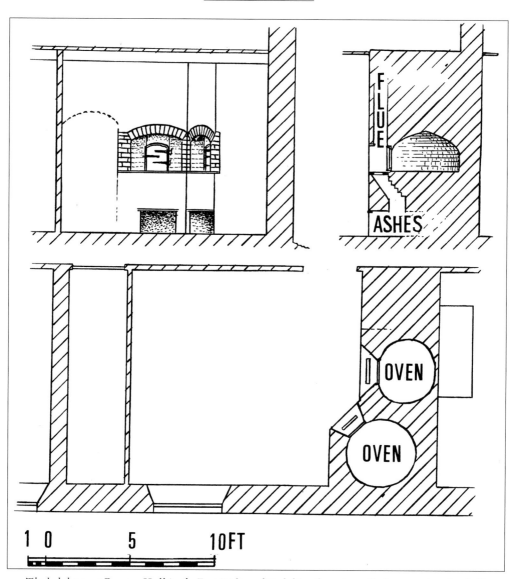

FLUE

ASHES

OVEN

OVEN

1 0   5   10FT

The bakehouse at Boynton Hall in the East Riding of Yorkshire, forms part of a large service wing built c. 1770. The two domed brick ovens, with their iron doors and with ash slots in their thresholds, are typical of this period.

Firstly, to prepare the flour, it was processed through 'the Baker's Ark, with its Lid or Leaf open, the Wheel set therein (which is a long Beam with Hoops, Cross pieces and Ribs, set at a distance from it, and covered with a kind of Canvas) with its Hopper set upon it, into which the Bolted Meal was put to fall into the Wheel, and so from the Wheel, the Bran to run out at the [bottom] into Vessels set to receive it; and the pure Dant, or second sort of Meal to fall into the Ark . . . by the help of this Engine more meal will be taken from its bran in one hour, than a person will searce or sift in a whole day.' A 'Bakers half round shovel, or a Meal shovel, being a shovel with rising sides [and] no head or cross piece at the top, as others have; for there needs none such, being it hath no strength laid to it, to go into any hard thing' was used to take the flour from the ark, and transfer it into 'a Kneading Trough, being made all of Plank or strong Boards; in this they knead all their Dough, or mix it in the Trough'. When the dough was removed from here, a 'Dough scrape, or a Grater' being 'a kind of Paddle with a Bended handle set into a Wooden haft', was used to clean all the dough from the sides and bottom of the trough. Next the 'Brake . . . a thick plank set upon four or more strong feet at the farther side of [which] is fastened a thick Pole fixed with a Bolt into a turning Staple, so that the nearer end of the Pole (which is made small to hold it by) may be turned to any side or part of the Plank', was used to knead and beat the dough until it was ready to be moulded into loaves. An alternative type of pole or baker's break took the form of 'a long round Rowler with Rings and Staples fastened at each end', but if this was not available the dough was wrapped in a cloth and kneaded underfoot.[4] The next operation took place on a separate 'Moulding Board or Moulding Table . . . a Tressel or Plank set upon strong feet, upon which Loaves of Bread are made or molded up' using a 'Dough Knife . . . a long Bladed Knife, with a very long Haft, half a Yard or three quarters long, with which Dough is cut into smaller pieces from the large Lump.' Wooden dishes could be used at this stage to hold the dough while it proved, Eliza Smith instructing the baker to 'have ready six wooden quart dishes, and fill them with dough. Let them stand a quarter of an hour to heave, then turn them out into the oven.' These were the vessels which Sir Ralph Verney referred to in 1653, when he ordered that 'If there is not wooden dishes to make white bread, buy a dozen.'[5] If the bakehouse was a separate room, a 'Braide, or Braed, which is a broad long Board, with a hole in one end of it to hold it by [was used by the] Cooks, and all other Household Servants to carry Bread unbaked, Pies, Pasties and all other sorts of Baked Meats, to and from the Bake-house'.

In the bakehouse itself, the most important structure was the beehive 'Oven,

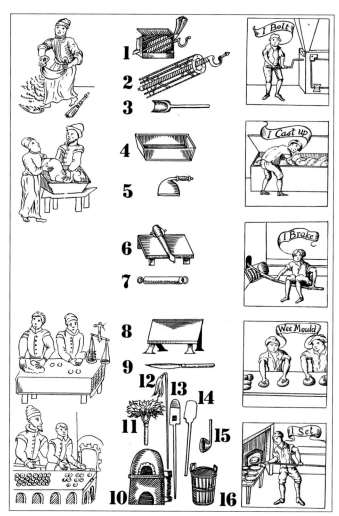

The art of baking. These illustrations, taken from the ordinances of the York Bakers Company of 1598 (left),
Randle Holme's Academy of Armory *of 1688 (centre), and John Penkethman's* Artachthos *of 1638 (right),*
provide a detailed picture of the traditional methods of baking bread, including (top to bottom): bolting, by hand
and by machine, using a baker's ark or flour dresser (1), with its internal wheel (2) covered in canvas, and a
meal shovel (3) for extracting the flour; kneading in a kneading trough (4), which is emptied using a dough
scrape (5); breaking with brakes (6–7); moulding, using a moulding board (8) and a dough knife (9); baking,
using an oven (10) heated with a kid of gorse on a pikell or pitchfork (11), the ashes being swabbed out with a
maukin or scovel (12), before the bread was inserted and later removed with either a shod peel (13) or a baker's
wooden peel (14), while custard coffins were filled with a custard filler or custard dish (15). Finally the loaves
were carried away in an open-sided baker's or bread basket (16).

with an Ashes hole under it; some term it a double Oven, or one Oven mounted upon another, having a stay or stand on the left side of it, to rest or set any thing out of the Oven thereon'. Like all ovens of this period, it was heated by thrusting bundles of fast-burning timber fuel such as cordwood into the oven-chamber itself, in order to thoroughly heat the surrounding masonry. Holme illustrates the iron 'Pikell or Pitchfork' mounted on its long wooden handle or shaft, by which a 'Kid of Gorse' is about to be used for this purpose. Having built up a sufficient temperature, the embers were scraped out and left to cool in the ash-hole below, the finer ashes being removed with a 'Maukin [or scovel] . . . a foul and dirty Cloth hung at the end of a long Pole, which being wet, the Baker sweeps all the ashes together therewith, which the Fire or Fuel in heating of the Oven, hath scattered all about within it'. He next used the peel, an instrument having a thin flat blade mounted at the end of a long handle, to insert the bread etc., and to remove it after baking. The baker's peel was all of wood, its blade being 'large and broad before, and narrow or round to the Staff', while the 'Peel shod, or a shod Peel' was 'a Peel made of Wood, but by reason Wood will not carry so thin an edge as to go under little things with tender sides and bottoms, therefore it is plated with Iron like a Shovel to take such things out without hurting them'. In addition, 'Peels are sometimes made of Iron Plate, fixed to a Staff by a Socket, having the further part made roundish'. The only other item used in the baking process was 'the Custard Dish or Custard Filler; by the help of this Custard Batter is put into the [pastry] Cases, as they are in the Oven, being no other than a Wooden Dish made fast upon the end of a Staff.'

Finally the bread was packed into either 'a round large Basket with Ears, or with Handles . . . called by the name of a Baker's Basket, or a Bread Basket', or into 'a flat Bottom Bread Basket, these are generally made of Osier Twigs with a close wound bottom, with a Wreath about the middle and top with two Ears, all the rest being so open, that any thing may be seen that is put into it.' Thus packed, the bread was carried away into the pantry, ready for use either in the kitchen, or on the dining table.

A study of country house inventories clearly demonstrates the continuity of the tradition of bolting the freshly-milled flour, kneading it into dough and baking it in beehive shaped masonry ovens, as may be seen in the following examples:

Sir Thomas Fairfax's bakehouse at Walton, Yorks, 1642[6]
'a meal sieve, a temsing tub, a tub for kneading manchet in, a dough trough, a coverlet for treading paste, a scraper, an iron peel and two bread baskets'

Sir Thomas Wentworth's 'boulting houses', Bretton Hall, Yorks, 1688[7]
'three meal arks, five dressers, two meal tubs, two kneading troughs . . . one pasty peel . . .'

Francis, Viscount Irwin's bakehouse, Temple Newsam, Yorks, 1808[8]
'. . . a meal bin and cover, a small meal chest, an old dressing mill with 4 sieves, a kneading trough, a Dutch oven set in brick . . .'

During the course of the nineteenth century, however, fewer and fewer houses continued to dress their own meal into flour, its place now being taken by ready-to-use supplies purchased from a commercial miller or grocer. As a result, most domestic dressing machines went out of use, although wire or horsehair sieves were retained for removing any lumps or foreign bodies from the flour. Other changes included the replacement of the break by hand kneading, and the use of German yeast instead of the brewers' or home-made yeasts of earlier generations. In addition, baking tins became much more popular, especially the rectangular tinplate bread tins which so effectively increased the capacity of the oven.

Despite the considerable improvements in the coal-fired iron ovens, it was still generally recognized that they could not rival the brick-built beehive ovens for baking bread. Eliza Acton stressed the problems of controlling the heat of iron ovens, and, along with Mrs Beeton, advised that they could be used effectively if their bases were lined with bricks and their doors left open when they became over-heated.[9] For these reasons, beehive ovens remained in use in those households which enjoyed sufficient skilled staff to operate them, but in most houses they had gone out of use by the time of the First World War, being replaced by the coal-fired iron ovens in the kitchens, back-kitchens or stillrooms; these in turn were replaced by electric or gas ovens, or by insulated closed stoves such as the Aga in the inter-war years.

NOTES

1. 'A Breviate Touching the Order and Governmente of a Nobleman's House &c', *Archaeologia*, 13 (London, 1800), pp. 315–84.
2. S. Whatman, *The Housekeeping Book of Susanna Whatman 1776–1800* (London, 1987), p. 43; 'Regulations for the Household of the Moore Family, Bank Hall near Liverpool, 1677', in M. Girouard, *A Country House Companion* (New Haven and London 1987), p. 131.
3. R. Holme, *Academy of Armory* (Chester, 1688), p. 315. For a description of bakehouse design

The bakehouse at Lanhydrock, Cornwall. The oven was supplied by Clement Jeakes, of Great Russell Street, London and incorporates a proving oven below the main one. This type of oven replaced the old beehive-shaped bread oven. (By courtesy of Country Life)

and equipment at the opening of the nineteenth century, see A. Eldin, *A Treatise on the Art of Breadmaking* (London, 1805), ed. T. Jaine (Totnes, 1992), pp. 72–6.

4.   G. Markham, *The English Hus-wife* (London, 1615), p. 126.

5.   Sir R. Verney to W. Roades, 1653, in Girouard, *Country House Companion,* p. 130.

6.   'Inventories made for Sir William and Sir Thomas Fairfax, Knights . . .', *Archaeologia,* 48 (London, 1882), p. 148.

7.   P. Brears, *Yorkshire Probate Inventories 1542–1689* (Leeds, 1972), p. 150.

8.   Inventory of Frances, Viscount Irwin, 1808. Yorkshire Archaeological Society DD54.

9.   E. Acton, *The English Bread Book* (London, 1852), p. 184 and I. Beeton, *Beeton's Book of Household Management* (London, 1859–61), p. 836. For detailed descriptions of the use of the beehive oven see Acton, *English Bread,* p. 180 and Mrs Loudon, *The Lady's Country Companion* (London, 1845), pp. 50–1.

CHAPTER NINE

THE DAIRY

Peter Brears

Although the primary function of the dairy was to provide the country house with high quality, unadulterated milk, cream, butter, buttermilk, cheese, whey, curds and numerous creamy delicacies, it enjoyed a social status quite unlike that of any other culinary department.[1] The main reason for this would appear to be the romantic view, popular from the sixteenth century at least, that milkmaids embodied the very essence of fresh, pure country beauty, health, innocence and virtue. In Shakespeare's *Winter's Tale* Polixenes describes Perdita as

> . . . the prettiest low-born lass that ever
> Ran on the green-sward: nothing she does or seems
> But smacks of something greater than herself,
> Too noble for this place . . . good sooth, she is
> The queen of curds and cream[2]

while Sir Thomas Overbury provides a fulsome account of the fair and happy milkmaid who rose with chanticleer and made the lamb her curfew, whose hands produced the sweetest, whitest milk, whose breath was scented like new-made hay, and whose every action was characterized by grace, decency and chastity.[3] An alternative view was presented by Henry Percy, 9th Earl of Northumberland, to his son in 1595: 'The kitching, buttery or pantry are not places proper for [great mens wyfes]; a dary is tolerable; for soe may yow have perhaps a dische of butter, a soft cheese, or somme clouted creme in a sommer . . . .'.[4]

Given these images, it is not surprising that dairy-work was recognized as a suitable activity for the mistress of the household, whether she be a Queen or a farmer's wife. During the seventeenth century her knowledge of its practicalities could be enhanced by reading the appropriate chapters in Gervase Markham's *The English Hus-wife* of 1615, or Robert Codrington's *Youth's Behaviour or Decency in Conversation Amongst Women* of 1672, while in 1685 Hannah Wolley provided her

In this fine watercolour of 1861, Hetty Sorrel and Squire Donnithorne in Mrs Poyser's Dairy, *E.H. Corbould shows Hetty Sorrel as the quintessential dairymaid, that unique blend of fresh rustic beauty and innocence which the upper classes, here represented by Squire Donnithorne, found so appealing. The painting also includes a wealth of fascinating detail, such as Hetty's quilted petticoat and pattens. The milking stool, the cream settling in its pans, the plunge churn, the bowl in which the buttermilk was beaten out, the scales and the wooden prints (round, with a cow, on the bench and the Welsh canoe shape in her hand) show the whole process of butter making. Cheesemaking, meanwhile, is represented by the lever press in the foreground, and the immense stone-weighted press in the alcove at the back. (Royal Collections © 1996, Her Majesty Queen Elizabeth II)*

with *Directions for such as desire to be Dairy Maids*.[5] In addition, recipe books now gave her access to the wonderful array of syllabubs, clotted creams, fruit-flavoured creams, fools, leaches and the richest of curds, cheesecakes and fine cheeses which were the great specialities of the country house dairy.[6]

In the eighteenth century it was still 'properly in the wife's province, if she were capable, lived always in the country, and liked to manage a dairy', to do so, and, as Stephen Tempest of Broughton continued to advise his son, 'you may be sure it would be in your Interest to provide her all conveniences'.[7] The virtuous aspects of the dairy became increasingly appreciated as the Romantic movement invaded every aspect of literature and the fine and decorative arts in the second half of the century. Idyllic rural scenes were now depicted both by painters such as John Constable and George Moreland, and by poets such as Robert Bloomfield, who told how, after milking, the mistress bore a bright-scoured brimming pail to the dairy door,[8]

> And now the dairy claims her choicest care,
> And half her household find employment there:
> Slow rolls the churn, its load of clogging cream
> At once forgoes its quality and name.
> From knotty particles first floating wide
> Congealing butter's dashed from side to side;
> Streams of new milk through flowing coolers stray,
> And snow-white curd abounds, and wholesome whey.
> Due north the unglaz'd windows, cold and clear,
> For warming beams are unwelcome here . . .
> Thus wastes the morn, till each with pleasure sees
> The bustle o'er, and press'd the new-made cheese.

Queen Charlotte, the Duchesses of Norfolk, Bedford and Rutland and numerous other titled ladies took the greatest interest and delight in their dairies, and also in their personal dairying skills.[9] When living in Brescia in Northern Italy, Lady Mary Wortley Montagu gained such a high reputation for teaching the local people how to make custards, cheesecakes and butter, that they actually proposed to erect a statue of her in her honour, but the highest accolade to the aristocratic English dairy came in 1783–6, when Marie Antoinette established her little model village

The dairy at Uppark, Sussex. Here the dairymaid, Mary Ann Bullock, was surprised speechless when her master, Sir Harry Fetherstonhaugh, appeared at the door and asked her to marry him. 'Don't answer me now,' he continued, 'but if you will have me, cut a slice out of the leg of mutton that is coming up for my dinner today.' When the mutton arrived, the slice had been cut, and so they were married in 1825. The dairy was renovated in 1832, when the stained glass and the white tiles 'with rich Enamelled Flower Border' seen here were installed by the London decorator Charles Pepper.

of Le Hameau at the Petit Trianon in Versailles. Here the Queen and her ladies adopted the role of dairymaids, using a clean dairy and a preparation dairy in the English manner.[10]

A similar, but more advantageous reversal of roles was occasionally enjoyed by a dairymaid. In 1825, when Mary Ann Bullock was working in the dairy at Uppark in Sussex, her master, Sir Harry Fetherstonhaugh, appeared at the door and asked her to marry him. After a little hesitation, she accepted, and, after education in Paris, she went on to enjoy almost fifty years as mistress of this great house.[11]

As the nineteenth century progressed, most aristocratic ladies appear to have lost interest in their dairies as a means of personal fulfilment, although their husbands still took pride in constructing fine dairies as part of their scientifically advanced model farms. The royal family clearly illustrate this change. Queen Victoria certainly tried to make butter in a silver-handled churn at Taymouth Castle, but it was Prince Albert who was responsible for creating the Royal Dairy at the Home Farm at Frogmore in 1858.[12] Measuring some 38 ft by 23 ft with walls and pillars lined with colourful Minton majolica tiles depicting the four seasons, agriculture, and portraits of the royal family, with stained-glass windows, and great rows of cream pans arranged on long marble tables, it represented the very peak of artistic dairy design in Victorian Britain. A number of other fine dairies were constructed in the latter half of the nineteenth century, but few of these could compare in scale and quality with their predecessors. Now the dairy was seen more as a specialist larder/preparation room, rather than as a setting for genteel dairy work.

Back in the sixteenth and seventeenth centuries, country house dairies, milk rooms and cheese rooms were often incorporated into the service wings of the main house, as seen in some of John Smythson's plans.[13] In 1650 Sir Roger Pratt moved the dairy at Coleshill into the north side of the basement, a place it frequently occupied up to the late eighteenth century, as at John Carr's Harewood House of 1759–71 (see the plans on pp. 67–8). Sir John Vanburgh's palatial houses had their dairies located in the wings which flanked the great entrance courts, a very convenient position, which was adopted in numerous country houses of the Georgian era. With the development of kitchen courtyards in great Victorian houses such as Mentmore Towers (1857) or Hempstead (1862), the dairies lay deep within the servants' quarters, close to the larders, where their produce would be readily accessible to the kitchen staff.

In many estates, the dairy formed part of the home farm, and during the late eighteenth and nineteenth centuries fine architect-designed dairies incorporating the most advanced sanitary and production features were included in new-built model farms, as at Bretby, Harewood, Sandon, Sezincote and Frogmore.[14] However efficient these might be, their location made them largely unsuitable for enjoyment by aristocratic lady dairymaids. They demanded that their dairies should lie beyond the range of farmyard smells, should make an interesting ornament to their pleasure grounds, provide the object for a pleasant walk from the house, make a setting for the display of their fine china, and be suitable for elegant informal entertainments.[15]

Given this brief, it is not surprising that country house dairies were built in the most fashionable of styles by some of the country's leading architects, the finest of them dating from the half century around 1800. The classical style was exemplified by Robert Adam's dairy built for the Countess of Derby at Knowsley, Lancashire, in 1776–7, its round dairy being flanked by wings and apparently containing accommodation for servants and an exquisitely decorated room where the Countess and her friends could take tea.[16] There were also Gothic dairies, such as that built by John Nash at Luscombe Castle, Devonshire, in 1800–4; Moorish dairies, such as the one S.P. Cockerell built at Sezincote, Gloucestershire, *c.* 1808; and Chinese dairies, such as the one Henry Holland built at Woburn Abbey for the Duchess of Bedford, *c.* 1790.[17] Other dairies took the form of thatched cottages to emphasize their rural purpose, John Nash's 1805 example at Blaize Castle, Bristol, forming a fine eye-catcher from the terrace of the main house.[18] Wherever possible, their construction included features such as wide eaves, verandahs, deep thatch, sunken floors and stained or ground glass windows which all helped to keep them cool and airy during the hot summer months.

Within, everything was designed for elegance and cleanliness, with floors of marble and walls usually lined with ceramic tiles, although the Shugborough dairy in Staffordshire was completely sheathed in Derbyshire alabaster. Around 1770 Josiah Wedgwood began to exploit the growing demand for dairy tiles, now producing them with painted patterns such as the ivy leaf design still to be seen at Ham House in Surrey and at Uppark in Sussex, or in imitation of marble, porphyry or jasper. Henry Blundell of Ince Blundell in Lancashire had no hesitation in contacting Wedgwood for advice, writing that 'I intend to fix up a dairy in a neat manner. If you have done anything of ye kind, or wd. tell me where I cd. see it, I shd. be much obliged'.[19] At this period Wedgwood appears to have dominated the dairy ceramics industry, but later nineteenth-century manufacturers also produced excellent wares, such as those made by Minton for Frogmore etc.

Niches or shelves arranged around the walls provided ample space for the display of Chinese porcelain or other fine ceramics, while below a range of marble-topped tables ran around the room, their supports being carved or cast in an appropriate design, such as imitation bamboo at Woburn, or even cow's legs at Ham. A matching table might also stand in the centre of the floor, but this could be replaced by a 'spring, fountain or *jet d'eau*' to give a highly agreeable effect, a cooling spray, and a ready supply of water for rinsing vessels etc.[20] This might be at

Dairies. Top: the Countess of Derby's dairy at Knowsley, Lancashire, was built to the designs of Robert Adam in 1776–7. The central rotunda formed the dairy, servants occupied the wing on the left, while that on the right, with its fine neoclassical plasterwork, offered a delightful room for the Countess. Bottom: the Chinese Dairy at Woburn Abbey was built by Henry Holland in 1790–1 for the Duchess of Bedford. Although the wide eaves, sunken floor, and glazed windows were designed to keep it cool for dairywork, the richness of the interior shows that it was also expected to perform an important social function.

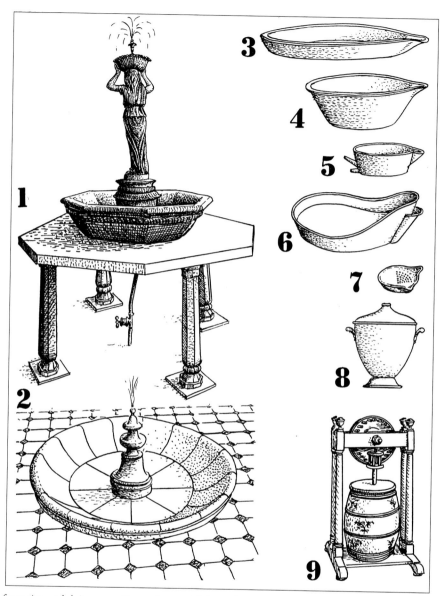

Dairy fountains and dairy ware. Fountains provided a cooling spray and a ready supply of water in the dairy, these examples being installed at Sezincote, Gloucestershire (1), and Cowdray in Sussex (2). Josiah Wedgwood & Sons, the great Staffordshire potters, made much of the white and cream-coloured ware used in country house dairies. Their range included shallow oval milk pans (3), deep round milk pans (4), cream risers (5), Fox's patent milk pan (6), cream skimmers (7) and cream vases or steins (8). The porcelain churn, with its contemporary walnut stand, dates from around 1800, and is now in York Castle Museum.

table height, as at Sezincote, where the fountain issues from a basket on the head of a draped female figure standing in a broad octagonal basin, or it could be set into the floor, as at Cowdray in Sussex.

The main purpose of the tables was to hold long lines of shallow white or cream-coloured earthenware pans into which the milk was poured and left to settle, so that the cream might rise and be lifted off using a pierced saucer-shaped skimmer. Sometimes the pans were beautifully blown in pale green glass, while other designs of earthenware, such as Fox's Patent Milk Pan had double spouts by which the cream could be poured separately from the milk.[21] After setting, cream was temporarily stored in urn-shaped cream vases or steins, these and their matching dairy wares sometimes being specially made by Wedgwood, an ivy leaf pattern being provided for Queen Charlotte's dairy at Frogmore, a bamboo pattern for the Chinese dairy at Woburn and an Egyptian pattern for the settling pans for the nautical Anson family's dairy at Shugborough, in celebration of Nelson's great victory at the Battle of the Nile.

Now the cream could either be used for a variety of culinary purposes, or be converted into butter, for which porcelain churns in walnut stands might take the place of the workaday plunge, box, or barrel varieties.[22] Skilled dairymaids and housekeepers would also model their butter freehand. The handsome 'Mrs' Wilmot of London's Oxford Market once called upon the great Georgian sculptor Nollekens bearing a butter-boat full of her butter lambs, sheep and pigs. 'I beg your pardon, Sir, for this intrusion,' she began. 'I am a housekeeper, in want of a situation, and finding the knowledge of modelling animals in butter would greatly add to my recommendation, I have taken the liberty of submitting the little things I have done for your inspection.' However, before 'Nolly' could respond to his charming visitor, Mrs Nollekens quickly arrived in the room, and rapidly removed the tempting butter modeller, informing her in no uncertain terms that 'Mr Nollekens will not suffer himself to be looked upon in the light of a pastry-cook!'[23] Finally, having been pressed into carved wooden moulds, it could appear in the form of a swan, fox, pineapple or heraldic device ready for serving in a dish of iced water garnished with parsley for the cheese course at dinner.[24]

After moulding, everything could be scalded clean and rinsed in an adjacent dairy scullery equipped with a copper for boiling water, sinks for washing, and probably all the cream separators, churns, butter-workers, cheese-presses and similar equipment which was necessary for the real work of the dairy.[25] The

A selection of designs showing how butter was moulded for the country house table. The crown is said to have been used at St James' Palace around 1820.

mistress of the house would then make careful note of what had been produced, and issue new instructions accordingly. In the spring of 1773, for example, Elizabeth Yorke of Erddig stated that she expected more butter from her eight cows, with the result that butter production soon increased. Later in the season she ordered that weekly records should be kept of the number of cheeses made, and their weight, that the whey should be used to make whey-butter for the use of the family, and that any surplus whey should be fed to the pigs, in order to fatten them.[26] As these records show, the country house dairy was by no means a mere plaything for aristocratic ladies, but it actually fulfilled a very real function in producing valuable supplies of food for the house, and hopefully surpluses which could either be stored for future use, or sold off to make additional income.

NOTES

1. It should be stressed that this chapter does not deal with the general practical aspects of the dairy, but only those which are peculiar to the country house dairy.

2. W. Shakespeare, *A Winter's Tale* (*c.* 1611), Act IV, Scene IV.

3. Sir T. Overbury, *Characters* (1614–16), quoted in J.D. Wilson, *Life in Shakespeare's England* (Cambridge, 1926), pp. 13–14.

4. James H. Markland (ed.), 'Instructions by Henry Percy . . . to his Son Algernon . . .', *Archaeologia*, 27 (1837), p. 340.

5. G. Markham, *The English Hus-wife* (London, 1615), pp. 104–20; R. Codrington, *The Second Part of Youth's Behaviour or Decency in Conversation Amongst Women* (2nd edn, London, 1672), pp. 97–100; H. Wolley, *The Compleat Servantmaid, or the Young Maiden's Tutor* (London, 1685).

6. For example A. Macdonell (ed.), *The Closet of Sir Kenelm Digby Knight Opened* (London, 1910), pp. 115–20; R. May, *The Accomplisht Cook* (London, 1685 edn), pp. 277–97.

7. Stephen Tempest of Broughton Hall, Yorkshire, advice to his son, quoted in J.H. Robinson, *Georgian Model Farms* (Oxford, 1983), pp. 92–3.

8. R. Bloomfield, 'The Farmer's Boy', quoted in D. Wright (ed.), *The Penguin Book of Everyday Verse* (Harmondsworth, 1983), pp. 387–8.

9. J.H. Robinson, *Model Farms*, p. 93.

10. Lady M.W. Montagu, letters to her daughter 1749 and 1751, quoted in B. Allen, *Food, an Oxford Anthology* (Oxford and New York, 1994), pp. 131–2 and C. Arthaud, *Dream Palaces* (London, 1973), pp. 247–8 and 254–5.

11. M. Meade-Fetherstonhaugh and O. Warner, *Uppark and its People* (London, 1964), p. 92.

12. See *Country Life,* 31 May 1979, p. 1733; Joan Jones, *Minton* (Shrewsbury, 1993), p. 173.

13. For example M. Girouard, *Robert Smythson and the Elizabethan Country House* (New Haven and London, 1983), figs 192 and 193.

14. J.M. Robinson, *Model Farms*, p. 94.

15. A. Rees, *The Cyclopedia* (1819) vol. 11, 'Dairy' and 'Dairying' describe these dairies as 'chiefly contrived as ornamental buildings', as well as giving some twenty-five pages on current good practice in the dairy.

16. D. King, *The Complete Works of Robert and James Adam* (Oxford, 1991), pp. 344–5. Other fine classical dairies were designed by James Wyatt for Dodington Park, Gloucestershire, by Samuel Wyatt for Shugborough, Staffordshire, 1803, and by Sir John Soane for Lees Court, Kent, 1789.

17. M. Mansbridge, *John Nash: A Complete Catalogue* (1991), p. 17; D. Stroud, *Henry Holland: His Life and Architecture* (1966), p. 37.

18. M. Mansbridge, *John Nash*, p. 64.

19. J.M. Robinson, *Model Farms*, p. 94.

20. A. Rees, *Cyclopedia*, 'Dairying'.

21. Josiah Wedgwood and Sons, *Illustrated Catalogue of Shapes* (Hanley, 1880), pp. 32–3.

22. P. Brears and S. Harrison, *The Dairy Catalogue* (York, 1979), front cover and p. 11, no. 114.

23. J.T. Smith, *Nollekens and his Times*, ed. G.W. Stonier (London, 1949). I am grateful to Mr Christopher Rowell for this information.

24. I. Beeton, *Beeton's Book of Household Management* (London, 1861), p. 814.

25. Dairy sculleries connecting directly with 'polite' dairies are still to be found in many houses, including Ham, Uppark, etc.

26. A. Wilson (ed.), *Traditional Country House Cooking* (London, 1993), p. 98.

CHAPTER TEN

LARDERS AND OTHER STOREPLACES FOR THE KITCHEN

Pamela Sambrook

Isabella Beeton did not underestimate the value of a good larder. She believed that:

> more waste is often occasioned by the want of judgement, or of the necessary care in this particular, than by any other cause . . . the utmost skill in the culinary art will not compensate for the want of proper attention to this particular.[1]

After all, larders were not just about food storage, important though that might be; they were also about food preparation and preservation and as such were central to the efficient organization of the country house. Foodstuffs coming into the eighteenth-century country house were usually unprocessed, perhaps even still alive. A number of procedures had to be carried out before the food was ready for the kitchen – in the case of meat this meant butchering, trimming, washing, hanging and salting.

The aim of this paper is to illustrate the role of the larder and other storeplaces. Firstly, drawing upon a mixture of contemporary manuals and actual examples, it will offer a sort of model of what the ideal country house larder might contain in the way of equipment for food storage and preservation. Using a few examples of country house inventories, it will then go on to make the point that techniques and needs changed over time.

The function of the larder takes us back a long way historically, to medieval traditions of household organization. The usual position of the main cooking area is still uncertain; some houses clearly had a specialized cooking room – a kitchen – perhaps in a separate building or shack; others had the main cooking space within the main living area – the hall place. It is probable that different cooking techniques – boiling and roasting – were carried out in separate places. Whatever the arrangement, specialized rooms were needed nearby in which to carry on the more noxious or basic functions such as food preparation, food preservation and butchery; these interiors were necessary adjuncts to both cooking and eating areas.

In modern parlance the words 'pantry' and 'larder' are often used interchangeably, but there is a clear distinction historically. Lard is a Middle English word meaning the back fat of the pig; the larder is therefore particularly associated with bacon, hence with preserved but uncooked meat. In Victorian times the name used for this room was wet larder. A pantry was originally a store for bread, grain and pastry; hence it became a store for cooked food. The Victorian equivalent was dry larder. Another term, still known in the north of England and the north Midlands, is spence, a place from where food or stores were dispensed; perhaps the later equivalent of this was the chef's or housekeeper's store, where dry goods were kept to be issued out to the household departments. The word buttery has an origin in common with the words bottle and butt; it was therefore a place to store drink, especially but not exclusively beer; casks in the buttery would be on tap, in contrast to the longer-term storage provided by the cellars. Napery was a place to store table linen. The functional equivalent to both these areas in Victorian parlance was the butler's pantry.

Butteries, naperies and butler's pantries were sited near to the main eating area, the hall place or dining-room. The larders and pantries, on the other hand, were more conveniently sited near to the main processing area, the kitchen.

This paper will concentrate mainly on the larder.

SITE FEATURES

The larder dealt with raw meat in quantity and so had the most exacting requirements. In the nineteenth century cooks and those concerned with food preservation were still groping towards an understanding of the processes of decay; without widespread appreciation or acceptance of the role of bacteria, people could judge only by what they could see. In 1860, John Walsh distinguished between two completely distinct forms of decomposition in meat – surface deterioration in which the parts exposed to air became 'putrid', even green, whilst the inside remained fresh and red; and decay from the inside, around the bone. According to Walsh, the first meant that the meat was still usable but the second rendered it unfit even for pigs or dogs.[2] Such theories might have been misled but the practical advice given was sound – the cook should beware of a tenderness or a giving way of the stiffness of the joint, as well as the more obvious signs of smell or discolouration. These were important considerations, for hanging meat was a basic function of the larder. With the exception of veal, poultry and fish, all meat was hung so that a certain amount of decomposition would tenderize the fibre. The period varied but could easily be up to three weeks. Even fish and poultry were usually kept for a day before use. But the temperature range for proper hanging was fairly exact: Walsh recommended keeping the larder considerably above freezing point but preferably below 50°F and certainly below 60°F. Because moisture accelerated the process of decomposition, storage conditions needed to be dry.

For these reasons the desirable characteristics of a larder were described by Robert Kerr as follows:

> The primary considerations in a larder of whatever kind are coolness of temperature, freshness of ventilation, and dryness. The aspect of windows must therefore favour the North and East; the transmission of heat through the roof must be prevented; floors and walls must be perfectly free from damp; a constant current of air must be promoted; and this must not be from any tainted, damp, dusty, or heated source, from ash-bin or drain trap, window of beer-cellar, scullery, wash-house, stable or anything of the sort. There ought to also be no fireplace or hot smoke-flue in its walls.[3]

It was a good idea to have a completely detached larder, on the north or eastern side of the house, and this was the policy adopted in some early houses where larders might be accommodated in outbuildings connected to the back door of the kitchen or scullery by a covered walkway. The larder could then be fitted with windows all round for good ventilation and an overhanging roof to give shade to the walls. Game larders are often like this – octagonal or round and fairly elaborate, with slatted wooden walls and louvres in the roof. Detached general larders have survived more rarely; there is one at Buckland Abbey in Devon, but even this may be a dairy in origin.

On the other hand, many early houses had sites constricted by walls or ditches, so even slaughter houses had to be incorporated into the house, fairly near to the hall. A good example is at Haddon Hall in Derbyshire, where the slaughter house

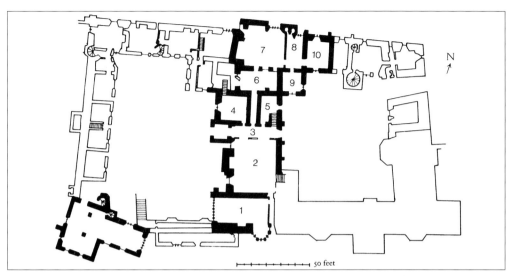

Ground-floor layout of Haddon Hall, Derbyshire, showing the pantry and buttery near to the dining area and the larder and slaughter house leading from the far end of the kitchen: 1. parlour; 2. hall; 3. screens passage; 4. buttery; 5. pantry; 6. court; 7. kitchen; 8. bakehouse; 9. larder; 10. butchery. (By courtesy of Mark Girouard)

is at the end of a run of rooms including larder and bakehouse, all leading off the kitchen which is separated from the hall by buttery, pantry and screens passage.

According to most contemporary authorities, a larder should be built on the north side of the kitchen court. Very often they were tucked away in the corner so they have two, or even three outside walls. To give even more shade, they might be heavily planted outside, or built partly below ground level with a sunken path paved around the walls. Wet and dry larders may be side by side, with the inner end wall backing on to a corridor which connected the inner court with the outside and which could be thoroughly ventilated – a layout like this was provided at Ormesby Hall, Cleveland.

A common alternative to corner larders was a corridor site. A row of larders were built backing on to a corridor with doors at either end, so a through draught could ventilate the rooms – a good example of corridor larders is at Lanhydrock, built in the 1880s. Here in line are the dairy and its scullery, the meat larder, the fish larder and the dry larder.

The dry larder or pantry might be situated next to the wet larder and each given

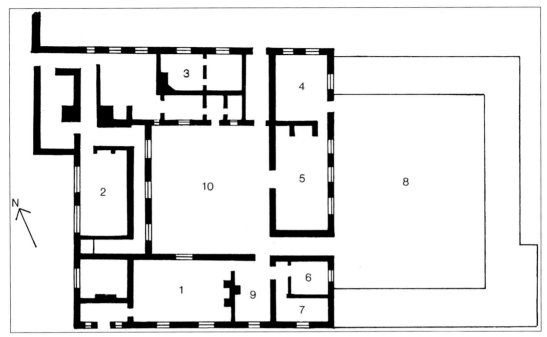

Ground-floor layout of Ormesby Hall, Cleveland, showing a wet and dry larder sited at the corner of the kitchen courtyard: 1. kitchen; 2. servants' hall; 3. housekeeper's room and store; 4. washhouse; 5. laundry; 6. wet larder or 'butchery'; 7. dry larder; 8. east court (single storey, timber yard etc.); 9. scullery; 10. kitchen court.

separate access. Often, however, the dry larder led directly from the kitchen; this was the case at Dunham Massey, where the dry larder doubled as a chef's pantry and contolled the access to both wet larder and game larder.

It has been pointed out by Edward Higgs, in a slightly different context, that looking at the domestic organization of country houses from contemporary instructional handbooks is rather like judging the average person's life-style today from the fashion plates of *Vogue*, and certainly one finds plenty of actual examples where the simple ground rules of Kerr, for example, have been ignored.[4] In the real world and as a response to the exigencies of site, larders have been built on the south side of houses or even backing on to the boiler house. The Ormesby larder, though occupying a classic corner site, is on the south-east side of the building, but screened by heavy planting. At Penrhyn Castle in Gwynedd, the south-facing

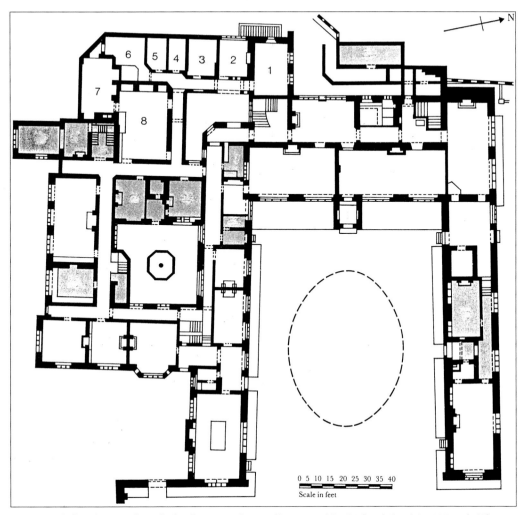

Ground-floor layout of Lanhydrock House, Cornwall, prepared by Richard Coad in 1881–4. The larders and dairy are arranged side-by-side, backing on to a corridor: 1. dairy; 2. dairy scullery; 3. meat larder; 4. fish larder; 5. dry larder; 6. bakehouse; 7. scullery; 8. kitchen. (By courtesy of the National Trust)

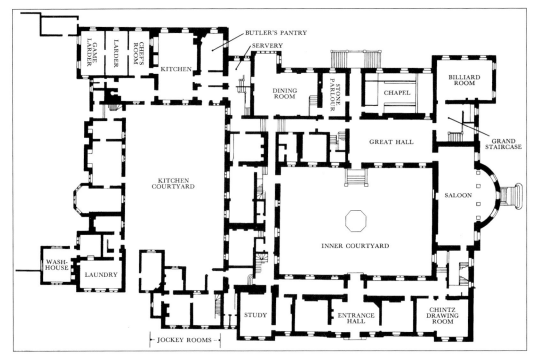

Ground-floor layout at Dunham Massey, Cheshire, showing corner-sited larders. The dry larder is called 'chef's room' and controls access to the wet and game larders. The kitchen court was built during the 1730s. (By courtesy of the National Trust)

windows of the larder are shaded by slate awnings. Perhaps this flexibility is testament to the well-known success of the builders of country houses in creating wind tunnels, deliberate or otherwise.

CONSTRUCTIONAL FEATURES

Ideally a larder should be single storey, with no roof lights or roof ventilation; in very hot weather in emergency, canvas could then be thrown over the roof and soaked with water. They needed a through draught, so two windows or a window opposite a door was usual. Windows in larders were filled with wire gauze to keep out insects and either not glazed at all, or fitted with hinged or removable glazing panels, in contrast to pantries which were often fully glazed.

Internal ventilation was important in temperature control. At Ormesby, pantry and larder are side by side next to a through passage; the upper part of the walls of both the passage and the intervening walls between larder and pantry are made up of panels of wire gauze, so that the breeze can circulate. This could get a bit too much of a good thing, so the passage wall has wooden shutters which can be let down in bad weather. Wooden shutters, sliding or hinged, are common in larders. At Dunham Massey, the intervening walls between dry larders, salting room and game larder are made up of wooden bars which allow internal ventilation.

The arrangements at Petworth were even more elaborate. The whole of one end of the ceiling of the wet larder is made up of lattice-work; this opens into a two- to three-foot deep void which runs the width of the building at that end and connects with grilles fitted in the outside wall.

Floors were usually of stone or paved with tiles, with a drain to ease washing down. Walls were tiled or whitewashed – the latter often blued with a dolly-bag to deter flies. The larder ceiling was fitted with strong hooks for hanging salted meat; or maybe thick iron rails stretched across the room, as at Lanhydrock and Dunham Massey.

Perhaps the most characteristic feature of larders and of some pantries was the stone, brick or marble shelving, slab or settle – often called a stillage or thrall – built around the wall, about two feet high.[5] This was used as a cold standing area for all sorts of baskets, bowls, pitchers or crocks as well as shallow pans for dry-salting meat. There may also be one or more large shallow stone sinks on which would fit a whole side of pork as it was washed, drained and dry-salted, or where dressed meat could drain.

Security was an important feature of larders and pantries. This was ensured by the provision of a stout lock and key, but in a large household which practised strict departmentalization of its staff, the actual dispensing of food could cause problems. For this reason, Petworth had a partitioned lobby area at the entrance to its wet larder, where meat prepared for issue to the kitchen could be left for collection, without giving access to the main store, which could be left locked. Similarly, Ruth Mott, cook in the BBC's 'Victorian Kitchen' series, remembered how supplies of dry goods were issued in the 1930s. Each week on Monday mornings, Ruth the kitchen-maid submitted an order for dry goods to last the week. Later in the day she went to collect the goods, not directly from the housekeeper, but left outside the locked store-room for her.[6]

FURNITURE AND FITTINGS OF THE WET LARDER

Both larders and pantries were fitted with pin-rails to carry hooks, built-in 'dressers' around the walls and a central work or 'dressing' table, often painted the ubiquitous country house colour known as drab. An important feature was the shelving built into the walls; at Pilgrim's Hall in Essex, Lesley Lewis remembered 'food stood out on the shelves, cooled by the north and east breezes'.[7] Many larders also had vermin-proof hanging shelves supported from the centre of the ceiling, not the walls, by iron rods or chains.

The wet larder provided specialist accommodation. Meat might arrive at the larder weekly, already cut up by the butcher, but it still needed to be weighed as a check on the butcher, so there was usually a large hanging balance or steelyard. Very often, however, meat came in whole carcases or sides and in houses which adopted this practice the wet larder was often called the 'butchery' (as at Ormesby). It would be supplied with a wooden beam where whole carcases could hang; sometimes this was in a special hanging area; a good example is in the corridor outside the larders at Painswick in Gloucestershire. Game larders were fitted with more elaborate racks for hanging carcases. Inside the wet larder there was also usually a chopping block and sometimes a pig thrall or bench; sometimes a shredding trough or board (the predecessor of the mincing machine). There was often a wire-fronted meat safe, varying in size, sometimes square and hoisted to the ceiling, sometimes floor-standing and on castors, sometimes lined with zinc or enamel. Sometimes the meat safe needed to be so large that it became a room in itself, partitioned off from the main area. Where space for uncooked meat was short, a large rectangular safe could be hoisted up in a nearby through corridor where the ventilation was good, as at Erdigg. Almost universal in either larder or pantry inventories was the pestle and mortar, mounted on a solid trunk of wood and common too was a pair of short steps.

The supply of some meat was seasonal, so keeping it over a long period was an ever-present problem. Equipment for salting was therefore important. Ideally the meat was brought in from the butcher early in the morning, before 6 a.m., then washed, carefully wiped dry and closely examined by the cook for signs of egg-laying by flies – 'fly strike'. The 'kernels' (bluish gelatinous masses of fat which would taint the meat) and pipes of individual cuts were carefully trimmed and sprinkled with salt, even the pieces needed immediately for roasting and boiling.

The trimmings were kept in a 'grease' tub for later rendering. The pieces of meat that were needed for keeping were either dry-salted or wet-pickled.

When dry-salted, the meat was rubbed hard with salt using the heel of the hand; it was then given several dressings of salt over a period as it lay on the salting stone; and finally packed tight in a deep salting or powdering tub; the prime pieces were packed at the bottom, a board on top and a heavy weight.[8]

Wet-pickle for meat could be made to a variety of recipes, usually containing bay salt, sugar, salt-petre, sal prunella, and even *in extremis* muriatic or nitric acid. Each type of meat had its own version of the pickle; a different recipe would be used for hung beef, tongues, or pork.[9] It was usual to have several pickles on the go at one time. Meat would be steeped in the pickle in deep tubs or earthenware crocks, some big enough to stand on the floor, the smaller ones on the settle. If salting or pickle tubs were made of wood they were usually lead-lined. Sometimes they were large enough to merit being described as troughs or a 'large lead cistern for salt meat' as found in the Petworth larder in 1764.[10] The Leveson-Gore's raw meat larder at Trentham in 1826 had seven slate salting tubs with fitted canvas covers.[11]

Meat could keep in wet-pickle for as long as twelve months provided the liquid was boiled, skimmed and strengthened with new salt every month. More usually the pieces were taken out after two or three weeks, drained and hung up to dry, sometimes pasted over with paper or muslin. The pickle could then be re-boiled and skimmed and reused. Many regions, of course, had their own versions of the pickle and their own methods particularly suited to local conditions. In parts of the Pennines, for example, after salting and a short hanging, pork or bacon was kept longer by burying in oatmeal; occasionally oatmeal kits or arks will appear in inventories, either in the larder or in the attic.

In houses near the coast, the fish larder was often separate, as at Lanhydrock, but otherwise the meat larder had to deal with fish too. In this case a marble or slate fish slab was fitted, which in some houses had a drain so the fish could be kept in a constant stream of cold water and the slab washed down easily. There might also be an ice tub; at Trentham this was a large leaden tub. Lesley Lewis remembered it at Pilgrim's Hall as being a huge zinc-lined chest, which was filled 'with a great slab of ice which used to be brought in sacking from the fish-monger's. On this the fish would be laid'.[12]

Ice tubs or chests were made of wood, double-walled, insulated with straw or hay and lined with lead or zinc, with containers for blocks of ice and a drain in the

Ice box showing the insulated food cupboard; the ice was put into the side compartment which is accessed from the top. (By courtesy of Staffordshire Museum Service, Shugborough)

bottom; periodically the chests had to be drained and cleaned out. They were used for general cool storage as well as keeping fish. Ice boxes or safes were also used in pantries – smaller upright cupboard-like boxes made on the same principle. Ice was useful in larders, of course, but it had the serious drawback of producing damp as well as cold. Damp was an ever-present problem in larders and ice safes; it made it much more difficult to control temperature and to avoid food spoilage. A rigorous regime of draining, drying and wiping food was needed; and generally, wiping meat with a dry cloth was emphasized by domestic manuals.[13]

GAME LARDERS

The storage of game of various sorts presented something of a problem. Special game larders were built, needing to be particularly well-ventilated and fitted with substantial racks in the centre. At Dunham Massey the rack is made of heavy wooden beams to accommodate deer carcases from the deer park. Alternatively several hundred birds might need to be hung at any one time, perhaps using a tiered iron framework which enabled birds to be hung in rows so as not to drip on each other.[14] Venison was usually hung for at least a fortnight in a cold place; after this, according to a servants' guide published in 1830, it was necessary to 'wash it with milk and water, and then dry it with clean cloths, till not the least damp remains. Pounded ginger or pepper should be applied to such parts as are attacked by the fly.'[15]

The problem of game bird storage became especially difficult towards the end of the nineteenth century, when some sporting estates had to find accommodation for thousands of game birds from a single shoot. One solution then becoming available was the installation of a cold storage unit. This consisted of a small refrigeration plant which used compressed carbon dioxide and circulating brine to cool a whole compartment or room – perhaps even two rooms, one kept below freezing point for the longer-term storage of birds or carcases, and a slightly warmer one for

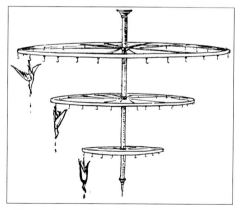

Hanger for game birds. (From Lawrence Weaver, The House and its Equipment, *1912)*

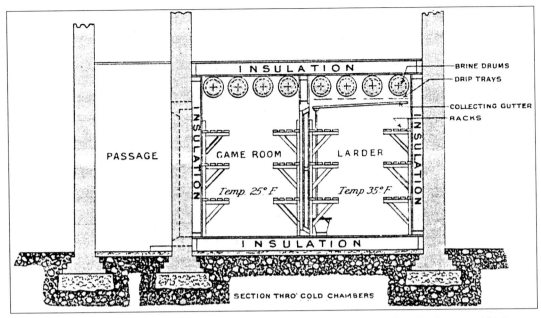

Larder and game room cooled by brine. (From Laurence Weaver, The House and its Equipment, *1912)*

keeping game for short periods for daily use. The compressor and pump were powered by a small electric motor or oil engine. The system was described and recommended in a book published for the proprietors of country houses in 1912.[16] At this date, certainly, Moreton Hall in Warwickshire had such a system in use and, with the spread of electricity, many houses followed suit. When Shugborough purchased an electrical generator in 1927 a refrigerated store was the second installation to be fitted after the lighting.

OTHER STORES

In the larger country houses cooking areas were highly specialized, so each would be fitted with a cupboard for the storage of appropriate dry goods – not only the kitchen but also the stillroom, pastry and bakery. There is great variety within different households as to the exact arrangements and the names given to different stores.

The kitchen required several stores besides a wet larder. Vegetable storage could be provided in the larder or the scullery but was often a small separate room fitted with wooden or, preferably, stone boxes divided into compartments. If wooden they were usually lead-lined. Whether in the larder, as at Harewood, or scullery, as at Dunham Massey, the boxes were usually fitted under the settle or sink; sometimes, as at Tatton, they were movable, on castors. Larger quantities of root vegetables were stored in cellars, embedded in sand or covered in matting and of course the more exotic vegetables and fruits grown in the walled garden had their own specialized stores as part of the garden complex, such as the shelves for grape-feeding bottles.

Pantries provided the storage area for prepared foodstuffs, bread, cold cooked meat, cheese, dairy produce and dry goods being used by the kitchen in meal preparation. They were usually fitted with dressers, cupboards and a table, pin-rails, hanging shelves and a stone settle. Some separate provision might be made for the cold storage of jellies, mousses, blancmanges and elaborate cold desserts: at Lanhydrock this was provided on a marble slab in the misleadingly named 'dairy'. Other houses provided larger versions of the ice box – full-height cupboards with insulated interiors. The kitchen also needed a chef's room – a combined office and dry goods store for highly valuable items. The pastry at Petworth has an excellent example of a specialist store – a cupboard with central shelving flanked by deep fitted drawers each labelled for its purpose.

The housekeeper also needed supplies of dry goods such as flour, rice, tea and coffee, for she was in charge of the stillroom as well as the distribution of servants' 'liveries' – individual allowances of tea, sugar, jam and butter. Much of the cupboard space in the housekeeper's room was devoted to china and napery rather than foodstuffs, but she kept smaller quantities of sugar, tea and pickles here. The stillroom itself was fitted with cupboards for the storage of jams and chutneys.

Bulk quantities of dry goods for both the kitchen and the housekeeper were kept in a separate secure store room or corridor, closely fitted with cupboards. Freedom from damp was here imperative, otherwise the loss of food through spoiling could be enormous: lump sugar would crumble into powder; moist sugar harden into lumps; bay salt turn to water; preserves grow mould; cakes turn soft; and linen become spotted with mildew. For this reason dry stores frequently back on to a kitchen flue or have a fireplace of their own. To make sure a wall was not damp, it might be lined with timber boarding; a cheaper alternative was a lining of battens and sheets of canvas nailed on to them – the same method as used in the harness room to protect horse collars. Goods were stored in canisters with tightly fitting lids, and, as in the larder, at the top level there may be a suspended shelf – here used for the storage of sugar cones. Cut lump sugar and powdered sugar was best kept in deep drawers, often internally divided. Ground coffee was stored well away from tea which it would taint. Soap and candles needed to be kept in a separate cupboard as did dried fruit; that used for cakes was kept in canisters and the better quality for dessert was stored in boxes.[17]

THE INVENTORY RECORD

Techniques of food processing and preservation changed and the function of larders changed with them. Rooms were used for purposes for which they were not intended originally or they fell into disuse and became little more than a store for junk.

The changing function of larders is discernible through room inventories. These are a notorious trap for the researcher – they may be incomplete or tidied up; and because of the tendency to accumulate unwanted equipment from elsewhere, larder inventories have to be used with special care; what, for example, are we to make of the inventory of the main larder at the Fitzherberts' house at Swynnerton, Staffordshire, in the 1820s, with its assortment of pepper mill, bread tins, salting tub and plate holders?

Inventory of Swynnerton, 1821[18]

Larder
Pepper mill and jelly stand, two bread tins, large marble mortar and pestle
Large drip pan and stand, four jars in basket cases
Tin fish kettle and cover, pair steps
Two round salting tubs, 1 cover
Two plate baskets lined with tin
Large painted cupbd. folding doors
Two tin bed candlesticks and candle back
Small tin can and cover
3 heights of shelves, rails and pigs, lock on door

Paste Pantry
Three large hair sieves
Marble slab, loose frame and stand
Two large square baskets, one oval [basket], small search
Pair brass scales, 4 lead weights
Japan spice box, mouse trap and rolling pin
Flour tub and cover
Dresser with 3 cupbds. under 1 cupbd. and 2 shelves above
6 jelly glasses 2 salts, lock on door

Lower Larder
Hanging shelf, 2 hanging rails and hooks
Chopping table, bench, 2 thralls, pair steps
Small deal table, shelf against wall
Cupboard lock and key
Iron lin'd lock and key to door, two coffers
2 wine stools

Throughout the last half of the nineteenth century, changing patterns of food availability and commercialization meant that many households no longer had a need for separate, highly specialized food-storage or processing areas. We can trace this change: a larder inventory taken at Temple Newsam in 1808 gives a conventional picture of a specialist larder well-equipped to deal primarily with meat and fish:

Inventory of Temple Newsam, 1808 – the Larder[19]

2 wood salting cisterns lined with lead
a grease tub
a salting tub
a deal safe
a wainscot table with stone slab
2 chopping blocks
a deal table with a drawer
an ash pasteboard

a pair of wood scales
a cleaver
a sieve
a pair of steps
a form
3 old drawers
a stone table for fish and a cover
a pair of steps

An inventory taken at Petworth in 1869, on the other hand, gives an example of how, later in the nineteenth century, a spacious larder could be used as a general-purpose food preparation or storage area. Theoretically a dry larder, it also had salting equipment as well as many spare kitchen utensils:

Inventory of Petworth, 1869 – the Larder[20]

Slate salting trough and cover	Tubs
2 saws	Small stand
Cleaver	2 Steaming kettles
17 Hair and other sieves	Large ice chest
Cake hoop	Box
Box	3 choppers
Mincing machine	3 knives
Candle box	2 steels
Glazed pan	17 Brown jars
2 Brown pans and covers	5 soup tureens
9 sweet bottles	2 Enamelled dishes
2 Tin cans	6 Ladles
Colander	14 Preserve pots
Cooler	Ware funnel
2 Jars Chilis	Bottle
Lead lined chest	8 White dishes
5 Brown crocks and covers	16 Plates
2 lead lined troughs	2 Deep basins
Pr 4 rise steps	Iron bowl

Baking dish

Brown pan

11 Pie dishes

2 Potted fish dishes

6 Enamelled basins

8 Stock basins

5 small "

2 enamelled basins

Hand bowl

21 Butter boats

4 Brown crocks & jars

2 Baking tins

Brown pan

Large square cutting table

Inventory evidence may be of particular use when inventories of the same room exist for different periods. Eighteenth- and nineteenth-century inventories of the larder at Ormesby show an emphasis on equipment relating to the processing and preservation of meat such as pickling and chopping; while an equivalent list of the 1920s shows a shift to the larder as simply a storage place, the pickling of meat being no longer of such crucial importance:

Ormesby Hall – sale inventory dated 1792[21]

Larder

a large chopping block

a large pickle tub, lined with lead, on castors

One smaller pickle tub

a pork pickle tub

a shredding board

a bread tub

a marble mortar, fix'd in a wood stand, and pestle

a chopping knife and wood steps

Ormesby Hall – household inventory 1853

Larder

large pickle tub (lead lined)

chopping block

shredding trough

Meat hook

pair scales wood bottom'd and weights

5 baskets

The larder at Speke Hall, Liverpool, in a run-down state in the 1940s. Are the barrels, with their slipping hoops, old pickle tubs? (By courtesy of Liverpool Record Office)

Ormesby Hall – household inventory 1924

Meat Safe
Meat safe 5' 9" × 2' 6" × 7' 2" high
Pair short steps
Lead lined vegetable trough on legs, 6' × 2' 6" × 1' 2" deep
4-ft chopping table, worn
2 sides bacon
4 hams

Perhaps the later Ormesby larder would have looked something like the larder at Speke, as photographed in the 1940s.

The decline in food-processing activities in the larder resulted in the decline of waste- or by-products. In the old medieval noble households, slaughtering produced much useful material which could be used around the house or sold for cash – skins, rugs, wool, vellum, hair, thread, tallow (i.e. rendered mutton fat), pig fat, gut for cord, bladders for waterproof containers have all been recorded.[22] The later country house was not so enterprising but it still produced rabbit skins, feathers, tallow for candles or dips, grease for lubrication and bladders for the tops of pickle jars. The change from food-processing to food-storage within the larder brought an end even to this. Larders on the scale of those at Lanhydrock or Dunham Massey stand testament to the scale and elaboration of country house catering. Yet they represent merely the end of a long tradition which stretched back to the specialized skills of the medieval pantler and larderer. The arrival of frozen meat and tinned salmon in the later nineteenth century was an indicator of fundamental change; from then on the domestic need was for food-storage rather than food-processing space.

NOTES

1. Mrs Isabella Beeton, *Beeton's Book of Household Management* (first published 1859–61; reprinted London, 1982), p. 37.

2. J.H. Walsh, *A Manual of Domestic Economy Suited to Families Spending Between £100 and £1000 a Year* (London, 1857), pp. 443–4.

3. Robert Kerr, *The Gentleman's House: or How to Plan English Residences from the Parsonage to the Palace* (London, 1864), pp. 214–15.

4. Edward Higgs, 'Domestic Servant Households in Victorian England', *Social History,* 8 (2) (May 1983), p. 203.

5. Jennifer Davies, *The Victorian Kitchen* (London, 1989), p. 15.

6. Davies, *Victorian Kitchen*, p. 18.

7. Lesley Lewis, *The Private Life of a Country House, 1912–39* (London, 1982), p. 130.

8. For details on methods of salting see several papers in C. Anne Wilson (ed.), *Waste Not, Want Not* (Edinburgh, 1989).

9. Jane Loudon, *The Lady's Country Companion* (London, 1845, reprinted Bungay, Suffolk, 1984), p. 98.

10. Egremont Mss, Inventory of Petworth, 1764.

11. Staffordshire County Record Office, Sutherland Mss, D593/R/7/10b, inventory of the household furniture at Trentham Hall, 1826.

12. Lewis, *Private Life of a Country House*, p. 130.

13. Anon., *The Servants' Guide and Family Manual* (London, 1830), p. 3.

14. Dudley G. Gordon, 'An Up-to-date Game Larder', *The House and its Equipment,* ed. Lawrence Weaver (London, 1912), p. 99.

15. Anon., *Servants' Guide*, p. 4.

16. Weaver, *The House and its Equipment*, pp. 93–9.

17. Loudon, *Lady's Country Companion*, pp. 34–7.

18. SRO, Fitzherbert Mss, D641/S/P(I)4, inventory of Swynnerton Hall, 1821.

19. *Leeds Art Collections Fund* (Leeds, 1987), p. 41, inventory of Temple Newsam, 1808.

20. Petworth House Archives, 10068, inventory of Petworth, 1869.

21. Cleveland Record Office, Pennyman Mss, U/PEN/9/8, inventory of sale, 1792; U/PEN/9/9, inventory, 1853; U/PEN/9/9/3, inventory, 1924.

22. Kate Mertes, *The English Noble Household, 1250–1600: Good Governance and Political Rule* (Oxford, 1988), pp. 99–101.

My thanks are due to Peter Brears and Diana Owen for suggestions and information about Petworth House; also to the Egremont Estate.

CHAPTER ELEVEN

SUPPLIES AND SUPPLIERS TO THE COUNTRY HOUSE

Pamela Sambrook

Country house documentation from the eighteenth and nineteenth centuries holds an enormous amount of information about the supply of food going into the household, yet it is an area which has been hardly touched as yet by the food historian. Detailed work on single households will no doubt help us to appreciate the individuality of their experience as well as the common features of a food supply which changed over time. Every house had its own requirements according to the family and their idiosyncracies. Food needs varied according to the status and wealth of the family, whether they entertained a lot or whether they had children. Incoming food supplies varied seasonally and at particular times amounts and variety could be huge. In this situation, the documentary record of individual households offers both potential and pitfall.

This paper aims to illustrate the type of information which was recorded, using a few examples from family archives of the Dukes of Sutherland, the Leveson-Gowers, now deposited in the Staffordshire Record Office and covering their households at Lilleshall in Shropshire; Trentham in Staffordshire; and Stafford House in London. Examples are taken from both the seventeenth and nineteenth centuries.

FOOD ACCOUNTS IN THE SEVENTEENTH CENTURY

The main kitchen accounts – often called food accounts – can help give some idea of the size of throughput of food coming into and going out of the stores. The Leveson family records for the 1640s show how even the organization of the tenanted estate and the method of receiving rents could affect this. As late as the seventeenth century, on feast days or rent days large quantities of food were brought in by the Levesons' tenants as 'expected presents', a relic of the days when rent was paid in kind. Part of the job of the clerk of the kitchen was to keep a record of these gifts. At the Levesons' house at Lilleshall in Shropshire on Christmas Day in 1643 the steward recorded gifts from the tenants; these varied from large farmers, able to send whole pigs or swans, to widows living on their own in small cottages, who struggled to send in a dozen home-made biscuits:

Presents to Lilleshall, Christmas, 1643[1]

1 salmon
138 chickens, pullets or capons
19 geese
5 turkeys
10 gamebirds
3 swans
22 pigs
35 and a half couple of rabbits
9 and a half veal carcases
1 mutton carcase
28 sugarloaves
11 doz of biscuit cakes
5 baskets of pippins
74 lbs butter
12 and a half dozen eggs
Gifts of wine, metheglin, sack, allegar and a gross of clay pipes

In November, Martinmas saw a similar situation. It is possible that some of these foodstuffs were sold on rather than consumed by the Leveson household; there is documented precedent for this practice from an earlier period.[2]

All this had to be processed at a time when we know, from the same record book, other large amounts of food were coming into store, both at Lilleshall and at the Levesons' other house at Trentham in Staffordshire. On a regular basis, grains and flours were recorded by the strike (bushel); they included wheat flour for the cook and the baker, malt for the brewer, rye, oats and maslin for the baker, and millcorn, oats, barley, light corn and pease for other consumers such as dogs, pigs, horses and poultry. Meat was counted in whole carcases (mutton, veal, pork, lamb and venison)

The well-stocked, though hardly well-ordered, larder was a favourite subject for the artist. (Unknown artist, by courtesy of Staffordshire Museum Service)

and in pieces (beef) and flitches (bacon). Poultry were kept alive and killed when needed – hens, capons, chickens, pullets, ducks, geese and turkeys. Within the kitchen court at Trentham, there were pens for these and perhaps, too, the larder was fitted with bird cages for larks, plovers, thrushes and sparrows, as at Dyrham Park in 1710. Certainly the Leveson kitchens kept a flock of twenty-five lapwings.

The Leveson kitchen record, kept weekly or sometimes fortnightly during 1646, also shows the extent of seasonality of food coming into the stores and kitchen: for example, cheese was entered into the record only during the summer and autumn, from May to November. Butter was made and used at home all the year round but there was a clear peak of production during June and July and supplies had to be

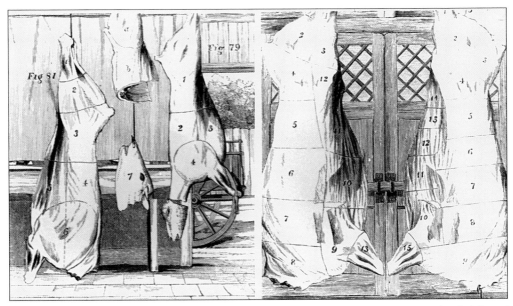

Illustrations from J.H. Walsh, A Manual of Domestic Economy, *1857, showing: 1. joints of veal (left) and mutton (right and middle); 2. country method of cutting up an ox (left) and the London method (right).*

supplemented by purchases from outside during the months December to April. The poultry supplies were complex: young stock – chickens and pullets – were brought in and eaten only during the summer months, while older birds – hens and capons – were available during the period from November to spring.[3]

In many cases seasonal variability was accepted and little effort made to spread out the supply, especially if the food was not a staple but provided a tasty change; in these cases it was eaten quickly, within a couple of weeks: mutton, lamb and venison was eaten fairly quickly as were the large numbers of rabbits and most fish, including skate, pike, salmon and crayfish. By contrast, some food was preserved for later eating: for example, neat's tongues came into the stores in winter, but were not eaten until May and June. Bacon came in only during winter (November to March) but was eaten regularly all the year; habberdines (salted cod) came in only during October and February but were eaten in small quantities all year round.

Beef supplies seem to lie somewhere in between these two patterns. Veal supplies show a clear increase in May, as one would expect with the usual spring calving, but veal was in fact available in smaller quantities throughout the winter from

November onwards. Beef came in and out during every month, but some months show a surplus of supply over consumption – October, January, March, April, May, July and August. The peak month for consumption of the whole year was June, followed by July, August and December. This may in fact reflect the presence of large numbers of family and guests and it may well be that even at this date the pattern of consumption relates as much to demand-led variability as to seasonal availability.[4] Much of the beef seems to have been consumed fairly quickly, or at least within a few weeks of supply, but some may well have been preserved for longer – perhaps in the seven slate salting tubs mentioned in the previous chapter from Trentham.

A few years later, during 1676, the grain book for the Leveson household records an annual consumption of 4,292 bushels of grain or flour of various sorts.[5] There are three records of bread flour – wheat, manchet and rye. The manchet probably refers to best quality finely-searched wheat flour, which made up the largest amount – 242 bushels for the year. In 1646, the household was making two qualities of bread on a regular basis – manchets for the family and guests and cheat loaves (made probably from coarser wheat) for the servants; the consumption of manchet bread shows a clear peak in June and July, probably related to the Levesons' pattern of hospitality. These two qualities were supplemented by occasional bakings of rye bread, mainly in the late summer when perhaps the wheat supplies were running low before the new harvest. This was still the case in 1676, but then the consumption of rye flour was greatest in October and here the record is unclear as to whether the bread was wholly rye or mixed rye and wheat. Barley was also used for bread-making, though in fairly small quantities and only from January till August; otherwise it was mainly used for feeding to poultry, pigs, dogs and pigeons. Oats were fed to saddle, coach and cart horses, poultry, pigs and swans, with a small amount going to the house in the spring and autumn. Pease seems to have been an important supplementary fodder crop for horses, pigs and poultry during the second half of the year.

FOOD AND EQUIPMENT BILLS IN THE NINETEENTH CENTURY

The Sutherland records of the nineteenth century give a completely different flavour. The emphasis has shifted away from a mainly internal supply of raw ingredients to commercial suppliers of high-quality foodstuffs and equipment. One of the benefits of the elaborate stores outlined in the previous chapter, of having 'a place for everything and everything in its place', was the ease with which supplies could be checked. This was not only to reduce pilfering and waste, but also to ensure the stores did not run out of essential goods. In most country households, the standard groceries were supplied by a good quality local firm whose manager or proprietor would pay a regular monthly visit to the housekeeper to check through her stores with her. In this way he could make suggestions of new products and the housekeeper could increase her expertise by keeping up to date – an important means by which new ideas came into the country house world. This system was recalled from before the First World War by the son of the manager of a fashionable grocery in Tonbridge.[6] His father would set out in the pony and trap, dressed in morning coat and top hat; sometimes he'd spend most of the day in a single house:

> I know of one big house where he went round with the housekeeper. They used to start in the kitchen or the butler's pantry and they generally finished up with the gardener or the coachman. He'd take his pencil out from over his ear and he'd tap all these drums they'd got on the shelves – rice, tapioca, semolina. 'That one's down a bit'. Seven pounds of that. 'Yes, that one's down. Better have fourteen of that'.

Account books kept track of purchases with individual suppliers. In 1864, for example, a firm called R. Nicholson, tea and Italian warehouse in Maidenhead, supplied on a monthly basis the Sutherland's house at Clivedon with soap, two qualities of candles, matches, emery cloth, bath brick, tobacco, blacklead, chair blacking, hearthstones, salt, pepper, sulphur and greaves (cakes of compressed fat used as dog food).[7] Some of these account books were elaborate leather-backed books, complete with advertisements and carefully interleaved with tissue and blotting paper. A milk account book from the Aylesbury Dairy Company to the Sutherlands in London shows how the system worked.[8] Amounts were entered every day for between eight and twenty quarts of milk and three to six shillings worth of cream; the weekly bill came to around two or three pounds. Each week the book was checked and an account sent out by the supplier; the bill accumulated to around forty pounds before it was settled.

The Aylesbury Dairy Company's elaborate account book gives an idea of the quality and range of the company's products and of the status of its clientele. From its elegant offices in Bayswater, it claimed to run the 'most extensive and complete Dairy Farm in England' at Horsham in Sussex, covering fourteen hundred acres and running a herd of five hundred head of dairy cattle, described as 'perhaps the most varied collection of well-bred cattle in the world' including Sussex, Shorthorns and Kerries. It had flocks of pedigree poultry, ducks and game birds, supplying both meat and eggs; and a herd of Royal Show-winning Tamworth pigs. It was also experimenting with milk products: it marketed a dietetic beverage called 'koumiss' a milk-based drink with a 'refreshing effervescence' designed for 'persons of delicate and fastidious digestion, the bilious, the gouty, the rheumatic . . .'; and it supplied artificial human milk for infants and older children; according to trials carried out at the British Lying-In Hospital, it had proved to be 'by far the best substitute hitherto discovered for the milk of the mother, and may advantageously supercede the services of the wet-nurse'. The firm also supplied pure whole wheat meal, ground especially finely and prepared so as to offer all the nutriment of a whole wheat meal but in a readily digestible and easily absorbed form for 'delicate persons'.

The reliance on seasonal mobility which is such a feature of country house life can confuse the record, if an account book does not make it clear when the household has moved to a different house. Each house usually had a hierarchy of suppliers, local merchants supplying ordinary quality staple products; a regional town supplying more expensive goods and services, even perhaps servants' clothing and uniforms; and major centres, notably London, for supplies of exotic goods and high quality luxuries. These would be ordered from a London supplier and taken to the country with the family. Equally, though, foodstuffs were sent from one country house to another, or from the country to the town; when a family was living in its town house, regular baskets of live chickens and dairy produce might be sent from their estates in the country. Before the advent of the railways, movement of perishables between houses was difficult but still common, fast posting services being used to deliver parcels of anything from sweets to oysters. The impression is given that in the 1830s and '40s country house proprietors were pushing the road transport system to its limit; the railways must have come as a godsend. Even then, sending food around the country with the family or guests was common practice. As part of the internal accounting system used, the Leveson-Gower meal books record foodstuffs issued from Trentham to be sent to supply other houses in this way. In April 1875, for example, the Duke of Sutherland travelled to his castle at

Dunrobin, north of Inverness, partly by train and partly by carriage, accompanied by hampers containing:[9]

1 ham 11 lb	14s 8d
12 lb bacon	14s 0d
Loaf sugar	5s 0d
Moist sugar	3s 0d
Coffee sugar	3s 0d
6 lb coffee	11s 0d
3 lb tea	12s 9d
2 pickled tongues	13s 0d
Anchovies, capers & vinegar	5s 6d
12 lb cheese	13s 0d
8 chickens	£1 12s 0d
French plums and figs	10s 0d
Harveys Worcester Sauce	3s 0d
Pepper and salt	1s 6d

Many of the fittings for stores and kitchens were supplied by the estate itself; shelving, pin-rails, tables and racks were made by the carpenters. This might also apply to the more complicated pieces of furniture, but the fitted cupboards, ice boxes or meat safes of the Victorian larders were bought from specialist suppliers such as Clement Jeakes, Great Russell Street, London, holder of the royal warrant and suppliers to Dunham Massey, Lanhydrock and many other great houses; or H.T. Ropes & Company, Ice Merchant, 34 North John Street, Liverpool and 17 Old Bond Street, London, suppliers to Speke Hall. Having the right name, even on your oven or meat safe, was important in the search for status.

Bills and books of trade vouchers record purchases and maintenance agreements. The firm of Johnson and Ravey, braziers and ironmongers to Her Majesty and the Royal Family, of 4 Conduit Street, London, carried an account with the Sutherlands throughout the 1840s. From July to November 1840, they supplied and fitted several pieces of new equipment in their houses at Trentham and Dunrobin, both of which were being substantially extended and modernized.[10] The total bill for an amazing amount of work at both houses came to £244 15s 0d. It is fair to assume that this equipment represented state of the art technology, yet it is combined with more traditional pieces in a way highly typical of the country house kitchen. At Dunrobin, it included 'making a very large and thick copper top for steam table, tinning and planished, copper tinned skirting slates, making a deep brass moulding, bevelled to hold down ditto, the whole screwed down . . . £55 10s 8d' plus '3 men's time 3 days each fixing above . . . £3 3s 0d'. At the same time the existing smoke jack was repaired and oiled and the back boiler to the range was altered and repaired. The existing *batterie de cuisine* was overhauled: a large number of copper stewpans, kettles, bowls and moulds had the 'bruises' taken out and were set flat on their bottoms and retinned. All the coppers were marked with a new ducal coronet and the letter 'S' and numbered.[11] New equipment supplied to Dunrobin included '12 town-made lark spits . . . £1 13s 0d' and a large number of smaller items such as four boxes of paste cutters, twenty-one larding pins, twelve steel trussing needles, a poultry chopper, twenty-four patty-pans, seven small fluted pie moulds. All were packed into large wooden cases, presumably to accompany the men who travelled to Scotland to fit the steam table. At the same time Johnson and Ravey supplied a large amount of copper utensils for the newly equipped confectionery at Trentham, a list which shows very well the sort of work carried on there, as well as the importance of ice at this time. The Trentham confectionery was highly specialized, for a wage list of the 1840s shows that the family employed not only a male confectioner but also two confectionery maids, one of whom was dedicated entirely to the Duchess of Sutherland.

For the Confectionery at Trentham Hall, 1840

6 copper sugar ladles	£4 9s 6d
4 wire egg whisks	15s 0d
Weighing machine	£1 4s 0d
Set of brass box weights	£1 4s 0d
5 square iron weights	12s 6d
2 copper egg bowls	£1 18s 0d
Large forged copper slice	8s 6d
2 forged punched spoons	14s 6d
Copper soup ladle	7s 6d
Tin bread grater	3s 0d
2 copper coffee pots and covers	£1 14s 0d
1 copper chocolate pot and cover	19s 0d

Large town-made coffee mill with fly wheel	£2 5s 0d
Pair of square wafer irons to pattern	£2 10s 0d
6 strong flat copper baking sheets	£6 18s 6d
3 tin candy pans	16s 6d
3 brass wire gratings to above	15s 0d
Copper jumble mould and 12 shapes	£2 5s 0d
2 corkscrews	3s 6d
6 square tin baking sheets	19s 6d
Oil and oiling smoke jack	5s 6d
Coffee roaster and frame complete	£1 1s 0d
Coffee measure and 2 coffee canisters	5s 6d
3 boxes of paste cutters	£1 5s 6d
36 queen cake pans	13s 6d
Square sugar tin marked with divisions	15s 0d
2 brick ice moulds with covers	7s 0d
5 pewter freezing pots and covers	£5 2s 6d
12 tin cake hoops, wired top and bottom	12s 0d
3 pewter icing bottles for water	£4 0s 0d
6 pewter ice moulds with covers	£3 18s 0d
6 kitchen knives	£1 18s 0d
6 French sheaths, 3 prs scissors	16s 6d
A turned, polished steel patterned roller	£1 4s 0d
Copper twine box, tin dredger	13s 0d
4 copper double spoons	£1 2s 0d
Paste roller, skimming pan	11s 0d
Copper soup pot and cover	£1 7s 0d
Toasting fork, 3 sponge tins	8s 6d
Tin shell, forged copper spoon	8s 0d
Oblong copper ice cave with 3 copper shelves and cover	£3 4s 6d
Forged copper ice shovel	12s 6d
Copper hand bowl, sugar chopper	15s 6d
Large tin coffee filter	18s 0d
Making a forged ring and socket for jelly bag	10s 6d
12 pewter ice moulds aportal	£1 16s 0d
Large oblong wood ice tub	£1 5s 0d

6 ice spatulas aportal	£1 13s 0d
Japanned inkstand	9s 6d
2 crumpet paste rollers	12s 0d
Engraving coppers coronet & numbering	£1 5s 0d
2 wood cases & packing	£1 8s 6d
New pan and fixing to kitchen shovel	4s 9d
Fixing up part of hot plates, burnishing, time	7s 3d

One final example will serve to illustrate the highly structured catering system which operated in the larger country houses. Meal books record not so much the food supplied but the numbers of meals taken each day, divided into separate categories such as the parlour (i.e. the family); nursery; steward's room; servants' hall; kitchen; and even included the number of dogs fed. For some periods the Sutherland households were so busy that separate books were kept for family, guests and servants – this is indeed bulk catering, though of a very high quality. Sometimes servants were simply totalled, sometimes they were described by their jobs. In the case of family or guest, individuals were named; it is possible, therefore, to identify the individuals who sat down to dinner in the great dining-room at Trentham on any given day – 13 February 1875, for example, was a day when no guests were present; even so the household fed thirty-seven people:

Parlour	*Value of food for the day*
Duke and Duchess	£1 12s 0d
Lady Florence	16s 0d
Steward's Room	
9 household servants	18s 0d
Maid's friend	1s 0d
Servants' Hall	
7 male servants	10s 6d
9 female servants	12s 2d
1 oddman	1s 6d
Garden boy	1s 6d

Clock man	1s 0d
Kitchen gardener	1s 0d
Kitchen	
3 male servants	4s 6d
4 female servants	5s 5d
3 dogs	9d

On many days sundry other entries were made, such as the supply of sandwiches to Mr Loch (the agent) for travelling, and donations of beef tea and jelly to a retired housekeeper and members of the travelling poor.

The meal books show how cheap servants' keep was in relation to family meals; in the case given above, only three out of a total of thirty-seven individuals account for almost half the cost. In the Sutherland houses there was an agreed allowance, to which the chef had to work and which was adopted for the purpose of the internal accounts. Breakfast varied from 2s 6d per head for the family and 1s for the nursery, to 8d per head for servants; dinner likewise varied from 14s each for the family, 2s for the nursery and 1s for the servants. Male servants were allowed twopence worth more food than females.[12] In other households the same sort of record kept track of the amount of meat used – at the Ansons' Staffordshire house at Shugborough, the daily target for the chef was one and a half pounds of meat per person per day, but the record shows it was usually nearer two pounds, though this figure was probably inclusive of fat and bone.[13]

The purpose of keeping such records was to keep control of costs. When catering on such a large scale and to very high standards, the potential for waste and dishonesty was huge. This is one reason why the household itself was so highly structured; as with the food stores, if everyone had their given place it was easier to keep control over them and to make sure they were not abusing their position. Even so the 'leakage' of food and drink from the great houses must have been very great. It was a continuous source of concern in household manuals, especially the consignment of good food to the 'washing' tub – the discarded bits and pieces which were allowed either to the kitchen staff or to the local poor. To some families living locally but connected with the working household, it could have made a considerable impact on their diet.

NOTES

1. Staffordshire Record Office (hereafter SRO), Sutherland Mss, D593/R/1/4/1, presents sent to Lilleshall Lodge, Christmas 1642.

2. Kate Mertes, *The English Noble Household, 1250–1600: Good Governance and Political Rule* (Oxford, 1988), p. 93.

3. SRO, Sutherland Mss, D593/R/1/4/2, kitchen accounts, 1646.

4. See SRO, Sutherland Mss, D593/R/1/5/6A, grain book for 1676 for records of feeding barley, oats and pease to domestic livestock – horses, swine, poultry, pigeons, dogs, swans; unfortunately the domestic record does not include farm livestock.

5. SRO, Sutherland Mss, D593/R/1/5/6A, grain book, 1675–7.

6. Michael J. Winstanley, *The Shopkeeper's World, 1830–1914* (Manchester, 1983), p. 127.

7. SRO, Sutherland Mss, D593/R/3/2/6/2, account book with R. Nicholson, 1864.

8. SRO, Sutherland Mss, D593/R/1/24/12, vouchers, 1889.

9. SRO, Sutherland Mss, D593/R/1/19, meal book for 1874.

10. SRO, Sutherland Mss, D593/R/2/22/1, bill from Johnson and Ravey, 1840.

11. Baron Gower was created Duke of Sutherland in 1833.

12. SRO, Sutherland Mss, D593/R/1/19, housekeeping charges, 1873.

13. SRO, Anson Mss, D615/E(H)35.

CHAPTER TWELVE

ICE-GETTING ON THE COUNTRY HOUSE ESTATE

Rob David

The fifteen gardeners at Holker Hall in Cumbria deserved their Christmas holiday in 1883. For the previous fortnight they had been involved in the seasonal task of ice-getting. Using a variety of implements they had cleared the frozen pond of its covering of ice, carted it the three hundred metres to the eighteenth-century ice-house, and begun to fill the enormous ice chamber. In recognition of the hard and unpleasant work that was involved, the gardeners were given a bonus of ale, bread and cheese 'for Ice getting'.[1] The Holker estate was large enough to employ sufficient gardeners to perform the annual chore of filling the ice-house. At Sedgwick House, a few miles away, in the period shortly before the First World War, when estate staff were already beginning to be reduced in number, the ice-house was filled by all the available estate workers; the few remaining gardeners were joined by the groom, the odd man and the chauffeur.[2] The annual gathering of the ice harvest was an unpopular and labour intensive part of that cycle of activities which ensured that the occupants of the great houses of Britain could maintain the lifestyle that they and their guests had come to expect.

The ice-house had emerged as a characteristic feature of the country estate during the seventeenth century, although there had been a few precursors constructed during Elizabeth I's reign.[3] Between 1618 and 1626 snow conserves, possibly following in the tradition of the Spanish in Grenada, who acquired snow from the mountains of the Sierra Nevada, were built at Greenwich Park in London, and at Hampton Court for James I. However, it was only after the restoration of Charles II in 1660 that the idea of ice-houses became more widespread. Charles had spent much of his time in exile at the court of Versailles, and on his return to England, he sought to make his court as elegant as that of the French, and since the sixteenth century ice had been an essential part of that elegance. The origin of French ice-houses, and therefore of those in Britain, can be traced to the Near East,

Entrance to the ice-house at Holker Hall in Cumbria. (Photograph Rob David)

and in particular Turkey. In 1553 Pierre Belon in *Les Observations de Plusieurs Singularitez et Choses Memorables . . . En Grece, Asie . . .* referred to Turkish ice-houses when he wrote: 'The Turks gather the snow, filling certain houses constructed like vaults or else like a hillock of earth . . . and expressly made for the purpose'.[4] Ice-houses were built at St James' Palace and Upper St James' Park in London, and at Castle Hill in Greenwich. It was not long before the courtiers who surrounded the king sought to emulate this new royal fashion. One of the king's many mistresses, Barbara Villiers, Duchess of Cleveland, had an ice-house built in the grounds of her London house, as did the Earl of Kent on his Bedfordshire estate.

During the eighteenth century ice-houses became a more common feature on the estates of the landed gentry, the fashion spreading from the immediate environs of London, to remoter parts of the kingdom; for example the ice-house at Holker Hall, referred to at the beginning of this chapter, had been built by 1732,[5] and the ice-house on the estate at Invereray in Strathclyde was built in 1786.[6] Only estates large enough to have both an ice-house and a lake to provide ice, could produce their own ice; the urban middle class and the gentry in their town houses had to rely on ice supplied by commercial enterprises, of which there were at least six in Edinburgh by 1800.[7]

During the Victorian era the ranks of the gentry were swelled by those who had profited from the commercial opportunities offered by the industrial revolution. Such entrepreneurs had to make an important decision, as Mark Girouard has pointed out: 'Once a Victorian merchant, manufacturer or professional man had made a sufficient fortune he was faced with the dilemma of whether or not to set out to establish his family in the landed gentry'.[8] For many who found themselves in this position this meant either purchasing an already existing estate with a country house built on it, or if no suitable ones were available, buying the land on which to build and create an estate. Either way, one of the features that was increasingly becoming a necessity rather than a luxury was an ice-house. This could involve quite considerable extra expense as the traditional subterranean structure could be expensive to build. In the early nineteenth century William Cobbett estimated the cost would be between £100 and £300.[9] However, lower-cost versions could be constructed. A handwritten manual which explains how to build an ice-house, dating from about 1825, commented that: 'In many cases the building may be completed for £10'.[10]

The traditional ice-house on a British estate was constructed of stone or brick. It consisted of a conical or cylindrical well sunk into the earth to a depth of four metres or more, surmounted by a domed roof. The whole structure was often built into a bank, in order to allow the melt-water to drain out from the bottom of the well, and was entered by a passage which was closed by a series of doors which could be made of wood or iron, and occasionally of slate. The ice was placed in the well and usually surrounded by straw, which helped to insulate the ice from the warmer temperature outside. An air vent was provided in the roof, because a through current of air helped to ensure that the ice-house environment remained as dry as possible. It was essential to keep the interior of the ice-house dry as dampness rapidly increased the rate of melt. Ice-houses were sometimes covered in clay and roofed in slate; free standing ones were occasionally thatched. There was some debate as to whether ice-houses should be surrounded by trees. Once school of thought suggested that the shade caused by the trees would provide a cool environment,[11] another felt that a covering of trees would increase the dampness, and therefore should be avoided.[12] Ice-houses are as likely to be found in open parkland as in wooded areas. This traditional type of ice-house was illustrated by John Loudon in the 1850 edition of his *Encyclopaedia of Gardening*,[13] and examples can be found throughout the country.

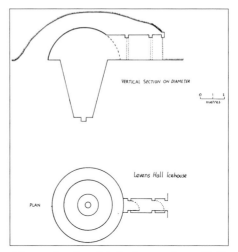

Plan and section of the ice-house at Levens Hall, Cumbria.

The range of ice-house styles increased during the nineteenth century, as technology changed and owners sought cheaper methods of ice storage. Sometimes ice-houses were little more than subterranean or part-subterranean rooms, or alternatively timber and thatch buildings of the type illustrated by Charles MacIntosh in *The Book of the Garden* in 1853. The storage volume of such temporary structures could be increased by placing the timber building over a hole in the ground. It was even possible to do without a building at all and to construct ice-stacks which consisted of a cone of ice placed on the land surface, surrounded by an insulating layer of straw or bracken. MacIntosh commented, 'In this way ice will keep a year, care being taken to expose it to the air as short a time as possible in

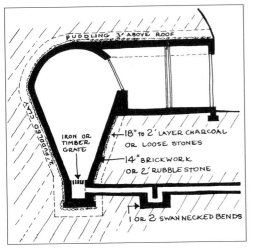

PUDDLING 3' ABOVE ROOF

PUDDLED CLAY 9"

IRON OR TIMBER GRATE

18" TO 2' LAYER CHARCOAL OR LOOSE STONES

14" BRICKWORK OR 2' RUBBLE STONE

1 OR 2 SWAN NECKED BENDS

Section through an ice-house. (From J.C. Loudon, An Encyclopedia of Gardening, *1850)*

taking supplies. A supply of ice is produced at little more than the cost of annually filling an ordinary ice-house.'[14]

Few ice-houses were conspicuous features of estates. Most were located in areas which would not be frequented by the owners or their guests. Often they were sited nearer the source of ice than the house. This was because the most difficult part of ice-getting was the transportation of the many tons of ice from the pond or reservoir to the ice-house in mid-winter. Only small quantities of ice were needed at any one time in the house during the summer, and because of melting the amount that was eventually carried to the kitchen was considerably less than the amount that had been harvested. However, there was a school of thought that favoured the construction of ice-houses as focal points of estates. The early nineteenth-century architect and landscape designer J.B. Papworth designed a number of ice-houses in the styles of Egyptian temples and country cottages.[15] The ice-house at Myerscough Farm in Lancashire is a small version of Papworth's Egyptian temple,[16] and those at Buckland in Oxfordshire and Newbattle Abbey in Lothian[17] were hidden behind classical façades. Some ice-houses were constructed as part of, or beneath, other estate buildings. The ice-house at Murdostoun in Strathclyde shared a building with a doocot, and that at West Wycombe Park in Buckinghamshire was built beneath the folly of the Temple of Venus.[18]

The ice was collected, as often as possible during the winter, from adjacent ponds and reservoirs, and occasionally rivers and canals. As the length and intensity of frosts was unpredictable in Britain, ice was usually gathered as opportunity arose, and therefore on several occasions during an average winter, and thus ice rarely achieved any thickness. The account book of Katharine Foulis[19] from the York area shows that she purchased nine loads of ice on 31 December 1825, a further nine loads on 11 January and twenty-seven loads on 16 and 17 January 1826. The accounts make clear that at least the last purchase was stored in a temporary thatched ice-house:

2 Men one Day at pond	4s 0d
Madders & His Partner 2 Days	13s 0d
4 Men 2 Days Each 2/0	16s 0d
ale &c Bread	5s 0d
for Diging the Hole	£1 13s 0d
for the Roof	
Straw – Poppleton 6 thrave	£1 1s 0d
D. Furnish 2 thrave	
D. Hornwins 2 thrave	
tar band	1s 3d
Wilkinson for Thatching	10s 0d
the Clark	3s 0d

[the thrave was two stooks or twenty-four sheaves of straw].

This temporary ice-house was built, stocked and insulated for less than ten pounds.

Even where a permanent ice-house had already been constructed, filling the building was a labour intensive occupation. In 1915–16 ice was gathered from the Lancaster to Kendal canal by the estate workers at Sedgwick House, in Cumbria. Mr W.B. Dawson, who was at that time a gardener at the house, has described the process involved. Initially two men broke up the ice on the canal, two more men pulled it along the canal to the ice-house, another two loaded it on to the chute, five men broke it into fragments and one man wearing boots and sacking around the lower legs for warmth, stood in the ice-house itself spreading out and compacting the ice.[20] A variety of implements were used for these tasks. Mallets and poles would have been used to break the ice, ice hooks were used to bring the rafts of ice into the bank and to pull them along the

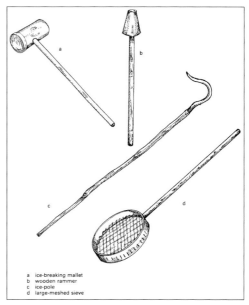

a   ice-breaking mallet
b   wooden rammer
c   ice-pole
d   large-meshed sieve

Examples of ice-harvesting tools found at Althorp House, Northamptonshire. (By courtesy of Routledge)

length of the canal, and pavement rammers were sometimes used to compact the ice in the ice-house. None of these tools was peculiar to ice-getting, so they were probably made by a local blacksmith and used for any appropriate tasks on the estate.

Occasionally, during colder winters, a greater thickness of ice became available. In 1905 Mr Donaldson's youthful skating trip along the Kendal canal was cut short by the ice-gatherers at Helme Lodge, Kendal, who were using saws to cut the ice for storage in the canalside ice-house.[21]

There was no shortage of advice for the nineteenth-century groundsman concerning the optimum way to fill an ice-house.[22] It was recommended that several days before the ice-getting began the doors should be opened and a bushel or two of unslaked lime be put in to dry the atmosphere, as a damp environment was most injurious to the survival of the ice. It was essential that the melt-water from the stored ice should be able to drain away, through the soak-away which can be found in all successful ice chambers. In order to permit a free flow of melt-water the drain was covered with an iron grating or, in chambers with a tapering pit, with an old cartwheel, covered with brushwood. The ice had to be insulated from the surrounding stone or brickwork, and this was usually done by placing sheaves of straw at the bottom and up the sides of the ice-pit. Sawdust, charcoal and occasionally bracken were alternatives. Some ice-house builders adopted the principle of cavity wall insulation. This was either achieved through constructing a double wall around the ice chamber, or placing an inner wooden wall inside the wall of the chamber and filling the space between with sawdust or charcoal.[23] These preparations had to be undertaken in advance of the first frosts so that the ice-house was ready as soon as a sufficient thickness of ice had formed on the adjacent water source. On the appointed day all the estate's outdoor workers and sometimes the indoor ones as well, as has been shown, were involved with the gathering of the ice. The ice was broken up into small fragments, and once in the ice-house was pounded into a solid mass by rammers. This was done because warm air trapped between lumps of ice would have increased the rate of melting. A solid mass of ice would last much longer. To reduce the temperature and help to consolidate the ice, John Loudon suggested pouring on quantities of salt water. [24] Charles MacIntosh, however, believed that such an act would be 'not only useless but injurious'.[25] The author of an anonymous book from the County Durham/North Yorkshire border written in about 1810 recommended the use of salt when constructing an ice stack:

'Beat the ice as small as possible, then place it in the ground . . . pour hot water upon it, & salt alternately with every layer of ice, each layer about a foot high the height of the pie [stack] to be about 4 feet or 5ft high. Thatch the same with rye straw a foot & a half in thickness. N.B. The ice being well beaten, add one stone of salt for every twelve load of ice & twenty gallons of hot water.'[26] In addition there were other debatable issues such as whether or not the ice at the top of the chamber should be left dome-shaped or saucer-shaped,[27] and whether or not a wooden floor should be placed over the ice.[28] The usual practice was to cover the ice with a thick layer of straw, and to fill the passageway between the doors with straw before sealing the ice-house. Once stored the ice needed little further attention.

The appearance of British ice was unattractive, and the purity, especially when gathered from canals, must also have been doubtful. MacIntosh warned his readers: 'The extreme impurity [of the ice in Britain] renders it unfit for any other purpose save that of merely cooling wines or other viands enclosed in bottles or well covered dishes.'[29] Food was not packed in the ice in the ice-house, although there is some evidence that fruit and game could be stored in the roof space of the ice-house.[30] At Crofton Hall in Cumbria the roof of the ice-house is lined with meat hooks and at Duddon Hall, also in Cumbria, a larder was constructed as part of the ice chamber.[31] However, a recent experiment carried out at Levens Hall ice-house in Cumbria showed that the temperature in the roof space reached over 11°C, even when the chamber below was full of ice insulated with its thick covering of straw.[32]

In most country houses the ice was collected from the ice-house as required and taken to the kitchen to be stored in bins, ice boxes or refrigerators.[33] The collection might either be performed by the estate staff or the kitchen staff. Once inside the house it became the responsibility of the indoor staff. Most of it was used for culinary purposes in the preparation of iced dishes, the refrigeration of fish, meat and other foodstuffs, and for cooling beverages. Confectionery and recipe books, the earliest of which had been published in the eighteenth century, provided many examples of iced dishes. Frederick Nutt in his *Complete Confectioner*, published in 1789, included instructions for making thirty-one different ice-creams,[34] but by the beginning of the twentieth century the range of exotic iced dishes had multiplied. Karl Scharrer illustrated such fancy concoctions as Congo Bombe complete with iced palm trees, and Othello Bombe in the shape of a crown.[35] Because of the filthy condition of the ice it was never allowed to come into direct contact with food or drink. The refrigerators of the period consisted of insulated boxes in which the ice was placed at the bottom, and the food placed on wire mesh trays above it. The ice was used to cool wine bottles, but was never placed in the drink itself. Ice could sometimes also be used for cooling rooms in hot weather, a primitive form of air conditioning, and for medicinal purposes. In the latter context it was used to control fevers and inflammation and for stopping bleeding. It was also sucked or swallowed to counteract disorders of the stomach, and applied externally to the head, chest or abdomen for internal disorders.[36]

Towards the middle of the nineteenth century those responsible for provisioning the town houses of the gentry and the wealthier middle class could take advantage of a new source of ice. In 1842 the first shipment of North American ice from Fresh Pond, Boston arrived in Britain aboard the barque *Shannon*.[37] Such ice from unpolluted lakes in New England had a depth and clarity that could never be achieved in Britain. It was so pure that it could be used in direct contact with food and drink. A presentation, by the importers, to the Fishmongers Association in London was not a great success as the guests were ill-prepared for the resulting coldness of their drinks.[38] However, this initial prejudice did not last long as people soon realized the advantages of such pure blocks of crystal ice, which opened up new culinary possibilities, as well as enabling the construction of the most exotic table decorations.

Ice from Wenham Lake, a few miles north of Boston, became the market leader. The Wenham Lake Ice Company prospectus revealed the company's intention to control all aspects of the market.[39] Not only did it own the lake and organize the collection of the ice in New England, but it established an office in the Strand in London and was in the business of filling ice-houses and retailing 'Portable Ice-houses' or refrigerators. An advertisement on 13 February 1846 indicated that the Company was 'ready at once to contract to fill ice-houses on moderate terms in Town or Country'.[40] Although initially only estates in the environs of London could take advantage of this facility, it was not long before the Company opened agencies in other cities such as Liverpool, Birmingham, Manchester, Hastings and Dublin.[41] The Wenham Lake Company had its competitors who soon began importing and retailing American ice, so country estates adjacent to an ever increasing number of cities and ports found that they could purchase high quality crystal ice. The Wenham Lake Company was able to make deliveries across the London metropolitan area, through insulating the blocks of ice by wrapping them in blankets. Vans left the company ice-houses twice a day, at 8.00 a.m. and 3.00 p.m.

to visit every part of the capital.[42] Royal patronage of Wenham Lake ice helped to ensure its success, and its increasing availability began to change the British people's drinking and eating habits. American beverages such as mint-juleps and sherry-cobblers, where the ice was mixed with the drink, suddenly became popular. However, the availability of American ice did not cause the traditional ice-getting activities on the British country estate to be abandoned. The expense of Wenham Lake ice was such that only the wealthiest could afford it, and probably only on special occasions which demanded high quality table ice. The price depended upon the quantity bought. For customers without ice-houses, who relied on small frequent deliveries to fill their refrigerator, the cost, according to a mid-century advertisement, was two pence per pound.[43] For those with ice-houses it could be bought at ten shillings per hundredweight, but filling a fifteen ton capacity ice-house solely with Wenham Lake ice would have cost as much as £150. Few households, if any, would have been prepared to pay that price.

The situation, however, changed during the 1870s. The monopoly in supplying crystal ice that the Americans had enjoyed was under attack on two fronts: firstly from an alternative source of natural ice, and secondly from the development of new commercial processes for the manufacture of artificial ice. American ice was always vulnerable to competition from Europe, because the cost of shipping the cargo was the most significant factor in its high cost. Although Norwegian ice had first been imported into London in 1822,[44] regular deliveries only began in the 1850s. By the 1870s the quantity imported began to regularly exceed 100,000 tons per annum, and on occasions during that decade even reached 200,000 tons.[45] Not all the ice was destined for the domestic market, as commercial uses for ice had developed in the fishing, brewing and confectionery industries, but it was becoming increasingly attractive to the private consumer. This was because it was as pure as American ice, and therefore could have a similar range of uses; and it also had the advantage that it was considerably cheaper because the short sea passage from Norway kept freight costs to a minimum. During the 1870s the cost was around one pound per ton at the ports, and by the end of the century, when up to half a million tons were being imported annually, this had fallen to about twelve shillings.[46] Retail prices were obviously higher, but ice could be bought in Windermere in Cumbria, for example, for 5s 6d per hundredweight in 1871; a price which incorporated fairly substantial rail freight costs.[47] Wenham Lake ice had been nearly double that figure twenty years previously. The development of the rail network, and in particular specially insulated refrigeration wagons, enabled ice to be transported rapidly from the ports to many parts of the kingdom and gave the gentry access to the higher quality ice which respectability demanded. Although the cost of rail freight had to be included in the eventual retail price, the advantages of Norwegian crystal ice were so great that a ready market was found, not only among the country landowners, but also among the urban middle class, as well as in restaurants, hotels and clubs. Even though local ice-getting was continued, those responsible for provisioning the country house were as likely now to put in an order with the neighbouring ice stockist, who might be the grocer, confectioner, fishmonger, butcher or chemist, in order to provide the high quality crystal ice which was demanded. Imported ice also solved the problem, though at a price, of mild winters, when not enough ice formed on the local ponds to enable the ice-house to be filled. Earlier in the nineteenth century such a situation would have necessitated the gentry changing their eating habits, but by the latter part of the century they were no longer so dependent on the fickle British climate for their supply of ice.

The unreliability of the British summer also had an effect on the demand for ice. The summer of 1899 is a good illustration of the typical seasonal unpredictability. The month of May was cold and the demand for imported ice was small, as the stocks in the British ice-houses were adequate to meet the demand. June began cool, but towards the end of the month, and during July and August the weather became hotter, and the demand for ice was brisk. The remaining British stocks had to be supplemented by Norwegian ice, whose price increased by six shillings per ton at the ports. Fortunately the winter of 1898/9 had been severe in Norway so stocks were high.[48] Had it been a mild winter, with a poor harvest in Norway, the Norwegian ice-houses would have been only half full, and the price during a hot English summer would have become higher still, which explains why the British ice harvest remained important. Natural ice, whether harvested at home or abroad, was an unpredictable commodity, as the quantity available, and therefore the price, fluctuated wildly.

In 1899 over half a million tons of crystal ice were imported from Norway, the highest figure reached.[49] Much of the increased imports was being absorbed by industry and commerce, and a considerable proportion of the domestic needs was still being met most economically by the local harvest. In fact the traditional methods had had something of a revival as a result of a number of scares concerning the purity of the imported ice. One of the chief marketing opportunities for imported ice had been with regard to its purity which allowed it to be used in direct contact with food and drink. A number of cases of intestinal disorders in the United States had been reported in the press during the 1870s and circumstantial evidence suggested that filthy ice from industrial rivers might have been to blame.[50] This raised the question of the purity of the Norwegian sources. Although the lack of heavy industry in Norway ensured that ice supplies were more likely to come from uncontaminated sources, at least one company took the precaution of buying up the land surrounding the entire catchment area of its principal lake. Once the doubt had been sown in the public's mind the damage had been done. In spite of the ice importer's attempts at damage limitation, through quoting eminent scientists in support of natural ice, the London County Council's inquiry into the natural ice trade in 1904, led its chairman Dr W.H. Hamer, to issue the following statement: 'Having in view the nature of the risks involved in consuming natural ice, and the demonstrated insufficiency of the supposed safeguarding circumstances, the reasonable course would appear to be to abandon the use of such ice for consumption or for purposes which it is brought into direct contact with foodstuffs.'[51] From the point of view of those responsible for supplying the ice requirements of the country estate, the advantage of Norwegian ice, which had been thought to be safe when in direct contact with food, had now disappeared, so there was no reason why British ice should not continue to be harvested, as it was equally as good as a preserving agent, and was considerably cheaper, than imported ice. Traditional British ice harvesting had been given a second chance. However, the manufacture of artificial ice posed a new threat to both the Norwegian import trade and the traditional British ice harvest. This was ultimately to change the whole pattern of refrigeration and make the ice-house, and the process of ice-getting, redundant.

The manufacture of artificial ice on a commercial scale dates from 1855, when the Scots engineer James Harrison, invented, in Australia, the vapour compression machine using ether.[52] Earlier inventions had been limited to the development of domestic apparatus. Thomas Masters described in his 1844 *Ice Book*, his invention in which blocks of ice could be produced in conical moulds filled with water, and immersed in a freezing solution of snow or pounded ice, and salt. He went on to comment that the 'ice-wells of noblemen and gentlemen might be filled with the purest ice, without the trouble of skimming ponds'.[53] This was a laudable objective, but the scale of production using domestic machines such as these was too little to have any real effect on either ice imports or the ice harvest.

Initially artificial ice was not popular with domestic customers as little attention was paid to its quality, and consequently much of the ice so made was opaque. For domestic consumers the opacity contrasted unfavourably with the clarity of natural ice. The remedy, for which the technology existed, was to agitate the water during the process of freezing, in order to expel the air which formed the bubbles which caused the opacity. The health scares associated with the impurity of some natural ice, gave artificial ice an advantage, although the possibility that some of the urban wells from which the water was drawn were themselves polluted, led to the recommendation that the water used in manufacturing ice should be distilled.[54] Increasing numbers of ice factories were constructed from the 1880s,[55] and by 1907, 62 per cent of the total ice consumed in Britain was of the artificial variety.[56] Artificial ice had the enormous advantages of being available all year round and of being cheaper than imported natural ice. The majority of the ice was being used in commercial and industrial processes, and ice factories therefore were limited to areas with such markets. In London there was room for both the natural and artificial ice trades because of the variety of customers. In many towns, especially fishing ports, the mainstay of the artificial ice plant was the industrial customer; domestic custom was welcome, but not essential, and was in any case limited by the expense of refrigerators, which had the effect of severely limiting the number of potential customers. Most country houses did not have convenient access to an ice factory, and therefore remained dependent upon the more expensive natural ice from Norway, or their own resources from the estate. It is not surprising therefore that many of the estates in the deep countryside continued the annual ice-getting into this century, and only those with access to ice from the ports and other urban sources, abandoned the ice-house, preferring to acquire their ice in small quantities as required.

Few domestic ice-houses were used after the First World War. In the straitened inter-war years, estates no longer had the manpower necessary for the labour intensive process of ice-getting. The war had also caused the virtual demise of the Norwegian ice trade, a situation exploited by the artificial ice industry with the encouragement of the Ministry of Food, who saw the need for a rapid expansion of the cold storage industry during the war years;[57] and the industry's trade magazine which commented that 'the ice manufacturing trade as a whole devoutly hopes that the Norwegian import trade may never again find its legs. The issue really rests with the manufacturers'.[58] Even the emergence of the artificial ice plant was ultimately less important in the closing up of the ice-house than the development of gas and electricity powered domestic refrigerators, such as the American 'Domelre'. Initially these could only be used on estates with their own power source, but in the inter-war years they became essential domestic items, not only in the country house, but also among an ever widening section of Britain's householders.

The domestic ice-house had been the only year-round source of ice for the gentry from the sixteenth century to the mid-nineteenth century. At the very time when the number of ice-houses was rapidly expanding with the numerous new country house estates of the Victorian era, new sources of ice became available, and new technologies were developed, which were to lead to the abandonment, within the following seventy years, of the rituals surrounding the traditional ice-getting.

NOTES

1. Account book of Holker Hall Estate in the possession of Miss Doris Wright of Holker.

2. Personal communication from Mr W.B. Dawson of Heversham, Cumbria.

3. S.P. Beamon and S. Roaf, *The Icehouses of Britain* (London, 1990), p. 17.

4. E. David, *Harvest of the Cold Months: The Social History of Ice and Ices* (London, 1994), p. 41.

5. Personal communication from Mr H. Cavendish.

6. T. Buxbaum, *Icehouses* (Princes Risborough, 1992), p. 4.

7. A.N. Robertson, 'Ice-houses of the Eighteenth and Nineteenth Centuries in Edinburgh and the Lothians', *Book of the Old Edinburgh Club*, 27 (1953), pp. 145–51.

8. M. Girouard, *The Victorian Country House* (New Haven and London, 1979), p. 7.

9. W. Cobbett, *Cottage Economy* (London, 1822), pp. 183–91.

10. Lancashire Record Office, DDG a/17(21).

11. A number of ice-houses are located in woodland, and the woods are sometimes known as 'Ice-house Wood'.

12. See for example *Encyclopaedia Britannica* (London, 1797), vol. 9, p. 85.

13. Beamon and Roaf, *Ice-houses of Britain*, p. 61.

14. C. MacIntosh, *The Book of the Garden* (Edinburgh, 1853–5), pp. 502–3.

15. J.B. Papworth, *Designs for Rural Residences* (London, 1818), pp. 99–100; and J.B. Papworth, *Hints on Ornamental Gardening* (London, 1823).

16. R. David, 'The Ice-houses of North Lancashire', *Lancashire Local Historian* (1985), pp. 15–16.

17. Buxbaum, *Icehouses*, pp. 21 and 23.

18. Ibid., pp. 24–5.

19. Katharine Foulis account book. Personal communication from Mr P. Brears.

20. Personal communication from Mr W.B. Dawson of Heversham, Cumbria.

21. Personal communication from Mr Donaldson of Holme, Cumbria.

22. See for example, MacIntosh, *The Book of the Garden*; and J.C. Loudon, *An Encyclopaedia of Gardening* (London, 1834).

23. For examples see R. David, 'The Ice-houses of Cumbria', *Transactions of the Cumberland and Westmorland Antiquarian and Archaeological Society*, 81 (1981), pp. 137–55.

24. Loudon, *Encyclopaedia of Gardening*, pp. 611–13.

25. MacIntosh, *The Book of the Garden*, pp. 497–513.

26. Personal communication from Mr P. Brears.

27. Lancashire Record Office, DDG a/17 (21).

28. Ibid., and C.S.T. Calder and A. Graham, 'An Old 18th Century Ice-house in Midlothian', *Proceedings of the Society of the Antiquaries of Scotland*, 84, pp. 208–11.

29. MacIntosh, *The Book of the Garden*, pp. 497–513.

30. Beamon and Roaf, *Ice-houses of Britain*, p. 130.

31. David, 'Ice-houses of Cumbria', pp. 142 and 147.

32. R. David, 'An Ice-house Experiment', *Transactions of the Cumberland and Westmorland Antiquarian and Archaeological Society*, 82 (1982), pp. 191–3.

33. A selection is illustrated in *The Army and Navy Stores Catalogue, 1907* (reprint Newton Abbot, 1969).

34. David, *Harvest of the Cold Months*, p. 312.

35. Ibid., Plate 7, between pp. 238 and 239.

36. V.G.L. Fielden, 'The Pharmacology and Therapeutics of Ice', *British Medical Journal*, 1 (1905), pp. 1264–6.

37. F.H. Forbes, 'Ice', *Schooners Monthly*, 10 (May 1875–Oct. 1875), pp. 464 ff.

38. Ibid., pp. 464 ff.

39. PRO, BT41, 741/4002, Prospectus A.

40. PRO, BT41, 741/4002. The advertisement is in draft form only.

41. *The Times*, 8 July 1845, Supplement.

42. *The Times*, 8 July 1845, Supplement; and *The Times*, 1 August 1845.

43. PRO, BT41/4002. This advertisement is in the form of a cutting from an unidentified newspaper.

44. T. Ouren, 'The Norwegian Ice Trade', in D.V. Procter (ed.), *Ice Carrying Trade at Sea* (London, 1981).

45. PRO, CUST5.

46. PRO, CUST5.

47. *Westmorland Gazette*, 1 July 1871, p. 1.

48. *Cold Storage and Ice Trades Review*, vol. 2, no. 3 (June 1899), p. 32; vol. 2, no. 4 (July 1899), p. 48; vol. 2, no. 6 (August 1899), p. 77.

49. PRO, CUST5.

50. *Cold Storage*, vol. 11, no. 119 (February 1908), pp. 35 and 64.

51. The report is extensively quoted in *Cold Storage*, vol. 8, no. 82 (January 1905), pp. 4–11.

52. P.C. Smith, 'Some Pioneers of Refrigeration', *Transactions of the Newcomen Society*, 23 (1942–3), p. 103.

53. David, *Harvest of the Cold Months*, pp. 340–1.

54. *Cold Storage*, vol. 8, no. 82 (Jan. 1905), p. 11.

55. PRO, BT31. Index volumes.

56. *Cold Storage and Produce Review*, vol. 13, no. 152 (November 1910), p. 309.

57. W. Keilhau, *Norway in the World War* (New Haven, 1930), p. 401.

58. *Cold Storage and Produce Review*, vol. 20, no. 266 (January 1917), p. 2.

CHAPTER THIRTEEN

THE SCOTTISH COUNTRY HOUSE KITCHEN

Una A. Robertson

For centuries, Scotland was regarded as a wild and savage land and a procession of travellers came to see this 'terra incognita' for themselves and, once safely home again, to publish an account of their travels.

Many recorded facts about the inhabitants' diet. From Froissart in the fourteenth century, who described how the people made oatcakes on a flat iron plate, to the parish ministers who provided information for the First Statistical Account of the 1790s there was a certain consensus of opinion: that some folk ate very well indeed, but the common people were restricted to preparations of milk, oatmeal, kale and a few roots.[1] One of the best-recorded excursions must be that of Johnson and Boswell in 1773 and, as the pair headed northwards along the east coast before making their way towards the Western Isles, their journals frequently reveal comments on hospitality received and foods eaten. Even then, Dr Johnson felt that Scotland had already changed out of all recognition on account of the punitive measures imposed on the Highlands after the 1745 Jacobite Rebellion.[2] Unfortunately, rather fewer visitors thought to penetrate into the kitchen premises or took note of the plenishings there and evidence on these matters must be looked for elsewhere.

Scotland has never lacked for 'country houses',[3] although this study is predominantly concerned with those in the Lowlands. In many instances documentation survives and, where it is of a domestic nature, a vivid picture emerges of life 'below-stairs'; even more is this the case when this is set against external material from published cookbooks and travellers' recollections.

Scottish country houses could certainly match anything offered by their English equivalent in the way of domestic offices and the staff to carry out the work. Architectural plans are often available, even though the premises themselves have been demolished or converted to other uses. The sheer extent of space dedicated to

Early twentieth-century kitchen court from the west of Scotland, showing storage for meat carcasses, root crops and so on; the free-standing pillar in deep shade to the right houses the tiled fish safe and, below it, the meat safe.

domestic processes surprises us today when, in houses open to view, 'The Kitchen' is set up to depict a multiplicity of uses. Previously, the kitchen was merely a cog, albeit an important cog, around which revolved the full panoply of scullery, pantry, larders for different categories of goods, along with bakehouse, brewhouse and cellars for the storage of beers, wines and spirits. Not far away would be housekeeper's room and stillroom, and the housekeeper also had charge over the dairy and its products. Elsewhere would be stores for roots, potatoes and other garden produce, while further afield would be that necessary adjunct, an ice-house.

The Scottish kitchen resembled its English counterpart in many particulars, such as in the fireplaces, bread ovens and, latterly, the ranges, the pots and pans, the gadgets and utensils. Evidence on these matters is plentiful as many inventories made over the years contain detailed descriptions of the domestic offices, right down to the smallest and oldest piece of kitchen paraphernalia. One such kitchen

Octagonal Dairy, c. 1838, Hopetoun House, S. Queensferry.

was actually in advance of the rest, being equipped with the prototype of the spit mechanism subsequently installed in the Brighton Pavilion.[4]

Such items, along with printed references in cookbooks and so on, suggest that the kitchens were as well-stocked as any. So much was this the case that one author could remark: 'We have so often been taken in with wonderful newly-invented frying-pans and infallible gridirons, that we do not venture to recommend any form. We have collected half a garretful of those and other culinary inventions, and on trial found nearly the whole useless, or no improvement on the old-fashioned utensils.'[5]

Nor was the Scottish kitchen deficient as regards staff. The full complement of cooks, kitchen- and scullery-maids and housekeepers can be found, along with someone to do the baking or the slaughtering and the occasional 'kitchen-man'. It is often difficult to follow the rapid turnover of such staff, although other households kept their cooks for many years.[6]

At this stage, therefore, it would appear that the scenario in the Scottish country house kitchen was, by and large, similar to its counterpart in England in point of provision of domestic offices, working practices and servants employed therein. As to the meals we have the evidence of Dr Johnson, that severest of critics, who remarked: 'A dinner in the Western Isles differs very little from a dinner in England, except that in the place of tarts there are always set different preparations of milk.'[7] Here, presumably, the local fuel was peat which gives a slow, gentle heat, eminently suited to producing milk-based dishes but not so suitable for pastry or items that need a quick heat; the cooking pots, too, might well have reflected the use of such low-heat fuel.

However, on closer scrutiny some significant differences can be found as, for example, in the cookbooks used in the kitchens. From the 1750s onwards, a dozen or so of such books were published in Scotland, all claiming to be adapted to local needs and local ingredients: 'I have calculated the following treatise for the northern climate,' said Hannah Robertson in 1767, and Mrs Dalgairns said of her recipes and book: 'their economical adaptation to the habits and tastes of the majority of its readers.'[8]

The most famous is surely *The Cook and Housewife's Manual*, of 1826 by 'Meg Dods', alias Mrs Christian Isobel Johnstone, wife of Sir Walter Scott's publisher and a well-known author and editor herself. Many people detect the hand of Sir Walter in its pages and quote lengthy passages to support the supposition, but it should be remembered that 1826 was not the happiest of times for Sir Walter to be writing anonymous and light-hearted passages for a cookery book.[9]

THE

COOK AND HOUSEWIFE'S MANUAL;

CONTAINING THE

MOST APPROVED MODERN RECEIPTS

FOR MAKING

SOUPS, GRAVIES, SAUCES, RAGOUTS, AND ALL MADE-DISHES;

AND FOR

PIES, PUDDINGS, PICKLES, AND PRESERVES:

ALSO, FOR

BAKING, BREWING, MAKING HOME-MADE WINES, CORDIALS, &c.

THE WHOLE ILLUSTRATED BY NUMEROUS NOTES, AND PRACTICAL OBSERVATIONS ON THE VARIOUS BRANCHES OF DOMESTIC ECONOMY.

THE THIRD EDITION;

IN WHICH ARE GIVEN,

A COMPENDIUM OF FRENCH COOKERY,

A NEW SYSTEM OF FASHIONABLE CONFECTIONARY,

A SELECTION OF CHEAP DISHES,

AND ABOVE

200 ADDITIONAL RECEIPTS.

BY MRS MARGARET DODS,

OF THE CLEIKUM INN, ST RONAN'S.

EDINBURGH;

PRINTED FOR

OLIVER AND BOYD, AND BELL AND BRADFUTE; GEO. B. WHITTAKER, LONDON; ROBERTSON AND ATKINSON, GLASGOW; AND WILLIAM CURRY, JUN. AND CO. DUBLIN.

1828.

Title-page of Mrs Margaret Dods' ('Meg Dods')
The Cook and Housewife's Manual,
Edinburgh, 1828.

The popularity of Meg Dods has overshadowed not only her near-contemporary Mrs Dalgairns but also their predecessors. The earliest known Scottish book devoted to cookery is generally agreed to be Mrs McLintock's, printed in Glasgow in 1736. However, some fifty years earlier *The Scot's Gard'ner* included advice on using the products of the garden and added monthly lists as to availability, which must give the author, John Reid, something of a head start over Mrs McLintock.[10]

Before Scotland was publishing its own, which cookbooks were in use? Curiously enough, before the Union of 1707 the answer would seem to be either popular English authors or French works in translation. Foulis of Ravelston paid 'for markames works' in 1680 and 'for ye lady kents manuall of phisick and cookerie' in 1689;[11] a manuscript inventory of the same period listed the books kept 'In my Lord's Study' which included *May's Cookery* and *Digby's Cookery*;[12] while Lady Grisell Baillie, on setting up house in London in 1715, bought no less than three cookbooks: 'For the *Court and Country Cook* 5*s*; For *Howards Cookery* 2*s*' and, the following day, 'For a book of choise recepts 2*s* 6*d*', from which it could be argued that she felt unfamiliar with English customs. She certainly recorded in detail many dinners she ate in other houses and the way the dishes were arranged on the table.[13]

Did the recipes (or receipts) given in the Scottish cookbooks refer only to foods of a totally local nature? The recipes and suggested bills-of-fare indicate a wide range of food. Local ingredients such as kail, salmon, barley and mutton are also in evidence, as are some dishes thought to be particularly 'Scottish' as, for example, those encountered by Edward Topham in the 1770s.[14] He described a dinner which had left him 'almost famished with hunger, and tantalized to death by the enjoyment of other people; because my friend must needs entertain with dishes in the highest taste; and, what was worse, entirely in the Scottish taste . . .'. The party were served with 'Hagis . . . Cocky-leaky . . . Sheep's head . . . and Solan Goose [gannet]' and Topham gives a graphic description of his reactions to each one. However, some Scottish dishes won his praises, such as Barley-broth (of which Dr Johnson, also, was highly appreciative);[15] Cabbieclow; and Friars chicken: 'I know not what Holy Order, may have had the reputation of discovering this last dish; but, from the luxuriousness of it, it seems admirably adapted for the provision of a convent.'

From his tone, it might be supposed that the selection of dishes at the dinner party was unrepresentative of everyday foods. Certainly by 1826 Meg Dods considered it necessary to produce an especially 'Scottish' bill-of-fare for St Andrew's night or Burns' clubs in which the pedigree of the dishes was impeccable.

Many of the recorded bills-of-fare include numerous dishes of vegetables and some of fruit, even though it is often said that such things were not much eaten. The evidence for Scotland is confusing, with some visitors being somewhat cynical about what they found while others were greatly impressed.[16] The primary evidence suggests that for certain people and in certain places there was no shortage of such items throughout the year, nor of ways in which to dress them. While poorer folk might depend on leeks, kail or a handful of nettles as flavourings to their

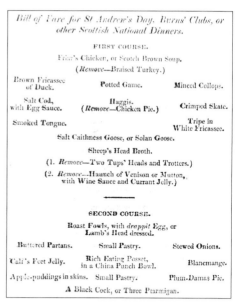

Bill of Fare for St Andrew's Day, Burns' Clubs, or other Scottish National Dinners.

FIRST COURSE.

Friar's Chicken, or Scotch Brown Soup.
(*Remove*—Braised Turkey.)

Brown Fricassee of Duck.	Potted Game.	Minced Collops.
Salt Cod, with Egg Sauce.	Haggis. (*Remove*—Chicken Pie.)	Crimped Skate.
Smoked Tongue.		Tripe in White Fricassee.

Salt Caithness Goose, or Solan Goose.

Sheep's Head Broth.

(1. *Remove*—Two Tups' Heads and Trotters.)

(2. *Remove*—Haunch of Venison or Mutton, with Wine Sauce and Currant Jelly.)

SECOND COURSE.

Roast Fowls, with *drappit* Egg, or Lamb's Head dressed.

Buttered Partans.	Small Pastry.	Stewed Onions.
Calf's Feet Jelly.	Rich Eating Posset, in a China Punch Bowl.	Blancmange.
Apple-puddings in skins.	Small Pastry.	Plum-Damas Pie.

A Black Cock, or Three Ptarmigan.

'Scottish' bill-of-fare from the 1842 edition of Meg Dods' The Cook and Housewife's Manual.

broth or porridge, accounts reveal that the head-gardeners of the country houses were ordering seeds of an impressive assortment of vegetables and buying in fruit stocks of every description.[17] Later in the eighteenth century there were those who said that Scotland had witnessed a great improvement in supplies in recent years,[18] although that possibly reflected greater availability to a greater number of people: the potential for supplying the country house kitchen had existed for many a long year. Garden books corroborate the picture, as do cookery books which give numerous recipes both for table use and preserving.

Just as it is often said that vegetables were not often eaten, so the Scottish country house varies from the norm in another respect. It is a much-quoted maxim that salt beef was the mainstay of the diet throughout the winter months, with the only fresh meat coming from the estate's doocot. This is wrong on both counts.[19]

Ownership of doocots was at one time limited to those estates producing a certain amount in rental,[20] the reasoning being that pigeons would then have no need to fly beyond the estate boundaries. A study of various eighteenth-century Diet Books revealed that, during the winter months, 'the Family' and their guests at the First Table dined off a wide variety of foodstuffs including freshly-killed

A simple doocot, an unusual Scottish example converted to use as a garden shed.

meat, game and poultry, while salt beef was noticeably absent. They did indeed eat pigeons, but not until the spring and early summer and then they ate them again in the autumn. This evidence is augmented by cookbooks which often specify 'squabs' for the recipes[21] as well as by agricultural manuals which confirm that two requirements are needed before pigeons can rear young: sufficient warmth and plentiful food.[22] Scottish owners might supply the one but the other was outside their control.

At the other end of the domestic hierarchy, the same Diet Books show that only when there was a serious glut of pigeon were they served to those at the Fourth Table; in contrast, these domestic servants were frequently eating salt beef during the winter months. To sum up briefly: those who ate pigeons rarely ate salt beef, while it was the exception for those eating salt beef to taste pigeon.

Pigeons may or may not have been introduced by the Normans but there is no doubt that 'the Auld Alliance' is still a matter for pride. This stems from the days when Scotland and France made common cause against a common enemy, England. The links forged then are reflected in numerous aspects of Scottish life, but the reverberations are particularly strong when it comes to the language of the kitchen. Four words in everyday use are 'ashet', 'petticoat tails', 'gigot' and 'the messages'; there is also the method of slow stewing, producing a dish known as 'stovies', and many other words are evident.[23] Examples are found in the Scottish cookbooks, as are dishes with French names or cooked 'in the French style'; while Meg Dods included a whole section devoted to French cookery and discussed its place in the national cuisine. 'The French', she said, 'are allowed to excel in soups and entrées, and in the refined preparation of their sauces. They have also more and better ways of dressing vegetables than are known to us.'[24]

ENGLAND.

Hind Quarter.	Fore Quarter.
1 Leg	5 Neck, scrag end
2 Loin, best end	6 Shoulder
3 Loin, champ end	7 Breast
4 Neck, best end	

SCOTLAND.

1, 2, 3 The Gigot	The two Loins joined together
4 The Loin	are called a Chine, or Saddle
5 & 6 The Fore Quarter	of Mutton.

Lamb.

In the fore quarter of lamb the vein of the neck generally indicates its state; if it appears of an azure blue it is fresh, but if greenish, or yellow, it is stale.

English and Scottish cuts of mutton and the names used. (From John Caird, The Complete Confectioner and Family Cook, *Edinburgh, 1809)*

Are there traces of French methods in food preparation? According to Meg Dods the very essence of French cooking lay in their many sauces and 'made dishes'; a gentle stewing over low heat was often the preferred method, in marked contrast to the great roasting fires of the English kitchen which caused so much comment. A contemporary of hers observed: 'The old English cookery was only roast & boil; blood and butter were the savage accompaniments of their cookery. Ours in Scotland was much improved by the constant communication and alliance with France. From France we got several excellent soups.'[25]

Not only the dishes upon the table but the entire meal was done as in France, according to one observer, and he was pleased to see napkins on the tables and noted that the Scots held their knives in a way that was familiar to him, whereas the English held them differently.[26]

Whatever form the meal might have taken, in the best houses it was followed by a course of sweetmeats and wine. At a time when England was talking of 'the banquet', was building 'banqueting houses' and making up 'banqueting stuffs', Scotland was taking 'dessert'. As early as 1594 one household had 'fine lame pottis for dessertis' and 'lyttil new plaitis for disertis'.[27] Accounts reveal many purchases of 'confections'; alternatively, a confectioner might be employed for a special occasion and might teach the ladies how to make these things. The Duke of Hamilton thought such an expense was justifiable, although Sir John Cochrane must have found the cost distressingly high when his 'House of Ochiltry was brunt by the negligence of on(e) that was making confections to his Lady in it'.[28]

No meal would have been complete without some form of drink to accompany it and, over the years, visitors often commented on the quality of the French wines they met with. In 1598 Fynes Morison had observed: 'They drinke pure Wines, not with sugar as the English, yet at Feasts they put Comfits in the Wine after the French manner, but they had not our Vintners fraud to mixe their Wines . . . the better sort of citizens brew ale, their usuall drinke.'[29] In the eighteenth century there was downright envy of the continued availability of French clarets and brandies, whereas the English had switched to drinking port on account of the punitive taxes levied on the French products. The Scots Parliament, shortly before the Act of Union, had taken steps to ensure continuing supplies of their customary wines. Not until the end of the century was there cause to change that policy.

It is no part of this brief survey to investigate whether such influences were the direct result of 'the Auld Alliance' or came about by a more generalized infiltration. However, it should be borne in mind that, at the time when such influences might well have been supposed to have been at their strongest, the Reformation was having a marked impact on the relationship between the two countries and on the character of the Scots themselves,[30] which would hardly be conducive to encouraging anything remotely French about the local cookery; while the general population, by all accounts, were existing on a limited range of foodstuffs. On the other hand, this line of argument is immaterial because, as Barbara Wheaten's comprehensive study shows, it was well into the seventeenth century before anything approaching a 'national cuisine' developed in France.[31] A later date for French influences in the kitchen would seem more likely, which would be in line with developments elsewhere.

Meg Dods pinpointed the culinary traditions of her day and described the 'Auld Alliance' as a living force. The book was published in 1826, and a persistent rumour links it to Sir Walter Scott, in which case its timing is even more significant. In 1822 he masterminded the visit of George IV, the first monarch to travel to Scotland for a hundred and fifty years. The country was acquiring a new image; the Jacobite Rebellions were in the past; and memories of pre-Union Scotland were fading. Interest was gathering momentum, assisted no doubt by the King's visit and Sir Walter's literary skills. If he did contribute to that cookbook then the emphasis placed on 'The Auld Alliance' and its all-pervading influence could have been his handiwork.

Regardless of the way in which they may have come about, the Scots are proud that they have these French elements in their history and that their lifestyle is based on a different culture to that of their southern neighbours. It would seem appropriate, therefore, to conclude this brief survey of the Scottish country house kitchen with an extract from the journal of a Frenchman, Faujas Saint-Fond, who arrived at Inveraray Castle in 1784, even before the rebuilding had been completed. He waxed lyrical at what he found:[32] 'At the Duke of Argyle's table . . . the different courses, and the after-meats, were all done as in France, and with the same variety and abundance . . . by most delicate water fowl, by delicious fish, and by vegetables the quality of which did honour to the skill of the Scottish gardeners.

'At the desert, the scene changed; cloth, napkins, and everything disappeared. The mahogany table . . . was covered with brilliant decanters filled with the most exquisite wines; comfits in fine porcelain, or crystal, vases; and fruits of different kinds in baskets.'

After such high praise there was one element, he had to admit, in which the Scots failed to follow their French mentors and Faujas Saint-Fond ended his eulogy on a slightly different note: 'We proceeded to the drawing room, where tea and coffee abound . . . the tea is always excellent; but . . . their coffee is always weak, bitter, and completely deprived of its aromatic odour.'

NOTES

1. E. (and J.) Chamberlayne, *Magna Britanniae Notia* (London, 1708), p. 523.

2. Dr S. Johnson, *Journey to the Western Islands of Scotland* (Edinburgh, 1798), p. 95: 'We came hither too late to see what we expected, a people of peculiar appearance, and a system of antiquated life. . . . Of what they had before the late conquest of their country, there remain only their language and their poverty.'

3. No real need here to differentiate between a 'country house' in the sense of the house which is

at the centre of an estate, and a 'house in the country' which might or might not have land attached to it but which, by definition, required a certain level of self-sufficiency.

4.   Callendar House, Falkirk, where the restored working kitchen opened to the public in April 1993.

5.   Meg Dods, *Cook and Housewife's Manual* (9th edn, Edinburgh, 1849), pp. 130–1.

6.   See, for example, *The Household Book of Lady Grisell Baillie, 1692–1733*, ed. R. Scott-Moncrieff, Scottish History Society (Edinburgh, 1911), pp. li–lii.

7.   Dr Johnson, *Journey*, p. 93.

8.   H. Robertson, *The Young Ladies School of Arts* (Edinburgh, 1767), Part II, p. xix; Mrs Dalgairns, *The Practice of Cookery* (Edinburgh, 1829), p. vii.

9.   Sir Walter Scott, 1771–1832; his enormous literary output led to ill-health from 1817 onwards and, in 1825, there were also the financial problems to contend with.

10.   Mrs McLintock's 'Receipts for Cookery and Pastrywork', Glasgow, 1736; J. Reid, *The Scot's Gard'ner* (Edinburgh, 1683).

11.   *Account Book of Sir John Foulis of Ravelston 1671–1707*, ed. A.W.C. Hallen, Scottish History Society (Edinburgh, 1894), pp. 21 and 115.

12.   Ms. inventory.

13.   Baillie, Accounts, p. 37.

14.   Edward Topham, *Letters from Edinburgh 1774–1775* (London, 1776), pp. 154–62.

15.   James Boswell, *Journal of a Tour to the Hebrides* (London, 1785), p. 88: 'At dinner Dr Johnson ate several plate-fulls of Scotch broth, with barley and peas in it, and seemed very fond of the dish.' When asked if he had not eaten it before Johnson replied: 'No, sir; but I don't care how soon I eat it again.'

16.   In 1498 the Spanish Ambassador could say, as quoted in Hume Brown (ed.), *Early Travellers in Scotland* (1891), p. 44: 'They have so many wild fruits which they eat, that they do not know what to do with them. . . . There are all kinds of garden fruits to be found which a cold country can produce. They are very good. Oranges, figs, and other fruits of the same kind are not to be found there.' On the other hand Sydney Smith said, as quoted in F.M. McNeill, *The Scot's Kitchen* (London and Glasgow, 1929), p. 13: 'They would have you believe they can ripen fruit, and, to be candid, I must own in remarkably warm summers I have tasted peaches that made excellent pickles.'

17.   Reid, *Scot's Gard'ner*, is corroborated by many Ms. sources such as garden accounts and diet books. See also E.H.M. Cox, *History of Gardening in Scotland* (London, 1935).

18.   R. Southey, *Journal of a Tour in Scotland 1819* (London, 1929), p. 76.

19.   Una A. Robertson, 'Pigeons as a Source of Food in Eighteenth Century Scotland', in *Review of Scottish Culture*, 4 (1988), pp. 89–103.

20.   In 1617 James VI restricted pigeon houses in both town and country to owners with adjacent

lands or teinds giving an annual rental of 10 chalder of victuals (1 chalder being 16 boll of 1¼ cwt. each) or lying within two miles of it.

21.   Squab pigeons are generally taken to be nestlings still being fed by the parent birds.

22.   C. Heresbach, *The Whole Art and Trade of Husbandry*, enlarged by Barnaby Googe, Esq. (London, 1634), p. 160; see also William Ellis, *Agriculture Improved* (London, 1745–6), p. 138; J.H. Walsh, *Manual of Domestic Economy* (London, 1859), p. 256.

23.   An 'ashet' is a serving dish; 'petticoat tails' are triangular-shaped shortbread biscuits; 'gigot' is a leg of mutton (or lamb); 'to go the messages' means to do the domestic shopping. See McNeil, *Scot's Kitchen*, pp. 241–6 for other examples.

24.   Dods, *Manual*, p. 373.

25.   H. Mackenzie, *Anecdotes and Egotisms* (Oxford, 1927), p. 59: i.e. Hodge Podge, Friars Chicken, Lamb's Stove, Hare Soup, Cocky Leekie, and a soup maigre called Pan Kail.

26.   B. Faujas Saint-Fond, *Travels in England, Scotland and the Hebrides* (London, 1799), vol. 1, pp. 252–3.

27.   John Warrack, *Domestic Life in Scotland 1488–1688* (London, 1920), p. 116: at formal or public events this course was sometimes called 'a banquet'.

28.   Sir John Lauder, Lord Fountainhall, *Historical Observes of Memorable Occurances in Church and State from October 1680 to April 1688* (Edinburgh, 1840), p. 121. Cookery schools in Edinburgh also taught confectionery.

29.   Fynes Morison, 'Itinerary 1598', in Hume Brown (ed.), *Early Travellers*, p. 89.

30.   Such influences would presumably be greatest when the links were strongest, such as during the time of Mary Queen of Scots or while her mother acted as Regent, 1542–60. The Reformation and its effects: just one example from John Nicholl, 'Diary', *Old Edinburgh Club*, 16 (1928), p. 38, 'it wes proclamed by beat of drum that that day, commounlie callit Crystmas day, sould not be observed . . .'.

31.   B.K. Wheaten, *Savouring the Past* (London, 1983).

32.   Faujas Saint-Fond, *Travels*, vol. 1, pp. 254–7.

CHAPTER FOURTEEN

HOUSEHOLD BEER AND BREWING

Pamela Sambrook

INTRODUCTION

Private country house brewhouses have long been neglected, both in reality and in the interest shown them. But they and their associated traditions of household ale and beer allowances are now beginning to be documented. The process of brewing and the buildings themselves have been described from Hickleton in Yorkshire, Calke Abbey in Derbyshire, and Chastleton in Oxfordshire.[1] A recent publication by the present author presents a detailed discussion of the brewing equipment found in country house brewhouses, the types of beer made and many of the issues involved in the beer allowance system, as it applied to country house domestic and farm servants.[2] These studies complement the wider context of brewing history, which deals mainly with the role of domestic brewing in the medieval household and early modern and modern commercial production and consumption.[3]

The background to this paper is provided by the restoration to working order of an existing brewhouse at the Ansons' country house at Shugborough, Staffordshire. During that programme a search was made through the family papers to find information about types and quantities of beer made, as well as methods of production and distribution.[4] The data available in the Anson manuscripts proved to be fragmentary; and both these and the restoration work itself threw up many questions about the wider context of country house brewing; it became increasingly obvious that a major long-term quest had started.

The main purpose of this paper is firstly to indicate some of the practical problems which the reconstruction of a working domestic interior can present; and secondly to introduce the historical context of the subject by summarizing the sort of issues which emerged from the research on Shugborough.

Basic to the understanding of the story of family beer, whether represented by documentation or brickwork, is an appreciation of the different malt liquors made.

The wealthy beer-drinking household required a minimum of three strengths: one fairly weak drink for everyday thirst-quenching; one medium strength for everyday mealtime drinking; and one strong drink for special occasions. In order to make these, the classic English method of brewing used a single charge of malt for two or three separate mashes, just as today it is usual to top up the teapot with a second lot of hot water. Often the wort (sugar solution) from the first mash was mixed with the second – this made the medium drink which was called 'ale' – but the weaker wort from the third mash was kept separate and variably called 'beer', 'table beer' or 'small beer'.[5] It was possible, of course, to change these combinations to suit the household: the first wort on its own would make a smaller amount of 'strong ale' and the second and third worts mixed would make an intermediate drink sometimes called 'strong beer'. To make a really strong ale for special occasions, the first-drawn worts could be passed through a second charge of fresh malt. Since one mash was usually made from one copperful of water, whatever the combination there were three copperfuls of scalding liquid to be moved around the brewhouse. These then are the very specific definitions which this paper attributes to the words 'ale' and 'beer'.

RESTORING A BREWHOUSE

The Ansons' brewhouse came into the hands of the National Trust in the 1960s, along with the rest of the site at Shugborough. Since then it has been administered by the Staffordshire County Council and in the late 1960s the brewhouse was opened to the public along with other domestic offices, but in a rather unsatisfactory way. The heart of the brewing process, the copper and its furnace, had been taken out long ago and without this it was a difficult room to understand or interpret to the public. In addition, the great oak mash tun, which had survived, had been hoisted high up on to a reconstructed timber staging, alongside a new and visually overpowering staircase, installed to give a one-way public access route through the building. The fermenting tun, the large timber cooling trays, the hoist and part of the older staging were left in their original sites. No records were kept of the work done in the '60s and the mash tun, hanging high over the rest of the brewhouse, was always a puzzle. The puzzle was resolved when the joiner who carried out the work in the '60s explained that no one had any real idea whether it should be like that, they just thought it looked good.

The brewhouse at Shugborough, Staffordshire, part of a range of domestic buildings built in the eighteenth century for the Anson family.

During the 1980s progress was made in restoring the Shugborough kitchen and laundry into something like working order. Attention was given to the repair of flues, so that it was possible to wash and iron in the laundry and cook in the kitchen. When it became obvious that the internal brickwork of the brewhouse badly needed re-pointing, it seemed a suitable time to do something about making the whole process of brewing more intelligible, in line with the rest of the site.

The Principle of Restoration

This, then, was the background to a number of decisions which had to be made. Most important of these was the fundamental issue of the extent to which the brewhouse was to be restored rather than simply conserved as it stood. Here the deciding factor was the incompleteness of the surviving equipment; lacking a copper, the brewhouse was without its most important feature. It was therefore a relatively easy decision to replace the copper and its furnace; since these had to be new it seemed reasonable to make them operable. On the other hand, the original mash tun, fermenting vessel and coolers were intact; these needed conservation rather than restoration. It was obvious that the original equipment was too precious an historical record to use for demonstration brews, so our aims gradually emerged: firstly to conserve all the original features; and secondly to replace the staircase and new staging by a small-scale copper, furnace, mash tun and fermenting vessel which could be used to produce beer and thus explain the process of brewing.

There was, of course, a third alternative – restoration of the brewhouse to what was thought to be its original state. This would entail replacing two coppers and their furnaces (see below), but since the original coopered oak vessels would still be in place, the system could not have actually been used to produce beer or even run water through. This was a very expensive option which would produce a wholly static display. Moreover, there already exists at Charlecote a more complete and original domestic brewhouse. For these reasons this option was not seriously considered.

The theoretical balance between conservation and restoration to working order is often difficult to achieve. In practice, the individual characteristics of each case often make the decisions easy. It would clearly be indefensible, for example, to consider making a brewhouse as complete as Charlecote or Lacock produce beer. In the case of the Shugborough brewhouse, the fact that the equipment was substantially deficient combined with the administrative context of the site; other

*The Shugborough brewhouse retains part of its original staging, with the tuns and coolers. A new copper and
mash tun are capable of producing beer.*

domestic interiors were partially 'working', so it was desirable to have at least some element of workability built into the restored brewhouse. This was especially the case as the process of brewing, though basically very simple, is difficult for a non-practitioner to understand. In the final analysis, moreover, the impetus given by the project towards the re-awakening of interest in the historical background of household beer and brewhouses can be judged to have been useful.

Research

Specifications for the new equipment and its fitting had to be worked out and a long process of investigation started. Wherever possible, decisions on how to restore were taken in the light of properly conducted research. Reference was made to contemporary printed manuals and inspections of the fabric of the brewhouse were carried out, looking for both problems and evidence of its former use. Visits to

The fire-box and ash-pit in the restored brewhouse at Shugborough. The ironwork came from the brewhouse on the Hickleton estate in Yorkshire, which was dismantled while the Shugborough project was taking place.

other surviving brewhouses took place, brewers were approached, and contact finally made with Lord Halifax's estate at Hickleton, near Doncaster.[6] The brewers at Hickleton, Ken Lindley and Dave Pickering, were then still working the old coal-fired copper and without doubt it was their practical expertise, and that of their consultant brewer from a nearby commercial brewery, which enabled the Shugborough project to get going.

At the same time, a search was made through the Anson manuscript collection to try to establish information about dates, processes and production. This last was only partially successful, as the brewing record was so fragmentary. It even proved difficult to date the brewhouse with any exactitude. A substantial rebuilding of the existing house and domestic offices was begun in 1694 by William Anson. He employed a team of bricklayers and labourers who were paid a daily rate plus beer money, which presumably indicates that the estate was then without a brewhouse. By 1708, however, William was definitely brewing, for he kept accounts of malt used and beer produced, but it is impossible to be sure whether this was in the present building.[7] If it was, it has certainly been refitted since that date, possibly around the same time as alterations were made to the kitchen in the 1790s.[8]

Practical Considerations

Of course there were many practical implications which followed from the decision to restore a working system. One disadvantage was that the original mash tun, though consolidated and treated for infestation, had to be moved from its correct site in order to make room for the new smaller system. Fortunately the brewhouse is fairly spacious and it was possible to move it over to one end, nearer to the coolers; but the fact remains that the original mashing vessel is not in its original site.

A second and very major problem had little to do with the brewhouse itself but had to be resolved before work could start – a lesson that it is often peripheral difficulties which eventually consume most time and money. A new staircase had to be built elsewhere in the building to replace the public access stair in the brewhouse. The new route required several new fire doors and proved more expensive than the whole of the rest of the entire project. To compound the problem, the main electrical substation to the whole site had been tucked under the old staircase; moving this was prohibitively expensive, yet this gradually revealed itself to be the site of one of the coppers and its furnace: demolition of the staircase revealed soot-blackening and an area of brickwork where the central chimney breast had been cut away to accommodate a flue coming into it from the side. Eventually a compromise site was agreed which involved moving the new copper and furnace by just over two feet out from the wall, enabling the substation to remain. The furnace was built on a raft of reinforced concrete and ducting was provided to allow future alterations or repairs to the cabling.

The most complex phase of the restoration work involved brickwork of various types. Some of the original brickwork was so crumbly it had to be replaced, especially over the old copper site; the rest was re-pointed. The main chimney and its flues were repaired, new soot doors provided and the whole tied into the wall behind, making it safer than ever before. The chimney had been capped off and roofed over in the 1960s, so a replacement stack had to be built. A new inclined flue from the copper to the chimney was built over a new segmental arch and a removable slab built into it to enable cleaning.

Building the furnace support was the most difficult part of the work. An eighteenth-century open brewing copper was 'set' or 'hung' from its lip within a brick or stone tower and supported at its bottom by short internal brick piers; there was thus a void around the base of the copper which allowed a circular 'wheeldraught' to form. The bottom of the void was provided by the fire-box which was usually fitted at something like shoulder height above a large open ash pit. The fire-box itself was fitted with a cast-iron door. At appropriate times, as the copper was emptied, the fire needed to be slackened very quickly to avoid burning the copper bottom; this was done by raking out the fire into the ash-pit. The height of the copper base and thus the fire-door was dictated by the positioning of the mash tun and its draining vessel, the underbuck. In the end, the furnace at Shugborough was designed using Hickleton as a model; before work was completed the Hickleton coal-fired copper was abandoned in favour of a gas-fired copper on a new site and the old brewhouse was gutted, so the original fire-bars and fire-box door were fitted at Shugborough.

A brand new copper and its piping were commissioned from a brewing coppersmith in Burton. A stainless steel mash tun which doubled as a fermenting tun was fitted, covered on the outside with timber cladding; a movable false bottom doubling as a hop sieve, a small milk cooler, an electric pump and a wooden malt hopper were also installed.

The health and safety aspects of the project were difficult but not insuperable. The brewing process required prolonged boiling of the ingredients, producing an inherently sterile product. There were three main problems: falling dust from the internal brickwork; drainage in case of loss of the brew or spillage; and the nature of the working utensils.

The first of these problems was eventually resolved by sealing with a modern matt-finish bonding solution, which proved effective and virtually undetectable. The drainage problem, too, was resolved fairly easily, by making a new connection to an existing foul drainage system. The utensils were a different problem. The rakes, stirrers and shovels would originally have been wooden, but this was totally

Engraving of a small eighteenth-century brewhouse. Although a commercial establishment, this level of equipment was also typical of a gentleman's brewhouse. The water was heated almost to boiling point in the copper which occupies the top half of the brick tower or underworks (A), with fire-box beneath (C); the water was then mixed with malt in the mash tun (D) where three men are shown stirring the mash with oars; a tap from the mash tun allowed the mashed wort to run down into the underback (F); from here the wort was pumped back to the copper for boiling with hops; the worts were then run into shallow wooden cooling trays (H), before being filled into the casks. From Universal Magazine, *January 1747–8. (By courtesy of North of England Open Air Museum, Beamish)*

unacceptable. Copies were made, to original designs, in white nylon plastic – unpleasant to look at but unavoidable. The real problem came when the first trial brew took place; Ken Lindley plunged his stirrer in to the mash only to find that the heat made it far too flexible. Fortunately the handle had been made hollow and we were able to push a wooden broom stale down it as reinforcement – a practical but hardly ideal solution.

The brewing world was astonishingly supportive – brewers helped with the design and provision of equipment and officers from the Inland Revenue were patient in their explanations of the intricacies of gauging the vessels and estimating beer duty. With the help of Ken Lindley and his assistant a trial brew was carried out, ready for the opening party. Our samplers agreed on their verdict – highly successful, but a little on the strong side. Since then several successful brews have been made though brewing is no longer carried out regularly. But the brewhouse now has a story to tell and its system is ready and waiting.

The Shugborough brewhouse project took several years from conception to the first brew. Most of the work on site was carried out by Shugborough's own technicians and especially the bricklayer, Pat Pilgrim. The restoration project was headed by the then Assistant Curator, Adrienne Whitehouse.

HOUSEHOLD BEER: A SUMMARY OF ISSUES

Buildings and Fittings

Although intact externally, internally the brewhouse at Shugborough was incomplete: the original copper and its fire-box, ash pit and supporting tower had been removed, probably early in the twentieth century. This was important for the copper was the main fixed feature, used for the two stages of boiling – the initial heating of the liquor prior to mashing and the later stage of boiling the worts with hops. Evidence of soot-blackening indicated the position of one copper at Shugborough, but the situation was complicated when an inventory dated 1841 was found. This showed clearly that the brewhouse had been fitted with not one copper but two:

> Large hop bag, cleansing sieve, 2 wooden scrapers, copper pump, 2 mash rules, large mash tub, 22 tubs of different sizes, 5 pails, 2 tun dishes, 2 lade

gawns, 2 benches, pair of small steps, 4 beer shoots, 4 casks of different sizes, 2 trucks, 2 beer coolers, copper 432 gallons, with lead and underwork, copper 200 gallons and underwork.[9]

This immediately raised the question as to whether this size and extent of fixed equipment was usual in eighteenth-century brewhouses. More questions followed. Was Shugborough in any sense representative of other brewhouses? Was there some sort of pattern to them, some sense to their development both over time and regionally? Could one work out a typology of plan?

Most surviving country house brewhouses were built during the eighteenth century, though the provision of fixed equipment for brewing within the domestic household goes back to a much earlier date. Most of the earlier premises had a single brewing copper, but in the eighteenth century many brewing households fitted two coppers, one for each stage of boiling.[10] Brewing was much easier to handle when there was more than one copper – the worts of the first mash could be boiling with the hops at the same time as the liquor for the later mashes was heating. Fitting two coppers into the brewhouse, however, made flue-construction much more difficult. The number of coppers and the ways in which the builder solved the problem of connection to the flue therefore emerge as the main criteria for sorting types of domestic brewhouses.[11]

The layout of the Shugborough coppers was almost certainly a fairly common one: each copper fitted into a corner either side of a flue which ran up the centre of an end wall and was fitted with an open fireplace at its base; the copper flues connected into the chimney at first floor level. This was a layout seen at several other surviving brewhouses including Stanway in Gloucestershire where both coppers have survived. As far as size was concerned, the Shugborough coppers were large; many private brewhouses had coppers holding between eighty-five and a hundred gallons; only the elaborate brewhouses on estates such as Chatsworth or Woburn had a boiling capacity on the scale shown by the Shugborough inventory.

Technology

How did private brewing technology, its associated equipment and skills compare to those of commercial producers? This question was particularly important when it came to restoring a brewhouse, since many of the contemporary manuals of brewing related to commercial breweries. On the other hand, as far as bricks and mortar are concerned, private brewhouses of this primitive type have survived while their commercial equivalents have not. It was important, therefore, to question contemporary sources about the relationship between the two sectors; in this way we could perhaps clarify our view of both the commercial brewhouse and the private.

The question of the level of private brewing technology might also help illuminate an important issue within the country house world: did the country house act as an innovator or as a break on technical change? Were they in the van or the rearguard of progress? Did ideas, concepts, new ways of doing things really trickle down the social order or seep upwards?

The individual case of Shugborough threw a little light on such problems. The scale of equipment pointed to a large scale of production. This conclusion was confirmed by a cellar stock-take which recorded a total of 9,950 gallons of ale and 1,908 gallons of beer stored in the cellars at Shugborough in 1824.[12] Other households show that this level was by no means unique; similar amounts have been recorded or calculated from Calke Abbey, Chillington in Staffordshire, and Chatsworth. So some larger private brewhouses were brewing on a scale which fell little short, if at all, of that of a commercial producer.

Contemporary eighteenth-century writers on brewing, however, either stated or implied that most private brewhouses operated on a level far more primitive than their commercial counterparts.[13] With respect for the smaller private producers this was probably true enough; they operated a simple, unchanging technology which paralleled that of commercial breweries, though on a smaller scale. Improvements in brewing techniques during the eighteenth century were achieved slowly and painfully, as a result of pressures in the commercial market. To judge from inventory evidence, some of the earlier improvements such as hand pumps and the equipment needed to bottom-mash seem to have been provided in most private brewhouses by the eighteenth century;[14] but few of the later improvements adopted by the commercial brewers trickled downwards into the private houses. By the nineteenth century, the gap between the private and the commercial brewer grew even wider with the emergence of a large-scale brewing industry. From the end of the eighteenth century the London porter-breweries led the field in the adoption of a new and mechanized technology; thus by the 1860s the commercial brewing world was fairly well mechanized. By contrast, the only innovation which suited the scale of production of even great households like Petworth seems to have been refrigerators – early versions using *gutta percha* coils and, later, metal refrigerators. Further, country house brewers persisted with the old English way of running three successive mashes, a method which exactly fitted the requirement of the householder for both strong and small beer. On the whole, therefore, private brewers – or their employers – were remarkably resistant to change. After all, the old ways valued their own hard-won experience.

It was not just a matter of scale; the whole philosophy behind the country house brewhouse was at odds with the commercial ethic. Time and labour were less important than quality and supply. Labour-saving equipment was irrelevant when only two or three men were employed intermittently and when the throughput was finite. So however elaborate the capital outlay (and this could be anything from £200 upwards), the need to experiment and to improve was not pressing. The conservatism which was thus innate in the country house system is what makes private brewhouses so important today.

Seasonality

Modern brewing tradition has it that the old brewers could not brew in the summer because they could not control the process of fermentation during the periods of high ambient temperatures. Was this really so and how did this fit in with our perception of beer as a staple drink?

Brewers' records from many country houses show that, because of the retention of a simple technology, seasonal weather patterns exerted a hold over the private brewer right up until the present day.[15] Ale brewing was generally concentrated into the autumn, winter and spring months, using larger and less frequent brews than for beer brewing. This concentration was not, however, rigid or exclusive; it seems that before the eighteenth century most households brewed ale also in the summer, either regularly or intermittently. Moreover, small beer was brewed all the year round, often showing a peak of production in the summer, with a concentration of small, frequent brews. When necessary small beer could be brewed on its own, not after ale, as was the usual case at other times of the year. This was essential, for though the stronger ale would keep up to a year, small beer would keep only a few days in summer and a few weeks in winter.

It can be argued, indeed, that the influence of climate increased over time rather than decreased. Seasonality seems to have increased between the seventeenth and the nineteenth centuries – later records often show what amounts to a retreat into those periods of the year which offered optimum conditions. Twentieth-century Hickleton shows this pattern, for summer brews were only attempted on special occasions, such as twenty-first birthdays. In earlier centuries, of course, there were fewer alternatives and hence a greater pressure to provide a continuous supply; it seems probable that cloudy beer, suffering from secondary fermentation, was widely accepted in weaker beers. The retreat into spring and autumn brewing must reflect a reduced demand for the staple small beer, since this was the product brewed most in summer; it therefore illustrates an important change in the position of ale and beer within the household, away from their role as staple thirst-quenchers. The degree of seasonality of food supplies in the past is one of the most important debates within the study of food history. Here it seems that the production of beer was demand-led, regardless of the exigencies of weather.

Brewers

Brewing was an intermittent activity, so who brewed? How were they employed – were they full-time, part-time, casuals, or employed in other jobs? Both of the two parallel traditions of brewers – male and female – relate to the private-brewing world, characterizing it as transitional between commercial and domestic brewing. Although the overall responsibility for brewing lay with the butler, the actual brewing was often delegated to someone else; employment conditions for the brewer were generally casual and part-time, recruiting from labouring staff otherwise employed on estate farms or gardens. This was the situation in the early years of the nineteenth century at Shugborough, where a couple of outdoor labourers were paid per brew; in 1803 this amounted to £1 each for the whole year, a matter of twenty brews.[16] The great country houses of the titled aristocracy show a more structured employment of brewers, for there the job of brewer was either full-time or combined with another similar indoor post such as baker. The ability to brew was a valued extra skill for a servant who was hoping to be employed for other purposes. It is mentioned in newspaper advertisements for both female and male servants well into the nineteenth century, combined with a variety of positions such as housemaid, dairymaid, coachman or gardener.

Drinking

A question crucial to the interpretation of a working brewhouse is of course: what sort of beer was brewed? How strong was it?

Records of many brewing households in the sixteenth century show that routinely three strengths were made – ale, strong beer and small beer – with occasional special brews of strong ale; by the 1840s at the Staffordshire house of the Sutherlands at Trentham, these had diminished to two – ale and small beer; and by the 1880s often only one strength was made by the few households which continued the tradition – ale.[17] The Shugborough evidence shows that in 1824, the household was still making three strengths of malt drink:

Malt liquor, described as 'strong, very old' and bottled.
Ale, kept in huge casks in the main ale cellars. One cask, called Lord Anson, held 900 gallons and a smaller one, called Lady Anson, held 400 gallons. Much of this was over twelve months old.
Beer, kept in the small beer cellar.

The household also kept bottled stocks of *porter*, brought from the Ansons' London house in St James' Square. This was bought from a commercial supplier.[18]

Contemporary writers agreed that private ale and beer was stronger than the commercial equivalent and was therefore better keeping – hence the age of much of Shugborough's ale and strong ale. Waste was much higher than in commercial brewhouses.

How much of these various beers did people drink? Was beer a staple, drunk regularly, or an episodic treat for special occasions? Were there differences in drinking patterns which coincided with gender or status? There has long been a belief that strong ale and ale were the traditional drinks for adult men, whilst table and small beer were for women, children and servants.[19] Although clearly more detailed research on the consumption of household beer is needed, enough is known to conclude that this statement is something of a simplification. No doubt different groups within the household had different drinking habits and no doubt generally men drank more and stronger ale and beer than women. There are complications, however: though small beer was always important for servants, it was also consumed by the employing families, at least before the eighteenth century. Nor was ale confined to the upper classes or indeed to men; both male and female servants drank ale, though to an extent which was always more controlled than beer. Ale was generally rationed, beer was generally freely available. Women always seem to have been given approximately half the men's allowances.

Drinking patterns were seasonal, reflecting not only seasonal changes in individual requirements but also social and work responses to weather – the social round, the seasonal migration between town and country, and the necessities of harvest. Patterns of beer-drinking were part of the fabric of everyday life, helping to mark seasons and hierarchies and to maintain continuity within the household. Not surprisingly, large-scale consumption of ale and beer seems to have been the norm among country house servants, despite elaborate systems for the control and issuing of drink; this was true even as late as the nineteenth century, when public attitudes to drunkenness generally were changing. Some occupations were higher risk than others – notably butlers, coachmen and cooks.

Ale in particular was consumed in many different ways: it was drunk cold or hot or as a basis for a variety of made up drinks, herbal and flavoured beers, as well as household and veterinary medicines.[20]

Many issues relating to ale and beer-drinking in the English country house remain to be explored. An intriguing question is how drinking related to mealtimes and the distribution of work through the day. Most ale allowances were issued in the servants' hall, after the servants' dinner at midday; so what effect did this have on afternoon work schedules? Did ale have anything to do with rituals of rank either within the family or the servants? To what extent did it become a form of currency within the household or a reward for particularly unpleasant work, celebration or charity giving?[21] Do the records of the country house in any way chronicle the progress of beer-drinking away from its position as a staple element of the diet?

Questions about country house beer-drinking are important if only because they inform our interpretation of household accounts and wage levels and our appreciation of the relationship between servant and master. Beer and ale allowances were given not as a perquisite, but as a part of the wage contract; cash had to be paid if for any reason the agreed quantity and quality were not available. The nature of the beer allowance as a wage substitute has meant that a written record of beer consumption was often kept and that records of payment of beer money have survived. Further, such allowances and cash payments have to be taken into account when estimating wage levels of servants, especially when drawing comparisons with factory wages.

The provision of household ale and beer was an important feature of many country houses, long after beer had been replaced by tea as a staple and long after commercial supplies of ale and beer were available. The fact that so many houses persisted in the tradition until late in the nineteenth century speaks volumes about the nature of those households – their gender base, their patriarchal attitudes to employees and their systems of control over servants.

NOTES

1. Peter Brears, 'Brewing at Hickleton', in C. Anne Wilson (ed.), *Liquid Nourishment: Potable Foods and Stimulating Drinks* (Edinburgh, 1993), pp. 60–9; Gary Marshall, *The Calke Abbey Brewhouse: The Historical and Archaeological Evidence,* National Trust pamphlet (Calke, 1987); John Steane, 'Chastleton House, Oxfordshire: A View from Downstairs', *Folk Life*, 33 (1994–5), pp. 48–61.

2. Pamela Sambrook, *Country House Brewing, 1650–1950* (London, 1996).

3. See for example: J.M. Bennett, *Women in the Medieval English Countryside: Gender and Household in Brigstock before the Plague* (Oxford, 1987); Christopher Dyer, *Everyday Life in Medieval England* (London, 1994); Helena Graham, '"A Woman's Work . . .": Labour and Gender in the Late Medieval Countryside', in P.J.P. Goldberg (ed.), *Woman is a Worthy Wight: Women in English Society c. 1200–1500* (Stroud, 1992); David Postles, 'Brewing and the Peasant Economy: Some Manors in Late Medieval Devon', *Rural History*, 3(2) (1992), pp. 133–44; Peter Clark, *The English Alehouse: A Social History, 1200–1830* (London, 1983); H.S. Corran, *A History of Brewing* (Newton Abbot, 1975); T.R. Gourvish and R.G. Wilson, *The British Brewing Industry, 1830–1980* (Cambridge, 1994); Peter Mathias, *The Brewing Industry in England, 1700–1830* (Cambridge, 1959).

4. Pamela Sambrook, 'Home-brewing on a Grand Scale', *Folk Life,* 29 (1990–1). The Anson family papers are deposited at Staffordshire Record Office (hereafter SRO), D615.

5. Before the seventeenth century 'ale' was the traditional English unhopped drink, and 'beer' was the hopped drink introduced from the continent. By the end of the seventeenth century, both ale and beer produced in the country house brewhouses were probably hopped, but the former was stronger and brighter than the latter as it was made from the first-drawn worts.

6. See Brears, 'Brewing at Hickleton'; Clarence E. Hellewell, 'The Hickleton Brew' (unpublished memoirs, 1984).

7. SRO, Anson Mss, William Anson's notebooks, D615/P(A)1/10.

8. SRO, Anson Mss, bill from Samuel Wyatt, D615/E(H)2/5.

9. During the 1830s and '40s the first Earl of Lichfield, Thomas William Anson, entrenched

both himself and the estate so deeply into debt that in 1841 a writ was issued against him; bailiffs were sent out to Shugborough and inventories of the whole household were taken; hence the very detailed inventory attached to the assignment to creditors. SRO, Anson Mss, inventory of the Ansons' brewhouse at Shugborough, 1841, D615/E(H)11.

10.   The surviving brewhouse at Charlecote in Warwickshire is an excellent example of a brewhouse with two coppers, possibly installed at different times.

11.   See Sambrook, *Country House Brewing*, chapter 2.

12.   SRO, Anson Mss, cellar books, D615/E(H)37.

13.   The eighteenth century saw the publication of a large number of brewing manuals. For a detailed bibliography see Sambrook, *Country House Brewing*.

14.   The earlier 'top-mashing' method required the liquor to be poured directly on to the top of the malt or the two ingredients to be poured in together. The later 'bottom-mashing' method required perforated false bottom-boards to be fitted to the mash tun; the malt was laid on top of the boards and the liquor introduced down a chute fixed to the side wall of the tun; thus the liquor level rose slowly through the false bottom with its charge of mash.

15.   Sambrook, *Country House Brewing*, chapter 4.

16.   Sambrook, 'Home-brewing', p. 24.

17.   Sambrook, *Country House Brewing*, chapter 5.

18.   SRO, Anson Mss, cellar books, D615/E(H)37.

19.   Mathias, *Brewing Industry,* p. xxv.

20.   See Peter Brears, 'Celebrations in Hot Ale', in C. Anne Wilson (ed.), *Liquid Nourishment* (Edinburgh, 1993).

21.   Sambrook, *Country House Brewing*, chapter 5.

FURTHER READING

The Army and Navy Stores Catalogue, 1907 (Newton Abbot, 1969).

Beamon, Sylvia P. and Roaf, Susan, *The Ice-houses of Britain* (London, 1990).

Brears, Peter, *The Gentlewoman's Kitchen* (Wakefield, 1984).

Brown, Catherine, *Scottish Cookery* (Glasgow, 1985).

Buxbaum, Tim, *Ice Houses* (Princes Risborough, 1992).

Cobbett, William, *Cottage Economy* (1822).

David, E., *Harvest of the Cold Month: The Social History of Ice and Ices* (London, 1994).

David, Rob, 'An Ice-house Experiment', *Transactions of the Cumberland and Westmorland Antiquarian and Archaeological Society*, 82 (1982), pp. 191–3.

David, Stuart, *The Kitchen Garden* (London, 1984).

Davies, Jennifer, *The Victorian Kitchen* (London, 1989).

Eveleigh, David, 'Put Down to a Clear Bright Fire', *Folklife*, 29 (1991), pp. 5–18.

Franklin, Jill, *The Gentleman's Country House and its Plan, 1835–1914* (London, 1981).

Girouard, Mark, *A Country House Companion* (New Haven and London, 1987).

Girouard, Mark, *Life in the English Country House* (New Haven and London, 1978).

Girouard, Mark, *Robert Smythson and the Elizabethan Country House* (New Haven and London, 1983).

Girouard, Mark, *The Victorian Country House* (New Haven and London, 1979).

Hardyment, Christina, *Home Comfort: A History of Domestic Arrangements* (London, 1992).

Hecht, J.J., *The Domestic Servants in Eighteenth-century England* (London, 1980).

Hope, Annette, *A Caledonian Feast* (Edinburgh, 1987).

Horn, Pamela, *The Rise and Fall of the Victorian Servant* (Dublin, 1975, reprinted 1994).

Kerr, Robert, *The Gentleman's House: or How to Plan English Residences from the Parsonage to the Palace* (London, 1864).

Lewis, Lesley, *The Private Life of a Country House, 1912–39* (London, 1982).

Loudon, Jane, *The Lady's Country Companion* (London, 1845; reprinted Bungay, Suffolk, 1984).

Loudon, J.C., *An Encyclopedia of Gardening* (London, 1834).

Macintosh, C., *The Book of the Garden*, 2 vols (Edinburgh, 1853–5)

Markham, Gervase, *The English Housewife* (1615, reprinted with an introduction by Michael R. Best, Canada, 1986).

Marshall, Rosalind, *The Days of Duchess Anne* (1973).

Proctor, D.V. (ed.), *Ice Carrying Trade at Sea* (London, 1981).

Reid, John, *The Scot's Gard'ner* (1683, reprinted Edinburgh, 1988).

Sambrook, Pamela, *Country House Brewing, 1550–1950* (London, 1996).

Waterson, Merlin, *The Servants' Hall: A Domestic History of Erddig* (London, 1980).

Wilson, C. Anne (ed.), *Liquid Nourishment: Potable Foods and Stimulating Drinks* (Edinburgh, 1993).

Wilson, C. Anne (ed.), *Traditional Country House Cooking* (London, 1993).

Wilson, C. Anne (ed.), *Waste Not, Want Not: Food Preservation from Early Times to the Present Day* (Edinburgh, 1991).

INDEX

Page numbers in italics refer to illustrations